Masters of the Victory Garden

Masters of the Victory Garden

Specialty Gardeners Share Their Expert Techniques

Jim Wilson

Little, Brown and Company

Boston   Toronto   London

First Edition

Library of Congress Cataloging-in-Publication Data

Wilson, James W. (James Wesley), 1925–
    Masters of the Victory garden: specialty gardeners share their
expert techniques / by Jim Wilson. — 1st ed.
        p.   cm.
    Includes bibliographical references.
    ISBN 0-316-94501-3 (hc) — ISBN 0-316-94500-5 (pb)
    1. Gardening.   2. Gardeners—Interviews.   I. Victory garden
(Television program)   II. Title.
SB453.W5624   1990
635—dc20   89-49071
                                                            CIP

HC: 10   9   8   7   6   5   4   3   2   1

PB: 10   9   8   7   6   5   4   3   2   1

Designed by Dianne Schaefer

RAI-WI

Published simultaneously in Canada by
Little, Brown & Company (Canada) Limited
PRINTED IN THE UNITED STATES OF AMERICA

*To my friends on the **Victory Garden** staff, WGBH-TV, and especially executive producer Russ Morash, who suggested that I write this book from our experiences on location*

Contents

Jeanine and Rex Smith's passion for rhododendrons transforms a dense north-western forest into a landscaped showplace.

Jim and Jill Wilkins: a Michigan physician's dexterity and his wife's artistic eye team up to create new vistas for hostas.

In nearly seventy years of service to humanity, Brother Charles Reckamp lets his light shine through his love for daylilies.

Charles and Lee Jeremias's life is filled with roses: growing, showing, and sharing them with others.

Elwood Fisher, Virginia Renaissance man, "rescues the perishing" by finding and saving ancient fruit tree varieties for posterity.

Preface

*O*ften, when we are on location taping segments for *The Victory Garden*, the Executive Producer, Russell Morash, will say to me, "There's a lesson here, Jim: tell home gardeners what it means to them."

That's how this book came about. Over the years, as we visited gardens large and small, a "big picture" emerged, much more significant than the thousands of lessons we created for viewers. The revelation slowly unfolded that gardening is a two-way street. The accepted concept is that gardeners shape gardens. We believe that, even more important, gardens shape gardeners; it changes their personalities and their lifestyles, and all to the good.

We call such committed gardeners "Masters of Gardening," for, indeed, they have mastered so many of the elements that day-to-day duties are completed almost automatically. They are left with more time to enjoy their hobby, and it shows in their good nature, self-confidence, and feeling of oneness with Nature.

At some time in their gardening careers, Masters of Gardening take up a specialty plant as a hobby, and come to know it so well that they become enthusiasts, missionaries for their hobby. Their enthusiasm is infectious; they willingly share information and plants with novices and bring them into their circle of friends, usually within a specialty plant society.

Over the years, *The Victory Garden* has introduced its audience to many Masters of Gardening. We not only admire what these gardeners have accomplished, but we also like them as warm and sharing human beings. Russell Morash felt that other gardeners could benefit by reading about how they got into their hobby plant; their challenges, triumphs, and disappointments; and how plants changed their lives.

Russell asked me to write this book, and I jumped at the chance. Garden writing isn't new to me (I sold my first garden magazine article in 1956), nor is interviewing home gardeners and commercial growers. But, I can tell you that I never before learned so much about gardening and gardeners in such a short time. It was a tremendously exciting and inspiring time in my life. I have written the names and addresses of these Masters of Gardening in my address book because there is not a one of them I would not want as a close friend.

My job of interviewing these gardeners and accumulating and validating much information about their specialty plants went easily because of the affection and loyalty accorded *The Victory Garden*. It all started with James Underwood Crockett, the original host of the show. His depth of information, natural enthusiasm, and warm ways helped many a first-time gardener feel the delight of biting into a home-grown, vine-ripened tomato. A tragic illness claimed Jim's life in 1979, and it is a tribute to this remarkable man that his memory is still strong among gardeners across this great country.

Jim tended a made-for-television garden in a corner of the parking lot behind the WGBH-TV studios in Boston. It was built around large existing crabapple trees and expanded to include vegetable and flower gardens, landscaped seating areas, and a small greenhouse. Viewing these shows was a personal experience, like coming right into Jim's own home and garden. But, Jim's death meant a change for the show.

A new host was brought in, a well-established nurseryman and keen home gardener, Bob Thomson. Bob was given the almost impossible task of taking over for someone who had won the hearts of viewers. In time he, too, became a trusted friend and adviser, through his honest and unpretentious ways and mastery of gardening. Bob brought to the show a passion for tasteful landscaping; it came at a time when gardeners seemed ready to extend their horizons beyond the vegetable patch.

At that time, the program was being broadcast nationally on Public Television but had a distinctly northeastern focus. This was due partly to Jim and Bob's down east and Boston accents and partly to the timing of gardening projects, set by New England weather. And, even though good garden culture travels well to most parts of the country, the time seemed right to develop regional gardens. Utilizing local hosts and regional plants, and timed for the seasons of each region, such gardens could add credibility and enhance loyalty.

I came on board at that time. *The Victory Garden* knew me from a guest spot I had done with Bob. So, when a regional garden was projected for Callaway Gardens in Pine Mountain, Georgia, I was asked to serve as host. I had been in home and commercial horticulture for nearly forty years, grew up in the South, and still talked "southern." My wife, Jane, and I operated an herb farm just over the border in South Carolina.

My first appearance in March of 1984 must have been painful for the crew because I knew nothing about being in front of a camera. What saved me, I think, was years of experience in public speaking and exposure to all sorts of plants around the world. With the help of the crew, good gardeners all, I began to give southern flower and vegetable gardens their due. When this old Mississippi boy praises turnip greens, okra, and purple hull peas, he has been there!

Since then, we've expanded the show's outreach to include Victory Garden West at Rogers' Garden Center near Newport Beach, California. Bob Smaus, Garden Editor for the *Los Angeles Times*, does a great job of introducing to western gardeners the amazing variety of plants that will thrive in their mild climates. Rogers' is open year round and is nationally known for its creative uses of unusual plants and planters.

Two changes were made in Massachusetts. The parking-lot garden was moved to the grounds of a marvelous retail nursery and garden center, Lexington Gardens, in the historic town of Lexington. Bob Thomson introduces all programs from the quarter-acre garden, open to the public spring through fall. Also, a new "Suburban Garden" was begun on the outskirts of Boston, where enough open space exists to demonstrate major garden construction projects from start to finish. Roger Swain, Science Editor for *Horticulture* magazine, joined the team in 1986 and serves there as host.

Often, Roger will end a show by delivering fresh vegetables from the garden to Marian Morash, a bona fide chef. She never fails to come up with wonderful ways to prepare them.

In addition to taping segments at regional Victory Gardens, the show travels extensively throughout North America, giving each of us a chance to see what other gardeners are up to. And in recent years, we've roamed the world with British plantsman Peter Seabrook. Peter does a masterful job of presenting some of the great gardens of the world, sending reports from Europe, Asia, New Zealand, and Australia. How times have changed on *The Victory Garden* since our parking-lot days of 1976!

The one constant throughout this long history of service to gardeners has been Russell Morash. *The Victory Garden* was his vision and, to this day, he continues to impart his creative genius, keen eye, and talent for gardening to the show. John Pelrine, who began as the manager of the greenhouse in Crockett's days, has advanced to Producer. Another veteran is the Director of Photography, Dick Holden, the only person I know who can back uphill while taping, following a twisting, rutted path, and never bobble his hand-held camera. He translates Russell's ideas into vivid images.

We've been blessed with a great crew that you never see on camera: Chip Adams, Derek Diggins, Nina Sing, Sally Cook, and the technical staff at the studio who, within forty-eight hours of receiving our raw tape, can uplink a finished program to a satellite and transmit it to nearly three hundred PBS stations nationwide.

If I look good on TV, credit it more to the WGBH-TV staff than to my talent, and especially to my associates at Callaway Gardens, Bob Hovey and David Chambers. They work in Victory Garden South every day of the year and keep all 9,500 square feet neat and shining for visitors. It is a major attraction at this great horticultural center and 2,500-acre resort.

I am blessed to be in a position to work with gardeners all over the country and to record for you the stories of some of the best. When I think of these newfound but fast friends, a line from a hymn I learned in Epworth League these many years ago comes to mind . . . "Blest be the tie that binds."

Acknowledgments

I f this book entertains and enlightens you, it will be due more to the gardeners I interviewed and horticulturists I asked to help, than to what I know about gardening. If it fails, it will be because I was unable to absorb the huge amount of information involved, or to translate it into the working language of gardeners.

Most gardeners are generalists, and that includes me. In my years of gardening, I rubbed up against all sorts of hobby plant specialists, both amateur and professional, but never absorbed a great deal of information about any given plant. I don't mind telling you that I had to hit the reference books, the telephone, and the U.S. mail to write in depth about the eleven hobby plants featured in this book. I queried skilled amateurs, commercial producers, public garden curators, and plant societies in many states.

I am indebted to Christina Ward, my editor at Little, Brown, who would not let me stop short of delivering the best that was in me, and to my associates at *The Victory Garden*, who have unselfishly shared their rich experiences.

It is a marvel that the featured gardeners didn't run me off, or chase away the photographers—we took up so much of their time with interviews, correspondence, and phone calls. They gave us what we call in the South "a gracious plenty" of cooperation. Bless every one of them!

So many people helped on daylilies: Roy Klehm of Klehm Nursery, Van Sellers of Iron Gate Gardens, and John Elsley of Wayside Gardens, to name a few.

Susan P. Martin, Curator of Conifers of the U.S. National Arboretum, sent a list, compiled by Tom Dilatush, of conifer collections open to the public. Gwen Fawthrop, a fellow garden writer, advised me on collections in Ontario. Jeanette Windham of Greensboro, North Carolina, checked my hardiness data on dwarf conifers.

I would be remiss in not thanking my wife, Jane, for double-checking my memory on how herbs grow in the South, and our friend Tom DiBaggio of Earthworks, Arlington, Virginia, for information on rosemary, oregano, and lavender. The Executive Director of The Herb Society, Julie McSoud, and Bob Hovey, the Resident Gardener at Victory Garden South, kindly helped me.

Roy Klehm, Van Sellers, and John Elsley also helped me with hostas, as did Peter Ruh of the Homestead Division of Sunnybrook Farms. Gene Ellis of Tallahassee Nurseries and Ken Chatham of Crabapple Nurseries, Roswell, Georgia, helped me pinpoint the southern adaptation of hostas.

Dorothy B. Schaefer of the American Lily Society put her twenty-five years of experience at my disposal.

Elsley and Klehm read my copy on peonies. My information on peppers came partly from Dr. Jean Andrews Smith's book, partly from David Chambers of Callaway Gardens, and partly from my special interest in them.

Adele Jones, of the American Rhododendron Society, started me off on the right foot, and Fred Galle, "Mr. Azalea" himself, read my copy.

A fellow garden writer, Maggie Oster, led me to the Jeremiases, where I did the rose story. Anne Reilly counseled me on miniature roses and my friend of many years, Bill Fike of Jackson & Perkins, on rose hardiness.

Nell Lewis of Greensboro, North Carolina, let me shoot photos in her superb woodland wildflower garden and introduced me to Dr. Elwood Fisher, who is every bit as knowledgeable about wildflowers as he is about antique fruit trees.

Photo Credits

Half title: John Pelrine
Title page: Russell Morash
Preface: Stephen Butera
Introduction: Stephen Butera
Rhodedendrons: photos by Don Normark, except p. 21, by Erin Smith
Hostas: photos by Kim Kauffman, except pp. 33, 35 (both), 41 (top), by John Pelrine; p. 47 (all), by Jim Wilkins
Daylilies: photos by Roy Klehm
Roses: photos by Chuck Armour, except pp. 70, 76, 81 (left), by Russell Morash; p. 81 (right), by Stephen Butera
Antique Fruit Trees: photos by Robert C. Simpson, except pp. 93, 97, by Jim Wilson; p. 95, by Elwood Fisher
Herbal Arts: photos by Stephen Butera
Dwarf Conifers: photos by Ann Reilley, except p. 147 (all), by Jim Wilson
Peonies: photos by Roy Klehm
Wildflowers: photos by Beth Maynor, except p. 189 (bottom row), by Jim Wilson
Lilies: photos by John Croft
Peppers: photos by Larry Albee, except p. 229, by John Pelrine; p. 230 (top left and bottom left), by John Swan

Masters of the Victory Garden

Masters of
Gardening

*I*t was my happy privilege, for the better part of a year, to travel
across the U.S.A., interviewing some of the best gardeners I have ever
met. By design, these were all hobby growers of specialty plants. Most
were noncommercial and involved only in gardening. Others had taken
up plant breeding in addition to gardening. A few sold enough plants to
help support their hobbies. I chose to interview mostly noncommercial
growers because a person's attitude toward plants can alter when he or
she begins to sell them. Evaluation of plants can change from favoring
the traits the gardener likes to those he or she feels the general public
will like enough to cause them to purchase the plant. Some had been
featured on *The Victory Garden* program; others are scheduled for future
productions. For lack of a better name, we call them "Masters of the
Victory Garden." None has the hubris to proclaim, "I am the best!"
They flinch at the term "expert," and even grumble at being called an
"authority."

You see, what these seasoned gardeners have discovered is that no
individual ever completely masters gardening. Much of the fascination in
one of this country's most popular hobbies is that one revelation leads to
another, and another. Gardening is a lifelong voyage of discovery.

Early on, these Garden Masters confronted the fact that an enormous
amount of information had to be absorbed before they could become
knowledgeable about gardening. I think they reached that conclusion at
about the time they became pretty good general gardeners, capable of
raising vegetables and herbs, annual and perennial flowers, bulbs, roses,
and a few basic trees and shrubs. They became frustrated, I believe, at
the difficulty of advancing their knowledge of gardening on such a broad
front.

The Garden Masters I interviewed enjoyed learning about one plant at
a time, through reference books, discussions with fellow hobbyists, lectures by authorities, and actual experience in the garden. They felt "in

control" of the situation, instead of vaguely uneasy about the impossibility of absorbing the vast amount of information on general gardening. They felt, and I agree, that it makes good sense to narrow the amount of data you need to absorb to succeed at growing.

I expect you know what they are talking about. Just the process of learning where to find gardening information and how to winnow relevant and reliable guidance from the mass of often specious "facts" on general gardening is bewildering. Translating all that information into action is enough to intimidate anyone and to paralyze a few.

Some of the Garden Masters worked their way, at least superficially, through one or more hobby plants on their way to their present specialty. Others, having reached a high degree of competence with one specialty plant, retained it but took on one or two others as well.

It seems to me that most gardeners sort of drift into a specialty plant. It often starts with an affinity with a plant they have bought or received as a gift. The plant "grows on them," and they begin looking for more cultivars in the same genus or species, building little families of related plants. They buy garden books about their specialty and usually join a plant society. Some grow mostly for the enjoyment of friends and family, others not only for the challenge of growing new plants but of doing it better than anyone else in their area. Some work all season long at growing, mostly for the thrill of entering their handiwork in shows.

One commonality in backgrounds of these Garden Masters fascinated me. I encountered it in the first of the interviews, and my initial impression was reinforced with each succeeding gardener I came to know. It seems that every good gardener has a role model, a "mentor." With some, it was a parent or a grandparent. With others, particularly those who took up a specialty plant in later years, it was an advanced specialty grower, one who cared and shared.

That revelation speaks to every specialty plant society, every garden club, every horticultural society. It says, "Make a real effort to be friendly and sharing with newcomers." There is much more to this than merely perpetuating the organization. If you are the advanced gardener who reaches out to educate and inspire a newcomer, you may be amazed at the impact of your sharing. Without intending it, you may become a mentor. Just read the experiences of these Garden Masters and you'll get an idea of the place role models play in gardening.

I found all of our Masters of the Victory Garden to be decent, likable, intelligent individuals, sometimes eccentric, but always fun-loving. None sees himself or herself as a "Creator" but as a willing apprentice in the natural order of things. Some are aware that they have become role models to other gardeners and are humbled by that realization.

Another commonality among these Garden Masters is the need to control their garden. Gone are the days when, faced with weather or other environmental problems, gardeners would capitulate. Now, they seek out and use many means and devices to moderate the impact of weather, plant diseases and insects, soil deficiencies, and even space restrictions. Certain of these Garden Masters have realized that, in order to progress in gardening, understanding the environment is vital. They have become "Stewards of the Earth" or, at least, of that small part upon which they pay taxes. Two or three have become effective environmentalists.

Let me share with you one more observation about these Garden Masters, which is admittedly subjective and colored by my own approach to gardening. I realize the subject of the motives behind gardening is sensitive, so let me assure you that this observation is meant to compliment anyone who recognizes his own leanings. . . .

Some gardeners, I believe, use gardening as outdoor theater, with themselves as directors. Some prefer the security of repeating a similar production year after year; they thrive on the praise heaped on their efforts. Others prefer the challenge of new tableaux each year; the thrill of learning about new plants and how to fit them into the gardening environment is what gives them satisfaction. Some, in order to understand the plants who are players, imbue them with human characteristics. They talk to them, praise them, interact with them, move them around the stage, change the lighting . . . but, ultimately, if they fail to perform, they reach for the stage hook.

My new friends would be the first to admit that I would not have gone wrong had I chosen some other Garden Master in their specialties. The woods are full of good hobby gardeners growing specialty plants. I chose to feature these particular Garden Masters to present a cross section of backgrounds, ages, lifestyles, aspirations, and climates. I believe you will agree that they are the kind of gardeners you would enjoy meeting and learning from, even emulating.

I know I will get letters from advocates of other specialty plants. They are no less important than the few that could be featured in depth within these covers. If fortune smiles on this small beginning, perhaps we can cover other specialties in future books.

It is my hope that, in reading about these diverse plants and skilled gardeners, you may find intriguing possibilities and even role models. You may think of yourself as a generalist or "plain dirt gardener," and be happy in your situation. Well and good; you are among the majority of gardeners. But, should the day come when you feel flat and burned out with gardening, pick up this book and read how these Garden Masters rise above disappointments to wring more out of every day in their gardens.

Rhododendrons

Jeanine and Rex Smith's passion for rhododendrons transforms a dense northwestern forest into a landscaped showplace.

(Left) Jeanine's artistic talent shows in this landscape arrangement of R. 'Ken Janek' with sweet woodruff, Galium odoratum, *and London pride,* Saxifraga umbrosa, *around a weathered log.*

F ew other flowering plants have the visual impact of rhododendrons, not just in bloom, but in flower bud and new growth stages, summer foliage, and winter form. The flower buds remind me of a coiled spring, winding tighter and tighter, swelling and swelling until, on one happy day, they burst through their restraining bud scales to dazzle the eye and nourish the spirit. The flowers are anything but ephemeral; in cool climates they remain fresh and unfaded for many days. Through careful selection of cultivars, gardeners can enjoy rhododendrons in bloom over many months. After the flowers drop, and the plants have summoned a new burst of energy, colorful new shoots branch from vegetative buds to grow a new canopy of leathery, evergreen leaves. During the summer, rhododendron plants are like a corps de ballet ... beautiful, but subordinate to the principal dancers of the season. During the winter, in forest underplantings, the persistent foliage, dark green, often glossy, shines against the background of bare trunks, branches, and fallen leaves.

The history of rhododendrons is replete with stories of great sacrifices by plant explorers who braved harsh winters, nearly impassable terrain, hostile villagers, and venal officials to bring back species to enrich our gardens. In the early days of plant exploration, all members of the genus were called "rhododendrons." Later, certain species, some deciduous, some evergreen, came to be known collectively as "azaleas." Thus, all azaleas are rhododendrons, but only a few rhododendrons are azaleas.

Any attempt at a concise, precise distinction between the plants we call rhododendrons and the ones we call azaleas is doomed to failure. Yet, most experienced gardeners can tell garden cultivars of azaleas from rhododendrons at a glance. Most garden azaleas are hybrids between species, and come under such classes as Indian hybrids, Glen Dale hybrids, Kurume hybrids, Ghent hybrids, Robin Hill hybrids, and Shammarello evergreen hybrids. Many azaleas are deciduous, particularly the native American species and hybrids between them. Individual azalea flowers are shaped like funnels, sometimes fragrant, and are relatively slender, as compared to the more bell-like individual flowers of rhododendrons. A typical cluster or "truss" of rhododendron flowers is larger and denser than one of azaleas, and typical rhododendron leaves are much larger, evergreen, and usually glossy.

Generally, the species and hybrids we call rhododendrons, and the evergreen azaleas, occur in mountain ranges where cooler temperatures and higher moisture levels are kind to broad-leaved evergreens. By far the greatest number of rhododendron species are native to Asia, where they are most numerous on mountains and foothills that receive abundant rainfall and, often, snow cover. However, the tropical species of rhododendrons grow as understory plants in jungles. The deciduous azalea species generally occur at lower elevations and can thrive on drier soil. The species rhododendrons are more demanding in their soil and climatic requirements than the hybrids, yet are the favorites of many rhododendron enthusiasts because of their simplicity and grace.

Only in recent years have rhododendrons emerged as a major landscaping plant in the United States. Forty years ago, rhododendrons had established a foothold in three regions that were ideally suited to their culture, with relatively cool summers, mild winters, abundant rainfall, and acid soils. On the West Coast, the fog-shrouded or rain-washed coastal plain from Santa Cruz north into British Columbia provided the ideal site for growing the spectacular semihardy hybrids. On the East Coast, the temperate bays, estuaries, or islands from Boston south to the DelMarVa peninsula pampered a then-new generation of rhododendron hybrids hardy to 5 degrees F. Further inland, along the uplands of the Appalachian chain, the old Ironclad hybrids, based partly on hardy American native

R. 'Bow Bells'
has rather small
leaves and pen-
dant flowers
(left). The pale
yellow blossoms
of R. hanceanum
contrast beauti-
fully with its
smooth, dark
green foliage.

rhododendrons, endured great extremes in temperature and fluctuations in soil moisture and humidity. Wild stands of species rhododendrons could be found in roughly the same areas.

Rhododendrons held unimaginable potential for American gardeners, but it could not be realized without more adaptable hybrids, efficient production and marketing methods, and greater publicity. Around the country were immensely talented geneticists, taxonomists, nurserymen, and amateur specialists in rhododendrons, all working more or less independently. Largely, theirs was a work of love; no one made much money out of new cultivars and some producers went broke. No one knew much about propagating rhododendrons on a commercial scale, and plants could not be patented. It all began to come together with the formation of the American Rhododendron Society after World War II.

The early rhododendron hybridizers wanted significant improvements in cold tolerance and resistance to dry soil conditions. They wanted fuller plants, and greater variety in foliage and plant habit. Above all, they wanted new and clearer colors. Cherry and magenta reds abounded in hybrids, along with muddy pastels. Desirable colors were available in species rhododendrons, but thousands of crosses were necessary to develop desirable

Landscaping for
a succession of
bloom: the white
R. 'Alf Bowman'
will be followed
by the coral R.
'Paprika Spiced'
and R. 'Lem's
Cameo', right.
The yellow is R.
'Golden Witt'.

hybrids from them. Progress was slow because of confusion in nomenclature, duplication in naming, inadequate pedigrees on existing hybrids, and the need for a broader genetic base.

World War II had an unexpected and positive effect on rhododendron breeding. Servicemen sent back seeds of rhododendron species from the far corners of the earth, and these deepened the genetic pool. The Europeans, with their generally "softer" climate, had been ahead of us in rhododendron improvement for some time, but their hybrids weren't tough enough for our more variable climate. After the war, using new Asian blood and native American species, our breeders rapidly began developing hybrids that were hardy as a rock, and as beautiful as any of the temperamental hybrids from Europe. The hardy eastern *Rhododendron catawbiense* and *R. maximum* were their mainstays and the more tender western *R. macrophyllum*.

During the first flush of enthusiasm over improved rhododendrons, new hybrids flooded arboreta, parks, and estates. Years passed before the plants matured sufficiently that their form, endurance under stressful weather, and resistance to insects and diseases could be evaluated fully. Today, although some of the better old hybrids linger on, vastly improved cultivars are taking over the market, some from other parts of the world. Plants are being bred for attractive foliage and neat form as well. Leaves may be blue-green or silvery, or dusted with velvety tomentum, the undersides purple, rust-colored, or white. New growth can be bronzy red, or as pale and fuzzy as a bunny's ears.

Even before *glasnost,* the cultivar *R. luteum* 'Batumi Gold' reached the U.S. National Arboretum from Russia's Batumi Botanical Garden. Two outstanding breeders, David Leach and the late Ed Mezitt, took the obvious route of developing and evaluating new hybrids in severe winter areas and introduced new lines of compact hybrids for today's smaller gardens. The Leach Hybrids provide extended bloom along with more attractive foliage and crisp, clean colors.

The improvements in rhododendrons have greatly increased their adaptability to other regions of the country. Still, in all of North America, no area can match the Pacific Northwest, from southwestern British Columbia through western Oregon and Washington, for growing a wide range of rhododendron hybrids and species. A few rhododendrons are native to the mountains in this area. Particularly near water level, the climate is temperate, the air and soil are moist for several months of the year, and the soil is porous and acidic, due to the abundance of decomposing organic matter and the leaching action of winter rains.

At their hillside home in Woodinville, Washington, Rex and Jeanine Smith have capitalized on all these advantages to amass a spectacular collection of rhododendrons, not lined up like an ill-assorted guard, but tastefully blended into a stunning landscape.

Under the high canopy of shade, rhododendrons line the winding lane to the Smiths' home.

When I turned into the driveway of the Smiths' secluded home, I was struck by the abundance of color and variety of choice rhododendrons. Pastel colors predominated, with an occasional accent mark of dark or bright, or a highlight of cream, yellow, or white like a shaft of sunlight. Plants ranged in height from groundcovers to taller than my head. Although basically a rhododendron garden, the landscape included azaleas, groundcovers, and choice perennials. I parked some distance from the Smiths' house and walked in, so I could get an idea of the number of rhododendrons in their collection. There must have been a hundred rhododendrons or more in the front yard alone! Rex and Jeanine are still working on the back yard of their three-acre lot. Only a few months ago, loggers dropped and hauled away the last of the hundred-foot-high Douglas firs tagged for removal. The lot hasn't been stripped of trees; far from it—more than a hundred firs, western red cedars, and hemlocks were left standing both to provide the high canopy of shade that rhododendrons like and to block the view of homes beyond their back and side fences.

Along the back fence stand several head-high rhododendrons. Jeanine, the hybridizer and propagator in the Smith family, told me that these big plants date back to her earliest experiments in growing rhododendrons from seeds. She grew them from hybrid seeds brought to a Seattle Rhododendron Society meeting in 1971 by Dr. Ned Brockenbrough, an amateur hybridizer. Little did she dream that, out of the thirty-five plants which she grew to maturity, would come an award-winning cultivar, 'Apricot Fantasy'.

In 1987–1989, Jeanine served as president of the nearly 450-member Seattle chapter of the American Rhododendron Society. She has good reasons for feeling strongly that one of the most important obligations of experienced plant society members is to introduce novices to the joys of growing specialty plants. "It was at one of those first meetings," she related, "that I received the seeds from Dr. Brockenbrough and, following the instructions in David Leach's book *Rhododendrons of the World*, I filled a covered plastic shoebox with moist milled sphagnum moss, planted the seeds, and grew dozens of tiny rhododendron seedlings on the bright end of our kitchen counter, out of the direct sun.

"Succeeding at my first attempt at germinating rhododendron seeds was so exciting!" she said. "It started me collecting and propagating rhododendrons from cuttings and, over the next three years, hundreds of small plants filled our city lot. Rex and I began thinking about having a piece of property large enough to grow and display our collection of rhododendrons."

Then she laughed and said, "I didn't know it, but I was already a 'Rhodoholic.'" She passed me a short essay by Heidi Shelton, a member of the Seattle chapter of the ARS, entitled *The Five Stages of Rhodoholism.*"

1. Patient buys commonly available hybrids ('Elizabeth', 'Hon. Jean Marie de Montague', 'Scintillation', 'Gomer Waterer', 'Pink Pearl', etc.). Notices the pretty flowers and relatively easy care, goes on to stage 2.

2. Begins to comb more prestigious and out-of-the-way nurseries for more unusual varieties and smaller plants (keeping in mind that he/she will run out of garden space in the near future as this acquisitive habit continues unfettered). Throws out or gives away perfectly healthy plants (especially non-rhodies) to make room for more of his favorites. Buys every book on rhododendrons available. Plants trees whose sole purpose it is to provide just the right amount of dappled shade for rhodies. Begins to collect plants for showy foliage alone. Tries rooting some cuttings. Joins the Rhododendron Society. *The disease can be halted at this stage but not reversed.*

3. Starts to look at "real estates" (minimum three acres) in outlying areas because garden is at capacity. Builds a greenhouse and makes some crosses, "just to see what happens." Dreams about owning a rhododendron nursery. If financial and physical resources are adequate for realizing this dream, patient may live out his/her life growing, hybridizing, exhibiting and selling rhodies and sharing experiences with like-minded people. All the while he/she harbors the secret hope to be the hybridizer of the next 'Lem's Cameo', i.e., a plant that will take the rhody world by storm and bring if not fortune, at least fame to its creator. *Recovery at this stage is difficult if not impossible, due to the fact that the patient sees the disease as entirely benign, even pleasurable.*

4. Admiration for rhododendron species, which began late in stage 2 or early in stage 3, begins to take over now. Patients will travel long distances to seek out unusual plants. Beauty of flowers or even acquisition of plants matters less and less; rarity is what patient is after. May sell house and car to finance a trek to the Himalayas. *Patient's family, if still intact at this point, gives up on his/her sanity.*

5. Patient shaves his head, dons a yellow robe, and becomes a Tibetan monk to live among his beloved species. It is not known how females cope with this stage; possibly they disguise themselves as mountaineers, naturalists, or missionaries. *As no case of recovery from stage 5 is known in the literature, it is generally considered terminal.*

At this point, Rex was smiling broadly. He likes rhododendrons, too, but the malady has not progressed as far in his case.

Jeanine continued her story. "Rex was gone from home a great deal as a pilot with Northwest Airlines and, in the evenings, I would pore over the rhododendron literature, which always filled my nightstand. The breaks between Rex's flights give us the time to pursue our projects.

"In 1973 we purchased three acres of land, in what was then a rural area northwest of Seattle. In 1976 we completed our present home and moved in with our daughter, Erin, then eighteen months old, and our sons, Greg, nine, and Kirk, seven years old. Building and moving at that time was difficult and it derailed my rhododendron hobby. Nevertheless, when we moved to our new home, we brought along several favorite large plants and countless small 'rhodies' including, of course, my treasured seedlings. We planted these in nursery beds. After the house was made livable, we began to tackle the vast project of clearing trees and brush, burning stump piles, designing gardens, building decks, and preparing soil.

"Actually, before I caught the rhododendron bug," Jeanine said, "I was interested in gardening and in landscape design. I have a background in art, and would have liked to have spent more time painting, but found that, while raising three children, the uninterrupted blocks of time weren't available. However, I could garden with children around me, and arranging plants in pleasing landscape designs fulfilled my creative instincts. Rex trusts my judgment about landscaping and never complains if a rhody has to be moved. I couldn't ask for a more supportive partner, in all things. Rex worked long and hard to clear this land of salal, brambles, brush, and tree trimmings after the loggers left. He built the service building, greenhouses, and cold frames and is now installing a sprinkler system."

Rex looked a little embarrassed when she told the following story about his willingness to help. "When we were about to move into our first home in 1968, I wanted to take a course in landscape design but was very pregnant with our second son. I knew I wouldn't be able to finish the class before delivery. Rex went instead, took notes, and reviewed them with me after each session."

Asked if he does any hybridizing, Rex smiled and answered, "No. I know how to hybridize but Jeanine knows why. I get my kicks out of helping her succeed, but I also enjoy building and heavy gardening. I guess that growing up around farms in Montana accustomed me to it. I'll tell you one thing: when I get out of that cockpit and rest up a little to get over jet lag, I enjoy the relaxation I get from building and gardening. Jeanine and I like working together on my days at home."

I like the way the Smiths defer to each other's strengths. When Rex finished talking about his involvement, Jeanine took over to show me

Rex and Jeanine mulch around a choice rhododendron hybrid that was grown from seed. This one has survived the evaluation process.

the steps of propagating rhododendrons. She began by demonstrating how to take, root, and "grow-on" cuttings to a size that can safely be transplanted to a nursery bed or border.

Jeanine showed me that, with the aid of rooting hormones, potting soils, bottom heat, and cold frames, increasing rhododendrons by taking cuttings is easy and almost foolproof. Now that their space is filling up rapidly, she has little room for plants other than her own seedlings, and has virtually discontinued growing from cuttings. It is quite a sacrifice because, as Jeanine puts it, she "likes to put roots on things." Nevertheless, she won't turn down a cutting from a rare rhododendron, and she will clone her own hybrids by cuttings when required.

Space limitations are also forcing Jeanine to be very selective about hybridizing. Long past the learning stage of making random crosses, she directs each cross toward what she sees as attainable goals, mostly new colors and improved growth habits. Through her ARS connections, Jeanine can receive pollen from species and hybrids not in her collection, even from foreign countries. In return, she sends pollen from her plants on request. Records of crosses and pollen donations are kept in what she calls her "stud book."

Jeanine is particularly fond of the plant habit and foliage of hybrids based on *R. yakusimanum* and, along with other hybridizers, is incorporating this species into her breeding program. The species is low growing and its rather slender leaves with truncated ends clothe the plants densely. New growth is colorful. The undersides of leaves are felty and give a bicolor effect when they blow in the breeze. The lack of a wide range of natural colors doesn't bother Jeanine, because she can cross *R. yakusimanum* with other species to get the colors she wants. She is aiming for full yellow, apricot, or orange trusses on compact, low-growing plants with attractive foliage.

I was struck by Jeanine's confident approach to difficult hybridizing goals. She explained how she got started: "I was inspired to try hybridizing by a dear lady, Elsie Watson, who taught me the techniques of crossing and encouraged me to join the hybridizers group of the Seattle chapter. She was my role model and her lovely hybrids gave me the assurance that, with a little luck and a lot of hard work, I might do the same. Elsie has several of her creations in the commercial trade, but is still searching for the elusive 'true blue' rhododendron, with no trace of purple color in the flower."

She showed me her pollen bank. Nestled in dozens of neatly tagged gelatin capsules were anthers and pollen grains, not only from her garden but also mailed from elsewhere. Pollen must be gathered from unopened or freshly opened blossoms. Wind and insects can vector in foreign pollen soon after blossoms open and contaminate hybrids.

Jeanine prefers gelatin capsules because moisture can escape through them and be absorbed by the layer of calcium chloride desiccant in the bottom of the sealed storage jar. She cools fresh pollen for two or three weeks at 40 degrees F. before transferring it to the freezer. Rhododendron pollen can keep for about three years when frozen.

I learned that rhododendrons set prodigious numbers of seeds as fine as petunias. Jeanine germinates hybrid seeds in one-pint plastic freezer containers filled to within one inch of the top with moist milled sphagnum moss. She showed me her bank of three fluorescent light fixtures that illuminate a table with a surface area of sixteen square feet.

In this restricted space, she could grow plants in one hundred containers, without sunlight. Each container could hold fifty to one hundred seedlings, but there is no way her outside production and display area could absorb so many. So, Jeanine uses 75 percent of the lighted area for growing on transplanted seedlings of choice hybrids which she wishes to accelerate.

When the seedlings are ready to transplant, she transfers them to plastic flats filled with a mixture of peat, perlite, and finely ground fir bark. These are kept under fluorescent lights until time to transplant again, at which stage they are moved to their lean-to greenhouse. There, they are

(Right) On the deck behind their home, Jeanine and Rex enjoy the fruits of their labors, surrounded by the variegated Japanese maple, Acer palmatum *'Ukigomo', the pale yellow* R. *'Butterfly', a pink rhododendron the Smiths hope to identify, and the large coral* R. *'Fabia x bureauvii'.*

acclimated and transplanted to six-inch pots. The seedlings are fed periodically with a weak solution of water-soluble fertilizer.

Under such forcing, the seedlings can put on several flushes of growth and reach a height of six to eight inches the first year.

The first winter, the potted seedlings are protected in the greenhouse or cold frame. Root growth continues during the winter, and new top growth will begin the following spring. If a branched plant is desired, Jeanine will pinch or snap out the center bud to force side buds to develop. At each transplanting, Jeanine culls out the seedlings that show poor foliage.

"I can hardly wait to see the first blooms appear on my seedlings," Jeanine said. "By that time, at least two years will have passed since I started seeds of the hybrid under lights. Some seedlings will keep me waiting for as long as five years before they will bloom!

"First bloom is the moment of truth for hybrid seedlings. I have to be ruthless about eliminating those which are deficient in color or form: only about one out of one hundred seedlings makes it past this stage of evaluation. Even so, Rex has to condense the few survivors of trial rows to make room for new seedlings. As soon as they grow enough to take shape, I evaluate them for landscape potential. Perhaps one out of fifty may survive the second screening."

From the plants grown to this stage, Jeanine will choose the most promising for moving into a landscaped border for growing on to the next "go or no-go" stage. Each seedling is tagged with its heritage. Within a year or two, any shortcomings of the few surviving seedlings will be evident. It is painful to have to dig these up and give them to friends after a gestation period of up to ten years, but that's what happens to all but the crème de la crème. Jeanine asks her friends to grow her discards as "unnamed seedlings" and occasionally revisits them to double-check her judgment.

Jeanine's goal is to produce hybrid seedlings that are not just good, but distinct from and superior to both parents. That may qualify the seedling for registration with the ARS, provided no one else has beat her to the punch with a similar cross. Qualifying for registration is difficult; technically you could win a red, white, or blue ribbon in a prestigious show and still not have a cultivar worthy of introduction.

After this relentless scourging, only one out of one thousand hybrid seedlings may remain in the landscape border. At this stage comes the moment that Jeanine and Rex have been working toward; judgment of their work by their peers in rhododendron growing and hybridizing. They cut a large truss of blossoms, stick the stem in a bottle of water, and take it to the annual show of the Seattle chapter of the ARS. Every hybridizer's dream is to win a "Best New Hybrid" ribbon, for it can catch the attention of commercial growers. It is gratifying to develop a new

1)

2)

3)

4)

5)

6)

Hybridizing Rhododendrons

Here, Jeanine takes me through the steps involved in hybridizing rhododendrons. To prevent self-pollination, the blossom of the female parent is (1) emasculated by removing the anthers. Anthers and pollen are stored in gelatin capsules (2) tagged with the name of the donor cultivar and the date of collection. The pollen is transferred (3) by inserting the receptive stigma into a gelatin capsule containing pollen from the male parent. Jeanine uses fluorescent light fixtures for germinating and growing rhododendron crosses and species from seeds (4). In the greenhouse (5), potted-up seedlings and cuttings are grown to sufficient size for transplanting. Rex covers overwintering young plants (6) with a poly "tunnel," which is removed when the weather warms in the spring. Root growth continues over the winter, with new top growth appearing in the spring. At least two full years will have passed before the seedlings' first bloom.

Jeanine gathers rhododendron trusses for a show. Rear, left to right: R. augusti- nii, R. luteum, R. oreotrephes. Front, left to right: R. 'Hotei' x 'Tropicana' seed- ling, R. 'May Day', R. 'Hotei', R. 'Paprika Spiced'.

seedling that tops all others in shows, but even more fulfilling to see it increased for many home gardeners to enjoy.

Jeanine is not discouraged that, after so many years of educating her- self in hybridizing and showing, she has only one seedling that has been registered and has commercial potential. 'Apricot Fantasy' won the "Best New Hybrid" award in a Seattle chapter show and was increased for introduction on a limited basis for spring of 1989 planting. I understood the reason for her optimism when I saw some of the beautiful seedlings in her landscape borders. She has the touch!

While we toured the evaluation trials and borders in the back and side yards, Rex told me some of their secrets for growing rhododendrons in the landscape. "In our climate," he said, "proper soil conditioning and mulching can influence a rhododendron's ability to perform in full sun. I've tried several kinds of soil amendments and prefer to add pulverized fir bark when preparing the soil. I'm lucky to have a small diesel tractor with five chisel points on a drawbar. I can gear down and loosen the soil to a depth of twelve inches. Chiseling breaks up soil compacted by the log trucks, and drags out tree roots. I spread a three- to four-inch layer of bark and about four pounds of ammonium sulfate per one hundred square feet, and mix it into the soil with a tiller. The nitrogen speeds the conversion of the raw bark into humus.

"I work three other organic materials into the soil when I can get them: wood shavings, stable manure, and chipped wood from the power company and road maintenance crews. We supplement sawdust with nitrogen to avoid nitrogen drawdown. Sawdust breaks down quickly, but I think it is worth the effort of application. We have purchased topsoil occasionally, but it always seems to bring in weeds. Consequently, we prefer to amend the existing sandy soil with organic matter. Cheaper to do it that way, too!"

I like the setup Rex has for lining out hybrid seedlings in rows for first and second evaluations. He has installed a solid-set sprinkler irrigation system with 36-inch risers pinned against posts to hold them erect. Looking ahead to possible water conservation restrictions, he used water-conserving micro-sprinkler heads. Combined with organic mulches, the efficient sprinklers should minimize water use.

Rex feels that they are blessed with not having many insect or disease problems. Root weevils can become a nuisance but are controllable. Mildew sometimes appears on susceptible types, but he controls it quickly with mild fungicidal sprays.

I spent three days with Rex, Jeanine, their daughter, Erin, and the photographer, dodging in and out between rain showers. It was a

The Smiths show me the cold frame they use for winter protection and for hardening off seedlings.

Jeanine's prized creation, 'Apricot Fantasy', won the "Best New Hybrid" of the ARS.

delightful time because, with their cool spring weather, the rhododendron buds seemed to take forever to open. It gave me an opportunity to appreciate the great show that rhododendron buds can put on, and to enjoy the changing moods created by sun, shade, and showers.

Rex and Jeanine garden on a scale that would intimidate most gardeners. I asked how many hours Jeanine spent in the garden per week, on the average. "Oh, ten to fifteen hours a week," she answered; "more in the spring, less during the rainy winter season. Actually, I spend a lot of time in the garden just looking. I appreciate the principles of good garden design and have tried to express them in the front and side yards, and around the deck in the back. But, I believe the main purpose for a garden is to provide enjoyment for the owner, and should reflect his or her special interests. Good design can suffer when a person grows large numbers of a specialty plant. We've solved the old 'design versus plant collection' dilemma for now by locating our breeding and production grounds on the back of the property.

"I still have time," she said, "for my duties with the Seattle chapter of ARS. I feel I have benefited from the organization and should give something in return. We in the chapter are especially proud of our contribution to Meerkerk Rhododendron Gardens on Whidbey Island, near Seattle. It was given to the chapter a few years ago by Anne Meerkerk so that her large collection of rhododendrons and companion plants could be preserved. A hybrid test garden has been established for rating the performance of new hybrids in our climate. There are acres of woodland gardens for strolling and enjoying mature rhododendrons and towering forests. This large garden is open to the public during the spring and summer and should continue to improve with the work of the chapter."

Rex was less definite about how much time he spends in the garden. It was as if I had asked him which leg of his pants he pulls up first. He thought for a while and said, "I really can't say for sure. I'm usually home four days between trips and put most of my spare time to building and gardening. We have the opportunity to travel but, at this stage in our lives, most of our leisure time is spent gardening. We like it here. We've put a lot of ourselves into this home and garden."

He looked off into the distance and mused, "Then, again, Jeanine and I have talked about visiting the rhododendron gardens in Great Britain and perhaps New Zealand. . . ."

Something tells me that, in a few years, when Erin has flown the nest, Rex and Jeanine will be looking for a larger piece of property, nearer the water for frost protection. If only one of each one thousand hybrid seedlings she now has under way makes it to the landscape border, they will soon run out of space. It appears that Stage 4 of Rhodoholism is about to set in!

More about Rhododendrons

To grow rhododendrons that remain beautiful and flower-filled from youth to old age requires more attention than growing, say, vegetables or herbs. Climate is the principal success factor, for without a hospitable balance of humidity, protection from intense sun and temperature extremes, and acid soil, even the hardy new cultivars will not flourish.

Purchasing Rhododendrons

To determine how rhododendrons will do in your area, make a few excursions to large home gardens in the vicinity, gardens with a few years behind them. Rhododendrons increase in beauty and stateliness with age. The garden owner can tell you if your climate is so fickle that it will damage or destroy rhododendrons periodically. Take note, especially, of his siting of rhododendrons in respect to shade, drainage, wind flow, and adjacent trees or shrubs.

If you are persuaded to go on, check out the better retail nurseries in your area at peak rhododendron time . . . early through late spring. Members of local ARS chapters can steer you to them. If the nursery offers only a few plants of rhododendrons and other acid-loving species such as pieris, leucothoe, and mountain laurel, it is a safe bet that rhododendrons are only marginally adapted to your area. At that point, you may decide either to find a mail-order source of hardy modern hybrids, or transfer your attention to the more ubiquitous azaleas.

Next, write to a few of the commercial rhododendron growers for catalogs. Most are located in prime rhododendron-growing areas and have retail stores as well. At first, patronize only those in your part of the country because they can offer you sound advice on adapted cultivars and species of rhododendrons and azaleas. They can tell you how to prepare the soil, using locally available materials. They will tell you how to control the few insect and disease problems of rhododendrons and will usually offer you a broader selection of cultivars than most general retail nurserymen.

On the other hand, if you live in an area where rhododendrons are popular, by all means start with your local nurseryman. Certain retail nurseries offer extraordinary assortments of rhododendrons.

I love to read rhododendron catalogs. As with most horticultural catalogs, they describe cultivars so compellingly that you find yourself condensing your wildly optimistic "want list" to a "need list" and finally to an "absolutely can't do without" list. But, at the core of descriptions is rock-solid information such as the relative hardiness of the cultivar, its average height and spread at ten years of age, foliage characteristics, and preference for protection or exposure in your climate zone. It is hard to fit all that on a plant tag in a retail nursery.

Adaptability

Before you invest in the cultivars on your "absolutely must have" list, you might consider contacting the ARS to determine if a chapter is based anywhere near you. If not, the next best alternative is to visit the nearest botanical garden or arboretum. At the reception desk ask if they have plantings of rhododendrons, or literature on their culture. Another good information source is your local association of Master Gardeners, accessible through your County Extension Office.

Site Selection

Next, consider the sites you have for planting rhododendrons. Here's what they like:

● High humidity to balance evaporation from their broad leaves. If summers are dry or hot in your area, plan on installing sprinklers.

● Protection from intense sun, either by fog or high, filtered shade. Only in favored areas can rhododendrons thrive in full sun. Hybrids vary in their tolerance for sun; as a rule, the smaller the leaf, the more sun the plant can tolerate. The small-leaved alpine types are exceptions; they are native to misty mountain ridges and can't tolerate hot, drying sun.

● Protection from rapid, drastic fluctuations in temperature, either by proximity to bodies of water or provision of a favorable microclimate, where drying winds are blocked off.

● Porous, well-drained, highly organic soil, pH 4.5 to 5.5.

Soil and Planting

How you plant rhododendrons depends on whether you have sandy or clay soil. With clay or clay loam soils, till the soil and spread a 3-inch layer of coarse sphagnum peat moss, pulverized pine bark, or, in the West, composted sawmill waste. Work it into the soil.

Do not dig deep planting holes. Instead, make up a pile of planting mixture composed of equal parts of organic matter, sand, and garden soil pulverized by tilling. Set the new plant on top of the tilled soil. Tap it out of the container or, if the root ball is wrapped in burlap, remove the pins or ties and let it fall flat.

- Carefully scratch away the outer ½ to 1 inch of the root ball to expose root tips. This will help them grow into the surrounding planting mix rather than retreat into the old restricted root ball.

- Shovel the prepared planting mix around the root ball. Firm it down by hand. Be generous. Build up the soil level even with the top of the root ball, extending out at least 2 feet from the trunk. A skinny little cone of planter mixture will dry out quickly or wash away.

- Plant as described above if your soil is a shallow layer of sandy or loamy soil overlying clay. But, on deep sandy or gravelly, fast-draining soils a different approach is called for.

- Spread a 3- to 4-inch layer of organic matter over the soil and turn it under as deep as you can with a spade or tiller. Thoroughly mix it with the soil. Dig generous planting holes. Set the plant in place so that the top of the root ball stands 1 to 2 inches above the surrounding soil. Gently scarify all sides of the root ball to encourage rooting. Fill around the plant with the excavated soil and firm it down with your hands.

Watering and Mulching

Before mulching, set a sprinkler near the transplanted rhododendron and let it run at low pressure for an hour. Then, spread a 3-inch-deep mulch around the plant, extending out 2 or 3 feet. Finally, pull the mulch away from the trunk of the plant to eliminate the possibility of rotting.

You can select from many materials for mulching: pinestraw, shredded hardwood leaves, composted sawdust, woodchips, hardwood bark mulch, or forest floor leaf mold. Be sure to pile sawdust with a little manure or a sprinkling of ammonium sulfate and garden soil for a month or so before use. Wet the pile and cover loosely with plastic to hasten heating. Raw sawdust can cause recurring problems with nitrogen drawdown if not composted before mulching. Chipped green wood, pinestraw, shredded leaves, and bark mulches rarely induce nitrogen shortages.

Jeanine Smith advises, "Take care the first year that the newly transplanted rhododendron does not dry out. Until roots have spread out into the surrounding soil, the root ball is especially susceptible to drying out. When this happens, overhead watering can fail not only because the canopy of leaves tends to shed water but also because bone-dry soil can be difficult to rewet. You may need to lay a hose or a sprinkler directly on the root ball and allow it to run slowly until the dry soil is thoroughly moist."

Fertilizing

It is in feeding rhododendrons that many gardeners get into trouble; they apply too little or too much, too early or too late. Just remember that, in nature, rhododendrons get by with a low level of plant nutrients, mostly derived from rotting vegetation and ozone nitrogen from thunderstorms. Micronutrients are usually in good supply, due partly to the low soil pH in natural populations of rhododendrons. When the soil pH level begins to creep up, iron deficiency chlorosis can show up.

In most areas, two light applications of fertilizer per year are sufficient, but in coastal California, where there is little danger of cold-weather damage, three light applications may be made. Organic fertilizers such as cottonseed meal, soybean meal, or blood meal release nitrogen in the ammoniacal form preferred for rhododendrons. Or, you can use specially compounded azalea/rhododendron food. Application rates are one-third those for organic fertilizers: ⅛ cup for 18-inch plants; ¼ cup for 24-inch plants; and ½ cup for 36-inch rhododendrons. Top-dress around plants in early spring and again at blossom drop. In coastal California feed again just after fall rains begin.

The danger in feeding after midsummer comes from "tenderizing" the plants. They should go into the winter "hard," not growing rapidly.

The principal danger in overfeeding is the stimulation of overly long internodes, which results in lanky, sparsely leaved plants or, in extreme cases, failure to bloom. This can happen if organic fertilizers are applied in the spring when the soil is too cool for them to break down. The gardener sees no response to the fertilizer and applies more. Warm weather increases the soil temperature and the activity of organisms that decompose organic fertilizers. Suddenly, the plant is given a strong push into vegetative growth instead of a gentle, steady pull.

One of the most efficient feeding programs combines late fall mulching with an application of a slow-release plant food such as Osmocote 14-14-14 Controlled Release Fertilizer. Since Osmocote ceases releasing nutrients at soil temperatures below 40 degrees F., there is no danger of stimulating winter growth.

Spread Osmocote at the recommended rate and cover with 2 to 3 inches of organic mulch. Little or no nutrient release will take place until spring weather warms the mulch to the depth of the Osmocote. All the nutrients will be metered out within 90 to 120 days. The noted azalea enthusiast Fred Galle cautions that, because of the high percentage of nitrogen in the Osmocote formulation, application rates should be those recommended on the package for fertilizer-sensitive species.

You can opt to apply Osmocote at half the recommended rate and supplement with a top-dressing of organic fertilizer at half rate when the blossoms drop. The organic fertilizer should supply most of the micronutrients needed by rhododendrons except where the soil and water are limy or basic. There, chelated iron may be needed as well.

When it comes to mulching, you could do worse than to follow Rex Smith's example, but it is possible to overdo it. The idea is to simulate the layer of litter that carpets forest floors. If you lose plants to root rot, poor drainage and mulching may have to share the blame . . . for if you plant a rhododendron too deep, mulching will compound the problem.

Housekeeping

Ideally, you should aim for two flushes of new vegetative growth of moderate length followed by the formation of flower buds in late summer and fall.

When rhododendrons are small, and a dense, well-rounded form is preferred, the terminal buds can be pinched or snipped off to force more lateral buds to grow into shoots. Do this when new growth appears, or soon after blooming.

Cutting back forces more compact, less leggy growth. New growth will come from the buds below the shears.

Housekeeping should not be neglected; spent rhododendron blossoms should be picked up and composted and seed pods should be snapped off as they begin to form. With a little practice, you will learn to prune rhododendrons to produce more flushes of growth per season, thus shorter internodes and bushier, leafier plants.

Pests and Diseases

Rhododendrons have few serious insect and disease problems, but those need to be dealt with promptly and firmly. As with any broad-leaved evergreen, you don't want to risk allowing insects to disfigure leaves, because they are not replaced every year.

The rhododendron lace bug is probably the worst pest; the tiny nymphs suck plant juices and mottle the leaves, depositing unsightly black excreta on the undersides. You can't confuse their damage with that of the rhododendron bud moth; their grubs tunnel inside leaves, twigs, and the buds of flowers and new growth.

If you see sawdust around stems and breakage from the weakening, suspect the rhododendron borer; it is most troublesome in the East. Your State Cooperative Extension Service can suggest a spray program to control these and other local pests.

Diseases are relatively few; mildew on leaves is easily identifiable and dealt with. Root rots and the resulting wilting are symptomatic of poor drainage. Taking up and repositioning the plant may work, but usually comes too late to save the plants.

Once you have braved the mainstream of rhododendron growing, you may find yourself digging out, containerizing, and selling or giving away some of the more ornate rhododendron hybrids you acquired early in your hobby, to make room for less-formal species. A home garden can accommodate just so many prima donnas, each trying to upstage the other. But however your collection may evolve, the rewards will be gratifying.

Hostas

Jim and Jill Wilkins: a Michigan physician's dexterity and his wife's artistic eye team up to create new vistas for hostas.

Dainty, low-growing, edging-type hostas act as a foil for tall iris. H. 'Gold Drop' lines the path; at lower left is H. 'Princess Kara-futo', backed by Hosta longis-sima; at right is H. ventricosa 'Aureo-Margin-ata'.

*H*ow can it be possible? A foliage plant with only four basic leaf colors and unremarkable flowers has become the leading shade plant for American gardens. For the answer, all you have to do is see a well-grown collection of hostas. Plant breeders have achieved outstanding foliage color combinations in shades of green, gold, white, and blue-green, and fascinating leaf shapes. They have perfected plant sizes and growth habits for every garden situation.

Plant breeders understand that the true glory of the several species of the genus *Hosta* is in the size, shape, color, texture, and stance of the leaves, not necessarily in the flowers. You hardly notice that the basic foliage colors are rather ordinary because the variations are as endless as cloud formations on a June afternoon. The flower spikes of most hostas lack the visual impact of sun-loving flowers but are valuable because so few flower species will bloom in moderate shade.

Plant breeders are now working to increase the size and longevity of hosta flower spikes, and the range of colors. As they stand, today's simple hosta flowers, in shades of purple, lavender, or white, combine well with the strong foliage colors without clashing or competing for attention. Some hosta cultivars have a mild, pleasant fragrance, especially the hybrids derived from the white flowered *H. plantaginea*. When mature, hosta seed heads can be dried for use in winter bouquets and wreaths. Hostas begin flowering as early as June with some varieties, and flowering continues for several weeks.

One characteristic of hostas that varies dramatically is the "stance" of the plants . . . the angle at which stems and leaves are held. Some mature plants are tall, open, and airy. Others have huge, overlapping leaves that look like shingles on a roof and shed rain accordingly. Other leaves are like cupped hands; they hold enough water to attract birds for a sip. The visual density of plants is just as important as color and mature height and the little "added attractions" such as fancy leaf formations of certain cultivars.

Visitors to hosta collections are awed by the huge variation in plant sizes between cultivars. Some are man-high, with leaves as large as tobacco plants; others grow to a height of only two or three inches. The wee hostas such as *H. venusta* were so valued and jealously guarded in their Japanese homeland that introduction to the United States was delayed by many years.

We need only to look at the place of hostas in Japanese gardens today to predict a new use for them in this country. With little or no open garden space around homes, the Japanese long ago turned to growing hostas in containers. On the northern islands they move hostas indoors before cold weather comes, so that growth is not checked by a period of dormancy. The Japanese also chop and steam the petioles as we do asparagus, or sauté them. American gardeners may not be ready for hosta omelettes, however.

In this country, the popularity of hostas is greatest in the Midwest and lower New England, and decreases as you go south and west. Although they are valued for performance under conditions that would either kill or discourage most flowering species, they don't like hot, dry weather. They grow pretty well in the central and upper South and Northwest, but only a few rugged cultivars will survive in the deep South and dry, warm Southwest. Where adapted, hostas have the happy habit of quickly settling in and rounding into a colorful mound. A little plant in a four-inch pot can increase in size and beauty a dozen times over during the frost-free growing season. They look good from late spring into early fall; some cultivars are attractive when yellowed by fall cold but in hot, dry climates

merely look weatherbeaten. Hostas have few diseases and pests, except for slugs and snails. Hostas are very cold tolerant, yet can endure short periods of high heat and humidity such as occur during midwestern summers. They shade out weeds and require little maintenance. They give much but ask little from the gardener in return.

The dramatic increase in the popularity of hostas came late, in comparison with other perennials, and is largely due to enthusiastic promotion by the American Hosta Society. The United States boom actually began before the founding of the society in 1969. It may have been sparked by the need for more and better shade-tolerant plants. The many homes built during the decades following World War II are rapidly becoming shaded by trees planted by the new owners. As these trees grow, they complicate gardening with sun-loving shrubs, flowers, and food plants. Consequently, homeowners are looking for colorful, shade-tolerant plants. Potted hosta plants displayed in the shade plant sections of nurseries sell themselves.

The world of hostas is big, and can be bewildering to beginners. Hundreds of cultivars appear in catalogs of specialists, so many that commercial growers must drop obsolete varieties in order to add new ones. Still, the number of cultivars offered in catalogs is bound to increase substantially. It is rather sad that so many beginners plant their gardens with the limited selection of old varieties available from mass marketers because some are decades behind the times in plant density, color impact, and leaf elaboration.

To assist gardeners in learning about hostas, the American Hosta Society has divided the genus *Hosta* into four rather loose categories: "edgers": compact, rather upright; "groundcovers": low-growing, spreading mostly by rhizomes; "background": tall and rather massive; and "specimens": any size plant, but it must look exceptionally good when displayed alone.

No such categories existed when hostas first appeared in this country, probably in the early 1800s. No one knows for sure who had the honor of planting the first hosta garden in the United States. Plants and seeds came through Europe on their way here, but the genus is native to Japan, Korea, and China. Hosta plants are very long-lived and some eastern U.S.A. gardens could still be populated with descendants of the original imports. A second group arrived when the Japanese began trading with the occidental world.

Dormant hosta plants and seeds could be transported easily by settlers and, once established in their new homes on the frontier, could be divided and passed around. It is a testimony to the goodness of the human spirit that, amidst the confusion and apprehension of moving by wagon or riverboat to a hostile frontier, someone thought to bring starts of flowers.

A more significant avenue of entry for hostas opened during the nineteenth century, when advanced plant hobbyists brought improved selections here from England. "Hostamania" was epidemic there in Victorian days, not just among the wealthy, but among the inhabitants of cottages and row houses.

Today, hostas are second only to *Hemerocallis* (daylilies) in popularity among herbaceous perennials. Their fascinating diversity in the home landscape is abundantly demonstrated in the garden of Dr. James and Jill Wilkins.

The Wilkinses gave me a tour of their elegantly landscaped hosta collection during taping for The Victory Garden. *The Japanese painted fern,* Athyrium goeringanum, *right foreground, combines well with* Hosta 'Northern Halo,' *left front.*

Jim and Jill Wilkins's large and lovely garden is the display area for their hobby of breeding and growing hostas, and for Jill's growing collection of dwarf conifers. The garden provides a serene setting for showing about twenty-five hundred plants of seven hundred hosta cultivars. It is one of five large private hosta gardens in the Jackson, Michigan, area that drew the twentieth annual convention of the American Hosta Society to their city in June 1988. About two hundred hosta enthusiasts trooped through the gardens to see their favorite plant in imaginative settings.

Visitors to the Wilkinses' garden enter through a path that meanders around hillocks, peninsulas, and islands, and offers new vistas at every turn. Large conifers, remnants of the forest that once clothed their property, have been thinned and limbed up to provide light shade for hostas. All the free-form display beds are of generous size to accommodate many groups of the smaller cultivars, individual specimen plants of massive hostas, and edgings of miniature cultivars. While all the hostas are stairstepped by height, groups of taller plants are occasionally brought forward to interrupt the regularity. Colors and variegations are placed for greatest total effect. The cultivars with more white or light yellow in the foliage variegations stand farther back in the shade of trees and the green or blue varieties are brought out toward stronger sunlight.

It must take great self-control to restrain a hosta enthusiast from planting display beds solidly with hostas. The Wilkinses leave enough room between groups of hostas to plant complementary perennials and groundcovers. These make the hostas stand out from the background, and separate the groups visually. Jill has taken a special interest in astilbes, epimediums, and primroses, shade-tolerant perennials that look good interplanted among hostas. Some of these bloom before and after the peak season for hostas. Jill has a good eye for color and avoids the jarring hues that would conflict with hosta foliage.

The garden slopes down from the house to a large grassy clearing in the back, then upward to meet a looming wall of dark, tall pine trees. Considerable forethought and work capitalized on the site and broke it into a number of intimate vistas, while maintaining flow and integrity.

Hostas   **33**

Jim and Jill started by identifying the major "overlook" points into their garden. While one stood at an overlook, the other moved around the yard with a flag atop a tall pole for visibility. In this way, they identified the trees that had to be removed; the stand was so dense that nothing but moss would grow in the gloom. Once they completed thinning and limbing up the survivors to let more sun in, and to open up views, they used the flagpoles again to locate planting sites for choice trees or shrubs.

With the foundation of the garden established, they laid out a garden hose to outline "islands" beneath the shade of the large pine trees. They sprayed the area with a nonselective herbicide to kill broad-leaved perennial weeds and the invasive perennial quack grass. They had the soil tested, and spaded in the recommended nutrient sources and lots of organic matter. The islands became raised beds, 6 to 8 inches in height, which is just high enough to avoid their being flooded during thunderstorms.

To add interest, they sighted-in and laid out curving "berms," built-up hillocks that look perfectly natural. The berms serve to guide the numerous visitors into and through the back yard, and out the other side. They were major constructions and required severals loads of hauled-in topsoil to build them up to the desired height.

On the berms, they first applied a layer of chipped wood mulch to reduce soil erosion, then planted Jill's expanding collection of choice dwarf conifers. She placed the all-green types in full sun and the variegated, golden, and silver types where shade from afternoon sun would prevent browning and fading. Dwarf conifers are so appealing that you want to reach out and touch them; elevating them well above ground level lets you appreciate them fully. In sunny areas between islands and berms, a thick turf of bluegrass and fine-leaved fescue sets off the scene as would a pretty frame around a picture. Jim and Jill edge the turf with hoes, to keep it from encroaching on their ornamentals. Somehow, the natural line between turf and flower beds looks better than an artificial edging.

The Wilkinses have most of the heavy labor of garden construction behind them. After twelve years of work, their garden has expanded (to three acres), as has their enjoyment of it. They have added a service area well off from the side of the house, a large barn with an attached greenhouse, a new lath house for propagation, a food garden with numerous fruit trees, and a pen full of noisy "watch geese." Although each addition is functional, each is attractive, blends into the landscape, and agrees with the architecture of the home.

Both Jim and Jill came by gardening naturally. Born during World War II when money was scarce, Jim's birth was "paid for with gladiolus and Shasta daisies." In their Victory Garden, Jim's parents grew not only food for the war effort, but also flowers to cut and sell for extra income.

(Above) A tri-
color beech fills
the space between
the low hostas
and the leggy
pines. 'Gay-
feather' and
'Curly Top' in the
left foreground
are backed by
'Golden Cas-
cades'.

(Right) The
highly popular
and adaptable H.
'Frances Wil-
liams' is set off
by the yellow-
flowered peren-
nial Corydalis
lutea.

Jill's parents were good gardeners. At their home in Ann Arbor, they followed the traditional division of food gardening for men and flower growing for women. Her mother's specialty is roses.

During Jim's long years in pre-med and med school, Jill completed two degrees, in zoology and education. While both were putting in long hours at school and living in a low-income housing development, they found time to beautify their little home with flowers and shrubs. Neighbors saw what they had accomplished and began to plant surrounding yards. Now, after more than twenty years and countless occupants, that little cluster of houses still boasts remarkably beautiful plantings. Their gardening had to be curtailed while Jim served his residency and completed a tour of duty in medicine with the U.S. army, but resumed in earnest upon his return to civilian life. Three daughters blessed the family; all are interested in gardening and environmental preservation.

Jim and Jill recall fondly the day they became interested in hostas. They were already good gardeners but their efforts lacked focus. Then, they visited the garden of a man who was to become their friend and mentor, Herb Benedict. He grows and breeds hostas at nearby Hillsdale, Michigan. "Herb gave us a start with numerous cultivars of hostas, convinced us to join the American Hosta Society, and showed me the elements of hybridization," said Jim.

"Hostas got us so fired up that we have persuaded a number of friends to take up gardening as a hobby and, in particular, with hostas. We are involved in several community projects, but bringing others into gardening may prove to be our most important contribution."

At Hosta Society meetings Jim listened closely to experienced hybridizers to learn their techniques and to get ideas on areas of hosta improvement that are within the reach of amateur plant breeders. Hosta breeding isn't a simple "A + B = C" proposition; the parentage of modern cultivars is so complex that it is impossible to predict what will come out of crosses. Success has a lot to do with the number of seedlings a breeder can grow and evaluate.

In selecting parent plants, breeders look for unusual color combinations and patterns, and graceful plants with an attractive ratio of leaf size to plant size. They lean toward hostas that emerge later in the spring and so avoid frost damage.

I asked Jim for some of the goals of hosta breeders. He said, "I think that more attention will be paid to hosta flowers and fragrance, which are now considered distinctly secondary to the colorful foliage. And, with the gardeners in the upper South using more hostas, I expect to see more sun-resistant cultivars. Not all cultivars are genetically stable and tend to revert to solid colors or throw color variations in the perimeter divisions taken from clumps. I think we will find ways to keep cultivars true to type. Now that we have learned from the Japanese how to keep hostas

Jill grooms a dwarf Alberta spruce planted among the hostas. The variegated border plantings are H. *'Louisa' and* H. *'Bold Ribbons'. At lower right is 'Gold Regal'; at far left,* H. *'Krossa Regal'.*

from going dormant, I think we will find ways to use them indoors during the winter as foliage plants. That is bound to have an effect on breeding programs. Certainly, we will see more hostas grown in containers, which will open up new applications for the small-framed cultivars."

Jim is by nature methodical and thorough; here's how he organized his hosta breeding program:

"First, I set up a system for record-keeping: good notes and labeling are essential. I use 4×6 cards to record crosses—one card for each plant. I also plan ahead which crosses I want to make, with a specific goal in mind.

"The night before I make the cross, I remove the petals from the pod parent's flower, that is, the flower that would be opening the next day. This prevents bees from being attracted to the flower and pollinating it instead of my doing it.

"The next morning, I remove stamens from the pollen parent and carry them to the pod parent. I hold the filament of the stamen like a paintbrush and literally paint the pollen from the anther onto the stigma, which is at the tip of the pistil. If the pistil is receptive, I can see the pollen stick to it and coat the tip.

"I use color-coded wire from telephone cable to mark the cross. When I have completed transferring the pollen, I loop a two-inch piece of colored wire around the stem (pedicel) below the flower. Then, I record the

Starting Hostas from Seed

Jim Wilkins explains how he starts hostas from seeds. Seedlings are started in cell-packs (1) like the one shown here next to dried seed pods. Later, the tiny seedlings are transferred to book planters like this one (2), where their roots grow long and strong. The book planters allow Jim

1)

2)

3)

to transplant the young hostas with little or no root disturbance. Three stages of seedlings are shown here (3): just after sprouting, about one month old, and seven months old, ready for transplanting. After a winter under lights (4), the seedlings are transplanted to the lath house, where Jim can give them concentrated attention for the first year. Optimum fertilizer, moisture, and drainage maintain vigorous growth until the plants are large enough to be evaluated.

4)

color of the wire on the index card identifying the cross by pod parent and pollen parent.

"When the seed pods are ripe, the seeds will turn black. I harvest the hybridized pods then, put them into small paper bags, and label them with the parentage of the cross. The seed pods will split open in a few weeks. I clean them by rubbing gently and carefully blowing away the chaff.

"The seeds can be handled in three ways: if I have room under the fluorescent lights, I will plant them immediately. Or, if the soil is in condition for planting, I will plant them in short, labeled rows in the garden. If not, I will store them in a sealed jar with a desiccant until spring. I have heard that hosta seed is difficult to carry from season to season, but this has not been my experience."

Normally, a time span of two years from harvesting hybrid seeds is required to produce plants large enough for evaluation of foliage characteristics and plant habit. After a few years' experience with the slow process of growing new hybrid hostas from seeds, Jim decided to see what he could do to speed it up. He installed a battery of fluorescent light fixtures in the basement and experimented with burning the lights for various time spans. "Actually, I stumbled onto the answer," he said. "I forgot and left the lights burning day and night over my flats of hosta seedlings, instead of the usual fifteen to eighteen hours. To my surprise, I learned that, in the seedling stage, hostas grow faster under lights that burn twenty-four hours a day.

"The fixtures are on chains and can be lowered to no more than two inches above the tops of seed flats. The gentle warmth and intense radiant energy from the tubes keeps the surface of the potting medium at 70 to 75 degrees F., the preferred range for germinating hosta seeds. The twenty-four-hour lighting not only causes seedlings to grow faster but also to form superior root systems."

Jim uses a standard seed flat mixture of peat moss and vermiculite to start hosta seeds and covers them to about three times their diameter with potting medium. Seeds come up within ten to fourteen days with the fluorescent lights lowered to where they nearly touch the tops of the seed flats. "The intensity of the lights falls off drastically as the fixtures are raised," he explained. "As the seedlings grow, I raise the light fixtures a link or two at a time on the supporting chains, but never higher than two to three inches above the tops of plants."

Jim also experimented with various sizes and types of pots for growing on the seedlings he sprouted and grew in flats of soil. He settled on a plastic "book" planter that opens into mirror-image halves, hinged on one side. The book has long concavities that are filled with moist potting medium. The small, rooted seedlings from under the lights are pricked out from flats and positioned so that their tops protrude from the book when it is closed and snapped shut. The planted book is tipped up and stood on edge in holding trays, plants up, of course.

I asked Jim why he chose the book planters instead of standard pots. "The secret of the book planters," he replied, "is that the long, cylindrical root balls hold more soil than small pots of the same diameter, and give roots room to grow long and strong. When spring frost danger is past and hostas can be planted outside, the books can be popped open and the plants tipped out with little or no root disturbance. I feel that the long, strong root systems get my seedlings off to a faster start.

"I move the trays of plants in books out to the solar greenhouse in March, where I have black-painted drums of water against a reflecting wall. Even at that early date, the drums will have absorbed enough heat from the sun to protect plants from freezing at night. Ours is a south-facing, lean-to greenhouse with a slanted glass front. Nothing would be gained by moving plants there earlier because winter days are short and dark at our latitude. By April, hostas in the greenhouse begin responding to the increasing heat and longer, brighter days. I want them to grow rapidly and to be ready for transfer to the lath house or garden spots by late May. I wouldn't dare put hostas into an unheated greenhouse in March were it not for the tempering effect provided by five 55-gallon drums. They absorb daytime heat and radiate it at night to hold temperatures at 45 degrees Fahrenheit or higher. I have a backup gas heating system but have never had to use it."

As the last stage in accelerated propagation, Jim takes the now-sizable seedlings from the greenhouse and sets them in deep binlike planting beds of potting soil under shade in his lath house. He has one hundred square feet of these waist-high planting bins, space enough to plant three hundred hosta seedlings.

"The lath house is much more than a garden decoration," says Jim. "Beneath 50 percent shade from the lath, and protected on one side from wind, many seedlings will flower the first year. Controlled-release fertilizer, excellent drainage, and abundant moisure push the seedlings into optimum growth rates. I couldn't give my seedlings that kind of attention if they were scattered around the garden or lined out in nursery rows."

The end result of the accelerated propagation is a time span of only ten to twelve months from harvesting and planting hybrid seeds to producing plants large enough for evaluation of foliage characteristics and plant habit. The old method of propagation required two full years. Through the American Hosta Society, Jim published a technical paper on the subject: "Accelerated Growth of Hosta" in *The Hosta Journal* (No. 55).

The few seedlings that survive Jim's rigorous process of selection for color, variegation, vigor, and uniqueness are grown in the garden for

(Above) Raised beds in the lath house are at a good height for evaluating hybrid seedlings.

(Below) Handsome hostas: the gold in the foreground is H. 'Ultraviolet Light', at the right edge is H. 'Fort Knox'. The green hostas are hybrid seedlings bred by Jim Wilkins and registered in 1989.

Masters of the Victory Garden

another year to note their flower color, size, and fragrance, and to measure the height and spread of the mature plant. If any are felt to be sufficiently good, and distinct from existing cultivars, they will be named and their parentage registered with the American Hosta Society.

"Out of every thousand seedlings I grow from crosses," said Jim, "perhaps one plant will be sufficiently novel to justify introduction. But, I don't throw the others away; I plant the other 999 in the vegetable garden. Jill and I grow them to use as gifts for visitors, family, and friends. Every now and then, we'll get sentimental, dig up an unregistered hybrid seedling, and plant it in the hosta garden. It may not be unique, but it is one I just can't bear to part with."

I asked Jim what he feels lies ahead for hostas. "Bigeneric hybrids could be possible," he said, "and who knows what can be achieved with gene splicing? My hope would be the addition of the red/orange spectrum to foliage colors. Now, we are limited to shades of green and blue-green, plus gold, yellow, cream white, and silver.

"Above all," he continued, "I expect to see the Hosta Society institute tighter controls on registration to discourage the introduction of cultivars that are similar in many respects to existing hostas. There must be two thousand named cultivars, but even the experts have difficulty identifying hostas when they venture beyond the five hundred or so most popular cultivars."

Jim and Jill are concerned that beginners might be put off by the sheer numbers of hosta cultivars. They suggested this "starter list" to fit a cross-section of hostas into a small garden. In their list, the initial "H" indicates the genus *Hosta*, "Aureo-marginata" means simply "gold-edged," and "nebulosa" means "cloudlike."

- *H.* 'Hadspen Blue': Groundcover type; blue foliage.
- *H.* 'Wide Brim': Specimen type; blue-green leaves, irregularly margined with cream.
- *H.* 'Gayfeather': White-centered green.
- *H.* 'Aspen Gold': Medium height; gold, highly seersucked plant; lots of substance.
- *H. ventricosa* 'Aureo-marginata': Groundcover type; large green leaves with irregular margins of yellow to white.
- *H. tokudama* 'Aureo-nebulosa': Rare; textured green leaves with blue streaks; short stems.
- *H.* 'Blue Umbrellas': Large-leaved, blue, background type.
- *H.* 'Tot-Tot': Dwarf, with distinctive wedge-shaped dark green to blue-green leaves.
- *H. montana* 'Aureo-marginata': Large background type; huge glossy-green leaves with irregular margins; award winner.

- *H.* 'Gold Standard': Groundcover type; pale yellow-geen with green margins.
- *H.* 'Krossa Regal': A popular background type; blue-gray leaves and very tall flower spikes.

The Wilkinses caution beginners that only a few of these select cultivars will be available in retail garden centers, which tend to offer the old favorites.

As for Jill's striking combinations of dwarf conifers that set off the hostas in the Wilkinses' landscape, she recommends the following cultivars in her garden:

Chamaecyparis (false cypress)
    C. obtusa 'Filicoides'
    C. obtusa 'Corraliformis'
    C. pisifera 'Little Jamie'
    C. pisifera 'Snow'
    C. pisifera 'Filifera Nana'
Microbiota decussata (Siberian carpet cypress)
Picea (spruce)
    P. abies 'Little Gem'
    P. abies 'Pygmaea'
    P. abies 'Conica'
    P. abies 'Nidiformis'
    P. abies 'Gregoryiana Parsoni'
Tsuga (hemlock)
    T. canadensis 'Bennett'
    T. canadensis 'Gentsch White'
    T. canadensis 'Jacqueline Verkade'
    T. canadensis 'Lewisi'
    T. canadensis 'Sargenti'

She also added, "Hostas look good, as well, with *Buxus, Ilex, Kalmia, Rhododendron, Azalaea,* and, I suspect, *Pieris.*"

"Given no more hostas than we have today," says Jim, "a home gardener just beginning to collect hostas for landscaping will find a lifetime of fun and challenge. As for me, I can come home from a frustrating day at the office, feeling out of sorts with the world, and just ten minutes in my hosta garden will straighten me out. During the winter, I can unwind by inspecting the seedlings in the basement to see if that one-in-a-million breakthrough has finally occurred. It's a good life, and I recommend it to everyone!"

More about Hostas

Climate has so much bearing on success with hostas that I called on friends who are commercial growers for advice, and asked the Wilkinses to put me through a short course on hosta growing.

Sources

Hosta plants lend themselves to both mail-order and retail sales. They can be shipped while dormant or grown in pots in greenhouses and sold as young plants. Local plant farms can dig up the hostas of your choice and sell them to you at any time during the growing season. Mail-order companies offer the newest cultivars, while retailers tend to offer mostly the old favorites, some of which are still highly rated.

Some producers grow plants in the field, others in greenhouses, still others by tissue culture. The advantages of tissue culture are that plants can be mass produced, thereby increasing availability and (eventually) lowering cost; systemic plant diseases such as virus can be eliminated, allowing healthy plants to reach their full potential. Someday, micropropagation may solve the problem of the color changes that come with age on some hosta cultivars: some take years to develop typical patterns, others tend to revert to the all-green color, especially in new growth coming from the margins of crowns. Tissue-culturing of hostas is now done mostly in the early increase stages of valuable new hybrids.

When ordering hostas, it is always a good idea to inquire if the varieties in which you are interested will perform well in your climate. While most cultivars are widely adapted, some, for reasons not clearly understood, have a distinct preference for certain areas of the country. One condition is universally liked by hostas, regardless of region: protection from wind. Windswept areas dry out rapidly and plants are subject to breakage of petioles.

Plant Performance

Experienced hosta growers know that catalogs should be used only as guides and that there is no such thing as a hard-and-fast description. For example:

Plant height and spread can vary considerably, due to the latitude of your area affecting day length, the amount and distribution of moisture, drainage, and the prevailing level of plant nutrients.

Flowering and foliage color can be affected by the degree and hours of shade. Beds in full sun and watered sparsely will flower more heavily and foliage colors will be richer, but there is always the chance of marginal scorch during extremely hot, dry, windy weather, especially on the lighter-colored cultivars.

The hostas with blue foliage prefer locations near a pool or on a streambank, where the high humidity keeps the air cooler. Some growers achieve this effect by modifying their soil highly with organic matter so that it can evaporate lots of moisture while retaining enough to meet the needs of plants' metabolism. In the South, growers employ sprinklers to keep the humidity high during hot, dry weather.

Shade Quality

The quality of sunlight and shade can differ from area to area. In some gardens, high humidity and or smog can cause refraction. Plants will perform differently in such locations than where the atmosphere is usually clear. The slope of the land can affect solar absorption. Fully exposed south- or west-facing slopes can stress hostas. Shade quality is determined largely by whether the shade comes in the morning or afternoon. In most climates, afternoon shade is preferred or, even better, high, filtered, daylong shade.

Considering the decided preference of many hosta species for high shade, you may want to limb up trees with low-hanging branches. You'll be surprised at not only the better growth of your hostas but also the brighter display provided by the stronger light.

Fragrance

Fragrance may depend not only on the species (*H. plantaginea* and its crosses are the most fragrant) but also on dryness, wind, and the time of day.

Soil Preparation

Take note of the advice in catalogs, or on packages, of the preferred site for the cultivar or cultivars you will be planting. Prepare the soil by mixing in a 1- to 2-inch layer of moist peat moss, pulverized pine bark, rotted sawdust or compost, and, if your soil is heavy clay, a similar amount of sharp sand as well. This will raise the level of the bed somewhat above the surrounding terrain. Hostas are not notably particular as to soil pH, but extremely acid soils should be limed to bring them up to about pH 6.0.

Planting

Planting should be delayed until about ten days after the average frost-free date. Watch out for low-lying frost pockets; if you have an option, plant hostas where they can get good air drainage. In such favored locations, hostas push up tender growth from their strong crowns in mid-spring, after frost danger is past. However, where cold air collects, new growth can be hurt by late frost. The plants are rarely killed but development can be delayed a month or two.

When setting-in hostas, leave room between plants for them to spread out to full size. (Some of the large background hostas can spread to 3 to 5 feet across.) Hostas display better if the outer leaves of mature clumps just touch adjacent plants. Groundcover types can be planted closer together.

Before setting your plants in the garden, the Wilkinses advise, soak dormant plants for a few hours in warm water, and trim off dead roots. Loosen the root system and spread it out when planting. Position the "crown" or top of the rhizome level with the surface of the soil, or about 1 inch below it if your soil drains well. In very dry soil, fill the planting hole with water and let it soak in. Then, pull loose soil in around the plant and trickle water around it to settle the soil and eliminate air pockets. Careful planting and watering-in can make a critical difference to the plants' survival.

Plant Care

Weeding is a problem only when hostas are young. As they mature, they crowd out, or shade out most weeds. Grass encroaching from turf pathways, or stoloniferus grass such as quack or Bermuda, can be controlled with edgings or spot treatment with a nonselective herbicide.

Water the new plants once or twice weekly until they are well established. After the plants have emerged, mulch around them. Once well rooted, hostas can go for two or three weeks without rain unless they are in soil that is invaded by tree roots. Experienced growers are careful about watering hostas.

1)

Dividing Hostas

Hostas benefit from occasional division. Unlike many other perennials, hostas can, with care, be moved at any time the ground is not frozen, though the optimum time varies according to region. Here, a crowded clump is taken up with a spading fork (1). The soil is rinsed from the roots in a bucket of water to make division easier (2). Then the clump is cut or pulled apart (3). The divisions are ready for transplanting in soil modified with organic matter and fertilizer. Complete the process with a thorough watering. If you divide in the fall, after the foliage has been killed by frost, mulch the new plants so that they will root well before the ground freezes.

2)

3)

They follow the "occasional deep drink" principle. They try to water before noon, which gives the plants time to dry off before nightfall. Sun-baked beds of hostas, especially those with a southern or western exposure, may need weekly waterings.

Give hostas light applications of fertilizer. For example, each year, just after shoots emerge, the Wilkinses work a phosphate and magnesium source, "MagAmp," into their soil and add greensand to provide potassium. The decay of organic mulches provides sufficient nitrogen. Farther south and west, or on lighter soils, two or three applications of dry granular fertilizer per season may be needed.

Maintain tight control of slugs and snails: the Wilkinses' garden is surrounded by forest, and is infested with 2-inch long gray slugs. They use bran cereal or wheat bran from a feed store, sprinkled lightly with liquid metaldehyde, to control them. By making their own bait, slug-control cost is kept at only fifteen dollars per year. If they relax the slug-control program for even a short while, damage quickly gets out of hand, especially in years with average or above-average rainfall.

Inspect occasionally for bug damage. Hostas have very few insect or disease pests in the North. Black vine weevils may periodically notch hosta leaves, but they can be controlled with one spray application of Carbaryl.

Division

Divide established hostas occasionally. While it is true that hosta plants can live for decades without being divided, certain clumps can grow too large for their sites. They can be taken up, divided, and replanted in soil modified with organic matter and fertilizer. In areas with severe winters, divide in late summer so that a strong root system can be established before the ground freezes. Hosta clumps are easy to pull or cut apart after soil has been rinsed off in a bucket of water. Unlike many other perennials, hostas can (with care) be moved at about any time the ground is not frozen. Therefore, they are not "set in concrete" and can be shifted around the garden to make just the right combinations of cultivars. Be sure to water divisions thoroughly after transplanting and to work rapidly to avoid their drying out during the process.

The admirable Graham Stuart Thomas in his book *Perennial Garden Plants* suggests a beautifully simple way for dividing large clumps of hostas. Quite correctly, he brings out the mixed feelings one has when approaching beautiful old specimens, with spade in hand. Rather than dig the entire plant up, cut out pie-shaped segments and use them as new starts. Fill in the hole with compost.

It has been my experience that you can take about half of a hosta crown in a single season without harming the established clump. I prefer to divide dormant plants in early spring. The growing season is so long in the Southeast where I live that hostas have plenty of time to establish themselves before hot weather. Up north, it seems that the new shoots begin popping up right after the soil has thawed and dried out. I hesitate to touch hostas then because the tender shoots can break so easily. If you divide in the fall, after the foliage has been killed by frost, you will need to mulch new plants to make sure they root strongly before the ground freezes.

In cold-winter areas where perennials are often damaged by heaving of soil, mulch established hostas after the soil has frozen and you have twisted off the dead tops. If you mulch too early, mice may invade the hosta beds and damage crowns.

Hybridizing

Jim Wilkins encourages hobby gardeners, and they don't have to be experts, to try their hand at hybridizing hostas. The individual flower parts are large and visible enough to be easily reached. He offers the following advice about selecting hosta parents for hybridizing, based on his own experience:

"In general, hostas which have solid central or marginal color variegation will produce only solid-colored offspring. However, a plant that is 'streaked' or 'splashed' with contrasting colors will often produce variegated offspring when it is used as the female or 'pod' parent." (The trait for variegation is carried in the chloroplast of maternal cells.)

"The offspring from crosses using streaked or splashed cultivars as the pod parent may eventually form stable central or marginally variegated plants. They need to be watched for a few years to detect solid color reversions.

"The pod parents I have found most reliable for producing variegated offspring are *H*. 'Dorothy Benedict', *H*. 'Northern Mist', and *H*. 'Color Fantasy'. Pod parents that give good solid gold-colored offspring are *H*. 'Aspen Gold' and *H*. 'Gold Regal'. Pod parents that produce blue offspring are *H*. 'Dorset Blue' and *H*. 'Blue Moon'. For breeding toward beautiful blooms I use as pod parents *H. kikutii* (a species hosta) and *H*. 'Maruba Iwa'. And, to produce beautiful leaf shapes I use *H*. 'Holly's Honey' and *H*. 'Donahue Piecrust'.

"If the beginning hybridist stays with these cultivars, he or she will avoid the hostas that are sterile, such as *H*. 'Krossa Regal' and *H*. 'Birchwood Parky's Gold'. If any fertile hostas are incompatible in crosses, I am not aware of them. One hosta species, *H. ventricosa*, is 'apomictic,' and produces offspring almost always identical to itself, without genetic input by the pollen parent."

Daylilies

In nearly seventy years of service to humanity, Brother Charles Reckamp lets his light shine through his love for daylilies.

In all its glory: Brother Charles Reckamp's unnamed hybrid seedling 86-123 shows the multiple branching and high bud count desired by daylily enthusiasts. Note the prominent ruffling.

Daylilies can be cast as the stars or the spear carriers of your garden grand opera. Massed in phalanxes or marshaled into small squads, they can back up or flank the stars on center stage. Like good troops, sturdy, adaptable daylilies can be moved about or dug in for a long occupation. Yet, among their ranks are individuals of such brilliance that they are destined to command attention. Daylilies are fast becoming the most popular herbaceous perennial in North America. Bright and bold, they require little care, can be planted at any time during the growing season, offer a broad variety of plant sizes, blossom colors, and conformations, can be tucked into niches in landscapes rather than requiring special beds, and thrive in containers.

Daylilies have long been beloved for their cheerful, sunny colors: yellow, gold, and orange. Plant breeders, however, were not content with such a limited palette and have added colors that, only a decade or two ago, would have seemed beyond the realm of possibility. Neither were the hybridists content with the rather brief shows of colors of the older cultivars, and they have significantly lengthened the duration of bloom. They have also stretched the season of bloom by developing early cultivars that bloom right after peonies, and late cultivars that bloom during the shortening days of late summer. They are introducing cultivars with remontant (repeat) blooming. They have increased the bud count to more than a hundred on well-established plants and have selected plants for precocious flowering. They have added peachy-coral pastels and somber dark hues, crystalline petal textures, broad petals, ruffled and waved.

If, when you hear the word "daylilies," you still think of the humble tawny daylilies that have naturalized along country roads over much of America, shake off this outdated stereotype. Today's cultivars are light-years removed from their country cousins. Entirely new colors and color patterns have been developed, entirely new classes of plants such as the miniatures and triploids have been introduced, the size and substance of blossoms have been improved, and the plants have been made more resistant to windstorms. If you have not recently visited a collection of modern daylilies at a public garden, you would hardly believe your eyes. You would recognize the new cultivars as daylilies—they still have the family resemblance—but what gorgeous creations they are. It would be hard to find another genus of plants so transformed in such a short time!

In no other plant specialty have amateur plant breeders contributed so much to the improvement of a hobby plant. (I'm counting as amateurs all who are not geneticists or who lack advanced education in the field of botany.) Back-yard plant breeders have contributed many of the twenty-five thousand or more cultivars developed during the past half century. The exciting part of daylily breeding is that much remains to be accomplished and that any reasonably intelligent, meticulous person might just be the one to make the next breakthrough.

Much of the potential for improvement lies in the deep genetic pool available to plant breeders. *Hortus III* lists about fifteen species within the genus *Hemerocallis*, all resembling typical daylilies enough to be easily identifiable. Even though there are differences in flower-head arrangement, foliage, and roots, the resemblance is strong between the species. Crosses between species, while difficult, are made with increasing frequency.

Long ago, civilized countries began planting daylilies for food rather than flowers. In their native China, gathered from the wild and eaten fresh or dried, daylilies were a staple in good times and a survival food during famines. Even now, dried daylily blossoms are exported in large quantities to be added to soups as thickeners or reconstituted to use as garnish. Curiously, it appears we are coming full circle: fine chefs in the U.S.A. are now using fresh daylily buds as an edible flower.

The bicolored Reckamp hybrid seedling 84-42 shows the broad, ruffled petals and striping favored by Brother Charles.

Daylilies deliver a lot of color for the small space they occupy and, during medieval days, were "naturals" to be taken from the wild and cultivated in the compact gardens of wealthy Chinese and Japanese. Early on, good plantsmen began making selections from the wild species. This caused considerable confusion among early plant explorers, who tended to assign a new name to every new acquisition if it differed from the norm for the species. Further confusing the issue was the tendency of daylily species to sport new forms in response to different environmental conditions.

It is believed that the first daylilies reached Europe in the middle of the sixteenth century. By the late sixteenth century, Dutch and English botanists were growing daylilies, but some of their early herbals posted confusing descriptions and inaccurate artwork. Little did the Europeans know that, because they were neither trusted nor respected in the Orient, the wealthy Chinese and Japanese held back their best developments and did not allow them out of their gardens.

The Western world didn't see the best daylilies from the Orient until Albert N. Steward, a botanist, and his wife, Celia B., taught there for many years and gained respect and trust. They sent to their friend, Dr. A. B. Stout, around fifty excellent cultivars and previously unknown species from private gardens on their travels in China. Their shipments set the stage for a quantum leap in daylily breeding. Perhaps the most important find of the Stewards was a seed-bearing plant of *Hemerocallis fulva:* previous introductions of this species were sterile and of little use in hybridizing.

Dr. A. B. Stout was one of the "greats" in horticulture, disciplined, insightful, and afire with a zeal for improving *Hemerocallis* and bringing order out of the chaos of daylily nomenclature. As director of the laboratories at the New York Botanical Garden and a colleague of many of the leading horticulturists between the two world wars, he was in the right place at the right time for his crusade. More than any other person, Dr. Stout set the course for daylilies and gave them a flying start to their present place as a bright star in the firmament of plants.

The very best cultivars developed by Stout were named and farmed out for increase. Some of his creations have stood the test of time and are still listed. He incorporated into new hybrids all but one of the traits he set up in his list of priorities: earliness, hardiness, higher bud count, showier (but not necessarily fancier) blossoms, new colors and variegations, greater extension of flower scapes above the foliage, and sturdy, blue-green leaves, not given to breakage or early yellowing. The one elusive dream? A pure white daylily: it remains to be found.

Since Dr. Stout's day, many hobby breeders of daylilies have upscaled to commercial production as they have developed an inventory of their own hybrid seedlings. They, along with less-advanced fanciers, keep track of the latest developments by visiting performance trials and by attending regional and national conferences of the American Hemerocallis Society. Just learning to recognize the thousands of cultivars by sight, and under different climate and soil conditions, requires several years of study. Fortunately, it is fun, and the advent of camcorders and videotape is accelerating the rate of recording and retaining information.

With most amateur daylily breeders, profit is a distinctly secondary consideration. Recognition from their peers in the daylily world is important, and a sense of contributing to the advancement of a plant they genuinely love. Brother Charles Reckamp is one of the world's foremost amateur breeders of daylilies, and is certainly not in it for profit. To see him at work evaluating his seedlings is to understand the satisfaction a person can realize from working to improve his chosen specialty plant.

Many of Brother Charles's seedlings don't make the "first cut," his evaluation in first-year seedling rows.

You may never be tempted to pick up a camel's-hair brush and transfer pollen from one flower to another. For some people, however, attempting to improve a species by hybridization is a natural step in learning about their chosen specialty plant. Some dabble in hybridization while maintaining large and beautiful gardens. Some become so wrapped up in plant improvement that they subordinate gardening to hybridizing and evaluating seedlings of their specialty plant.

If he chose to, Brother Charles Reckamp could grow the plants for a magnificent landscape. He has spent more days on the business end of a hoe than some of us enjoy on earth. But, more than fifty years ago, he made the choice to minimize gardening and maximize his efforts to improve daylilies through hybridization and selection. Long before I met Brother Charles, I had heard of his plant-breeding work. He, Dr. Robert A. Griesbach, and Nathan Rudolph are about the only survivors of the daylily specialists in the Chicago area who began revolutionizing the genus in the 1940s. Figuring that he had to be in his eighties, I expected to meet a frail, elderly man. When I arrived at the Society of the Divine Word U.S.A. headquarters in Techny, Illinois, I found how wrong preconceptions can be.

A brother at the residence pointed to a group of three men wrestling with transplanting a ten-foot-tall serviceberry tree. It had a root ball that must have weighed six hundred pounds. He said, "That's him over there, the one on the left." I went over and introduced myself to a bright-eyed, vigorous man who, while small in stature, was doing his share of the grunt work. Come to find out, he and an employee named Wally and a lay volunteer had transplanted several such trees in the heavy clay land around the campus. Wally and the layman appeared to be in their seventies. They courteously declined my offer to help, possibly because they considered me too old!

To understand Brother Charles's involvement in daylilies as a hobby plant, you need to know a little about his background. He came from a poor farm family who lived north of St. Louis, Missouri, near a town called Ethlyn. Times were hard and he never had a chance to attend high school, not unusual in those days. In 1927, as a young man, he was accepted as a working brother by the society, and, since then, has not ventured far from northern Illinois.

The Society of the Divine Word exists for educational and missionary work in some of the poorest districts of the poorest countries, as well as in the United States. Priests and brothers periodically rotate back to the headquarters for rest and medical treatment. Finally, when they grow too old to shoulder the load, they retire to the residence of the society at Techny.

Since its founding, the society has depended on working brothers to grow grain, livestock, vegetables, fruit, and bees to help feed the staff, visitors, and retirees. That was Brother Charles's first job but, soon, he became involved in growing nursery stock, garden plants, and flowers to cut and sell to the burgeoning suburban Chicago market. The society needed the income to augment that which they received from donations.

Among the flowers grown for cutting were gladiolus, peonies, and iris. At the time, Brother Charles was kept busy growing and harvesting and, during the winter, helping operate a large greenhouse for growing bedding plants. When I say "busy," you must understand that working brothers rise before dawn for devotions, labor hard through long days, and retire at dusk.

Two local men who went on to become legends in daylily breeding, Orville Fay and David Hall, took a liking to Brother Charles and showed him how to cross-pollinate and propagate iris from seed. At the time, Brother Charles had no idea that this newfound skill would lead to the second great love of his life. The mentor-friend relationship between him and established plant breeders opened the door to new opportunities and convinced this modest man that he, too, could make a success of plant breeding.

The good fortune then enjoyed by Brother Charles seemed almost inconceivable to him, but got even better. In the 1940s, Dr. Robert A. Griesbach began breeding "tetraploid" daylilies by treating seeds and seedlings with colchicine to double their chromosome number. He lived in the area and shared his techniques with Brother Charles. Also, James Marsh, a leading amateur plant breeder from Chicago, often came up to Techny. Concurrently, the developer of the famous 'Stella d'Oro' daylily, Walter Jablonski of Merrivale, Illinois, was making great strides in hybridization but was not part of Brother Charles's group.

Reckamp, Hall, Fay, Griesbach, and Marsh held long discussions on the improvements needed in daylilies, and how to go about achieving them. Even though Dr. A. B. Stout had made tremendous progress in improving the genus, he had only scratched the surface. The range of plant sizes, blossom colors and patterns, petal and sepal width and texture were still limited. Cultivars tended to hide their blossoms amidst the foliage, were rather shy bloomers, basically midsummer flowers.

It happens that daylilies are one of the easiest plants to hybridize; the reproductive parts are large and readily accessible. Anthers can be quickly removed from yet-to-open buds, and pollen transferred to the receptive stigma from a desirable pollen parent. Pollen from early bloomers can be dried and stored for crossing on later cultivars.

Brother Charles was still young and had the energy to keep up his food- and flower-growing duties while learning plant breeding. However, he decided to put iris breeding on the back burner because of his conviction that daylilies held greater potential for improvement, and greater possibilities as a landscape plant. He explained to me how daylilies came to be improved so greatly in a relatively short time span.

"It was the vast improvement in iris created by the introduction of tetraploids that convinced our little band of plant breeders to try the same approach on daylilies. When you double the number of chromosomes in a plant, a number of things can happen: its progeny can be dwarfed, with thicker stems, more massive flowers, and thicker petals. Hybrids between species are sometimes possible, when you work with tetraploid male and female parents.

"Dr. Griesbach had the scientific mind and equipment for the demanding task of experimenting with the powerful gene-altering drug, colchicine. He spent many hours in the lab at DePaul University, treating

Daylilies have come a long way in two decades. Compare the modern tetraploid seedling BC 88-6, left, with the diploid 'Mission Moonlight', introduced by Brother Charles in 1967.

newly germinated daylily seeds with various concentrations of colchicine to double the number of chromosomes within cells. The treatment is traumatic, very few seedlings survive, and those are slow to regain their natural fertility. All seedlings have to be grown to maturity in trials because many survivors will have the normal chromosome count but some will be crippled or deformed.

"Orville Fay worked closely with Dr. Griesbach, and they soon had a few tetraploid mutations that set marginally fertile seeds. It took several generations for the plants to regain full fertility. These tetraploids were hybridized to begin their daylily breeding program. It was like starting all over again; their tetraploid hybrids were like nothing we had ever seen before in daylilies.

"The price tag on the first tetraploid daylily introduced by Orville Fay was two hundred dollars per plant. It was the cultivar 'Crestwood Ann'. My superiors had confidence in me and purchased one plant as the start for a tetraploid gene pool of my own.

"I was fortunate to have working with me the young Brother Daniel Yunk. He had a good feel for daylilies and tried his luck with colchicine treatments. He succeeded in producing several nice tetraploids, which we restored to fertility and used in crosses with 'Crestwood Ann'. The resulting seedlings became the foundation stock for my future hybridizing. At this time, I also had access to valuable pollen from Orville Fay's collection, which included daylily cultivars I could not afford.

"During the 1950s, the five of us, while still friends, developed different goals in daylily breeding and began working independently. For example, Orville Fay was centering on wider petals and open-faced blossoms with ruffled edges. Griesbach was all wrapped up in creating new tetraploids, in which he did very well. One of his top achievements was a line of improved red daylilies with larger flowers, wider petals, and brighter, sunfast hues.

"I began finding extraordinary pastel shades amongst my hybrids and transferred the traits for ruffling and wider petals to them. My hybrids looked good and began to sell. I returned all the income to the society and they let me have a plot of farmland to evaluate my experimental seedlings.

"Gradually, my hybrids began to show a common 'signature'—a combination of wide petals and highly visible sepals. My latest hybrids show a tinge of gold around the ruffled edges. Most of my work has been with the creamy pastels, which, to me, seem richer than the straight pastels.

"For years I had searched for exceptional ruffling and found it in the hybrid I named 'Amen'. As a pollen parent, it passed on the ruffling to succeeding generations. Another turning point was the development of 'Milepost', a pastel pink. It became the source for an intensified pink blush color in my later hybrids.

"I've tried the red colors, but haven't produced anything to brag about. I haven't tried breeding miniature daylilies. Crosses between species are beyond my expertise in genetics. I haven't tried to pick up breeding lines from the evergreen *Hemerocallis*. I've stuck pretty close to the plants in the 20- to 36-inch class. Yet, there's still so much to be done in this category that I haven't felt at all limited."

In 1975, young Roy Klehm came over from nearby Barrington and offered to market all future Reckamp hybrids through the Klehm Nursery mail-order catalog. Brother Charles accepted; now, when you see the credit line of Reckamp-Klehm behind a cultivar name, you know it was introduced in or after 1975. Roy comes over to Brother Charles's plots, digs out most of the plants, and moves them to his own nursery for further evaluation and increase of promising lines. The only plants remaining are those Brother Charles tags to keep for use in his breeding work.

"At first," Brother Charles said, "Roy and I always saw eye-to-eye on the experimental hybrids. But now, thirteen years later, Roy has become more knowledgeable and a lot more critical. I like it because he makes

Masters of the Victory Garden

me defend my judgments. One thing we did agree on was to continue my practice of giving my introductions 'heavenly' names such as 'Amen' or 'Angel's Delight'. I don't consider myself any closer to the angels than anyone else, except perhaps due to my age, but 'heavenly' names come easily to me and I think they are memorable."

Brother Charles was experiencing long and dangerous delays in crossing busy Waukegan Road to reach the old daylily plots, so he moved his garden to a new location near the residence building. He showed me the new 85×125-foot trial garden. Klehm brought in a crew and large machines, and laid 900 feet of drain tile for it in a single day. After removing the sod from the garden plot, he hauled in an eight-inch layer of rotted leaves plus several loads of manure and turned them under with a chisel plow.

I think that Brother Charles has for so long given himself to serving others, that much of his life's pleasure comes from his ability to create beauty for others to enjoy. When asked what advice he could give to aspiring daylily growers, he said, "Visit demonstration gardens first, to find out which cultivars do well in your area, and which ones you like. Go on an early summer morning to catch most cultivars at their best. The hot, humid weather of late summer fades the colors quickly. The cultivars called 'rebloomers' offer a special advantage. When the first 'scapes,' or blossom sprays, have finished blooming, additional scapes develop to prolong the production of flowers.

"Unless you are making solid plantings of dwarf daylilies for groundcovers, plant them in groups of three or five of the same cultivar for best effect. Don't jumble up a bunch of different cultivars in the same bed; they will look like a hodgepodge. If you want to show several different cultivars in one bed, intersperse low-growing perennials between them, especially those with silvery leaves or blue flowers. Daylilies will take a half day of shade but the blossoms will face the sun. Keep that in mind when choosing a site for daylilies.

"Realize that individual daylily blossoms remain open only one day but are replaced by new flowers the following day. This is why planting a cultivar with a high bud count is so important. You may not be able to be home at ten A.M.; that is the best hour for freshness and color. Yet, some of the harsher colors look better to me when the afternoon sun has subdued them. Conversely, some of the dark colors lose a lot of character when faded by the sun. When evening comes, you will be glad for planting light-colored cultivars such as the creams and light yellows because they will show up better at dusk.

(Left) Brother Charles spaces his evaluation rows for easy cultivation with a small power tiller.

"If you can, plant daylilies in front of evergreens or deciduous shrubs. They display better with a green background. But, avoid planting them too near greedy, aggressive shrubs that will rob them of nutrients and water. Work organic matter deeply into the area to be used for planting, and don't set crowns any deeper than they grew in the container or nursery bed.

"If you have a choice, plant daylilies in September. They will bloom the next year. Spring-planted daylilies often are shy about blooming the first season. Large, containerized plants get off to a fast start but, often, only the old standard varieties are offered in containers. Some mail-order sources offer young plants grown in pots.

"Your plants may occasionally have problems with spider mites and various leaf spots. Neither is terminal, but both will disfigure plants. I have a thirty-gallon power sprayer and use captan, Benlate and malathion, but only when I see outbreaks.

"In my rich soil modified with leaf mold, I feed only once a season, in spring with 5-10-5, worked in. Our deep soil seldom requires watering, except for newly transplanted seedlings, but I did have to turn on the sprinklers during the 1988 drought. I get color from late June through September, counting the rebloomers. Few other flowers can match that. Home gardeners can get color over such a long season, also, by choosing cultivars for season of bloom as well as for color and height.

"I like to divide daylilies more often than other specialists because the young plants are so vigorous, and because I need to grow several plants for proper evaluation of a new seedling. Every second year, I dig up old crowns with a spading fork, wash them off with a sharp spray of water, and use a sharp, stiff butcher knife to cut the crowns into four pie-shaped segments. I don't separate crowns into individual plants or 'fans' because some would not bloom until the second year. If I miss a crown and it grows large and dense, I do the first dividing with a sharp spade, and then pick up the knife.

"On the deciduous daylilies, which make up most of my collection, the tops shrivel to practically nothing after a hard winter. I leave them in place and twist them off during spring cleanup."

I asked Brother Charles for a starter list of daylilies for beginners—cultivars he really likes. After much hemming and hawing, which is typical for anyone who has seen thousands of cultivars, he offered this list:

- 'Priceless Pearl': A pale yellow tetraploid with a pink blush. The petals are edged with a golden yellow band, and have lacy, ruffled margins. Individual blossoms can reach 6 inches in diameter on 36-inch plants. *A late bloomer.*
- 'My Sunshine': These tetraploid plants are somewhat shorter than 'Priceless Pearl', with yellow blossoms up to 7 inches in diameter, suffused with pink and cream. Ivory midribs and deep golden, heavily ruffled petal margins add character to the large flowers. The recurved sepals that back up the three petals are blushed pink toward the centers. *Midseason.*

● 'Heavenly Treasure': A most unusual tetraploid with a yellow-to-olive-green throat that sets off the apricot-melon petal color. The 36-inch-high plants sport blossoms of 6½-inch diameter. A thin yellow edge and tight, lacy ruffles dress up the petals. *Midseason.*

Brother Charles is a cheerful man who delights in recalling the many pleasant and humorous experiences he has enjoyed in daylily breeding. One of his favorite stories is the reaction of a fellow daylily breeder when he first saw the Reckamp cultivar 'Heavenly Treasure'. "Brother Charles," he said, "if this is what I can expect to see in heaven, I'm going to start leading a better life!"

If there is any connection between a hobby plant and one's reaching a serene, productive old age, I believe that Brother Charles has found it . . . in daylilies.

More about Daylilies

My first recollection of daylilies was of a clump thrown on a pile of coal ashes and clinkers in an alley in Paducah, Kentucky. I was only five years old, but can recall how impressed I was at how that plant took root, grew, and bloomed in that impossible situation! I wouldn't recommend such severe treatment for any plant, but daylilies are one tough flower. They will thrive in all but the most severe climates and on a wide range of soil types. You need to pay attention to one of their peculiarities. Daylilies are separated into two major categories: deciduous and evergreen. The deciduous types are adapted all across the North, New England, and the upper South. The evergreen types are preferred for the Deep South and warm West. The two types look and are grown much alike but the evergreen types die back only partially or not at all during the winter, depending on minimum temperatures.

Treat daylilies as a sun-loving flower. In the South and West, light afternoon shade won't hurt but, up north, shade can cause plants to stretch and to flower sparsely. You can tell when plants are receiving more shade than they like; flowering will be delayed and sparse.

Planting and Division

You can plant new daylilies or divide old crowns at any time after flowering. Containerized plants can be set in the ground in full bloom. Observe one precaution . . . up north, plant them by late summer. The crowns need several weeks to send out the anchor roots that keep them from being heaved out of the ground by frost. That complicates the dividing of late bloomers because some of them are still showing color in September. Wait out the blooming, and mulch the divided plants heavily to keep the ground warm enough for root formation well into the fall season.

Daylilies require dividing about every five years. First, cut off the top growth about 6 to 8 inches above the ground. Use two spading forks for dividing. Shove them deep into the middle of the crown, back to back and touching. Lever the handles to split the crowns, pull the spading forks out, and repeat the process crosswise to make four divisions. Uproot the crown with the spading forks, invert the segments, and blast off the soil with a sharp spray of water to expose the roots. You can strip individual plants, called "fans," from the segments but most gardeners prefer to plant the entire segment to get abundant color, and faster.

You can transplant crown segments or fans, water them in, and do nothing else . . . they will eventually get over the shock and regrow. The cut-back plants will bleach from the sun and suffer in silence. You can ease the adjustment and hasten recovery by mulching transplants with a light scattering of straw to cast shade and reduce evaporation. Common sense will tell you to water transplants well and frequently for several days.

I try to rotate daylily planting every four or five years when I divide the crowns. I plant the new crowns in soil that has been fortified with organic matter by tilling in green manure crops such as winter rye. Mulches of compost, rotted sawdust, or chopped straw help to maintain a high level of organic matter, which encourages beneficial predatory nematodes and predatory bacteria. I

Note the strong root system on these year-old hybrid daylily seedlings grown from seeds started indoors in late winter.

use organic fertilizers or concentrated manures to replace all but liquid fertilizers. This approach is too new to claim complete control, but it looks promising.

Rotating daylily beds in small gardens is, of course, impractical. There, the best approach, when daylilies begin to decline, is to dig up the crowns, divide them, and incorporate generous amounts of organic matter and organic fertilizers before replanting. Organic fertilizers are safer to use at planting time than dry granular chemical fertilizers.

Soil and Fertilizer

Despite the tolerance of daylilies for a wide range of soils, you need to add organic matter to the soil to get new plants or divisions off to a fast start and to get an acceptable show of color the first season after planting.

Add and mix in enough organic matter to build the beds up for good drainage in heavy soil, and to improve water-holding capacity in sandy soil: a layer of organic matter about 2 inches deep should be sufficient. Add and work in pelleted dolomitic limestone, if needed, to bring the soil pH into the 6.0 to 7.5 range. When planting, dig generous holes and make a mound of loose soil in the bottom of each. Spread out the roots of fans or segments and add or remove soil from the mound to position the crown level with the surrounding soil.

Don't add any fertilizer at planting time, except for a phosphate source. Young plants need to generate a new feeder-root system before they can take plant nutrients. Usually, two applications of balanced granular fertilizer per year will suffice for established plants: one in late spring and another just after blooming. You be the judge; if the foliage color begins to lighten (and it well might on poor, sandy soil), make a third application. Southern and western growers often make one or two applications of liquid fertilizer in addition to the granular feedings because of the length of their growing seasons. Be careful not to feed in the fall where winters are severe. Late fertilization can force plants to continue to grow later than they should, and delay the onset of dormancy. This makes plants vulnerable to injury from winter cold.

Hybridizing

Should you wish to cross daylilies to get a new seedling you can call your own, have at it. The odds of your finding a distinctive, different, and deserving seedling in the progeny of random crosses are about 1,000 to 1, but you wouldn't be ashamed to give any of the remaining 999 to your mother.

Start with valuable modern hybrids or tetraploids that differ considerably in color, blossom conformation, but that bloom at the same time. You can minimize seed sterility problems by crossing diploids with diploids and tetraploids with tetraploids. The flower parts are easy to reach and work with. I watched Brother Charles do it; here's how:

1. Select a female parent. Slit a flower bud that is about a day away from opening and trim off the petals so you can see the reproductive parts. Remove the pollen-bearing anthers. They are on long, translucent filaments that can be pinched off or tweaked off with tweezers. Tear off a square of aluminum foil and fold it to about half the size of your hand. Crimp it over the entire emasculated flower to exclude foreign pollen.

2. Within twelve to twenty-four hours, inspect the stigma of the covered blossom. If it feels sticky to the touch, it is receptive to pollen, ready for hybridization.

3. Select a male parent that is shedding pollen. Tap it into a small container such as a pillbox and transfer the pollen to the sticky stigma with a camel's-hair brush or a frayed toothpick. Pollen is large enough to be seen clearly; it should cling to the stigma.

4. Carefully cover the pollinated stigma to keep out insects, which could carry pollen from other daylily blossoms. If your timing was right, fertilization should take place and seeds should form. The first sign of success is a swelling of the ovary, behind the stigma. Label the cross in permanent ink with the names of the male and female parents and the date of the cross.

5. Watch the ripening seed pods. When they begin to turn brown, but before they split, gather them and put them in a warm, dry place to ripen. When the seeds are dry, shell them out and store them in a sealed bottle in the refrigerator until early the following spring.

6. Sow the seeds in vermiculite or in a special seed flat mixture and sprout and grow them under fluorescent lights. When the seedlings have four to six true leaves, transplant them to individual 2½-inch pots and grow them to a size large enough to move into the garden.

7. In late spring, harden off the seedlings and transplant them into a garden row, about 6 inches apart. Label the row with the parentage of the cross, date made, and date transplanted.

8. Although a few vigorous seedlings might form late-season blooms the same year, you won't be able to evaluate them properly until the second or third year. Discard or give away inferior seedlings or those which closely resemble either of the parents. Transplant any promising-looking seedlings to a flower border and invite a knowledgeable *Hemerocallis* specialist to see them in full bloom. They will probably tell you, "Close, but no cigar!" Don't be disappointed; beauty is in the eye of the beholder.

1)

2)

3)

4)

5)

Hybridizing Daylilies

Brother Charles's hybridizing process begins with these simple tools of the trade: cotton swabs, aluminum foil, scissors, scalpels, tags and marking pens, and envelopes for collecting pollen (1). The female parent is selected and tagged (2). Pollen-laden anthers and stigma of the female parent are visible in this photo of tetraploid seedling BC 87-15 (3). The anthers are removed and the flower protected from foreign pollen with a square of aluminum foil. When the stigma of the covered blossom feels sticky to the touch — within twelve to twenty-four hours — it is ready for hybridization. Pollen is applied from the male parent, and the cross is indicated on the tags (4), shown with these developing seed pods. The ripe seed pods of this tetraploid *Hemerocallis* (5) are at the prime stage for picking.

Weeding	Put away your chopping hoe when it comes time to weed around daylily plants. Daylily roots are shallow and deep cultivation can injure them. I prefer to use a push-pull scuffle hoe for weeding between plants and to hand-pull the weeds growing close to daylily clumps. Scuffle hoes slide just beneath the surface to stir the soil and uproot weeds without disturbing the roots of adjacent ornamentals. Mulching with pinestraw, composted pine bark, wood chips, or saltmarsh hay can greatly reduce the frequency of weeding.
Pests and Diseases	I haven't seen many insects on daylilies at the regional Victory Gardens. Occasionally, thrips or aphids will jump on weak cultivars as they begin to set blooms, but they are easy to control with botanical insecticides such as pyrethrum, or with insecticidal soap. Southern and western gardens occasionally suffer outbreaks of spider mites during hot, dry weather. Sharp sprays of water directed at the undersides of leaves will blast off many insects and mites, and a program of spraying with insecticidal soap should get rid of the rest. The important thing is to prevent small outbreaks of spider mites from spreading throughout your garden.

A serious problem with daylilies in the South and Southwest is with nematodes, especially on dry, sandy soils. The usual method of control is periodic fumigation of the soil with a chemical such as methyl bromide. I find that such drastic measures are self-defeating. A better approach seems to be using organic amendments and natural fertilizers to keep nematode populations at levels that create little or no injury to plants. Nematodes have always been present in warm-climate soils. They always will be and, in order to eliminate them, you have to kill every living thing in the soil.

Other than a few leaf spots, I have seen few diseases on daylilies. Good sanitation every spring, gathering and composting old leaves from deciduous species, seems to keep diseases in check.

Landscaping with Daylilies	Arranging daylilies in landscapes is not complicated. Heights range from about 12 to 48 inches at maturity; catalog listings are usually reliable. Your first consideration should be to place daylilies where they won't tower over plants growing behind them. Your second consideration should be toward selecting a range of blooming dates in cultivars to extend the season of color. Finally, look at colors, patterns, and fancy frills; lean toward the yellows and pastels, with just enough dark colors for a bit of variety. Too many dark hues can deaden a color scheme.

If you buy plants from a local grower or a mail-order source in your geographical region, you can count on getting adapted cultivars. Northern and midwestern growers will sell only hardy deciduous cultivars; southern and western growers will specialize in evergreen types.

A single, well-grown, mature plant of a tall daylily cultivar can make an impressive specimen. However, most daylily specialists prefer to plant individual cultivars in groups. If you have a large garden, you can plant three to five fans of the same cultivar in a circle about three feet across. In a small garden, where the impulse is to cram more variety into a given area, you can make up the group from different cultivars having related colors. Plants within groups should bloom together for impact; make up other groups from earlier or later cultivars to extend the season of color.

There must be more to this landscaping approach than the numerological significance of threes and fives. I see variations of such groupings used in many gardens. Grouping the same or related colors in threes or fives looks so much better than jumbling colors in a pastiche that gives the eye no rest and the stress-ridden mind no solace.

Miniatures and Dwarfs

You may want to try your hand at hybridizing "miniature" daylilies. They have been the center of the latest flurry of activity in daylily breeding, and interest is continuing to grow. Miniatures are distinct from dwarf daylilies. Surprisingly, the term "miniature," as applied to daylilies, doesn't necessarily pertain to the size of the plant. The American Hemerocallis Society classifies a miniature daylily as one having a flower of 3-inch diameter or less, with no mention of plant height.

If short daylily plants with flowers larger than 3 inches are not miniatures, what are they? They are dwarfs. You can buy dwarf species daylilies, dwarf diploid (normal) hybrids, and dwarf tetraploids.

The increase in interest in container growing has helped to further advances in miniature and dwarf daylilies. Full-size clumps, with crowns a foot or more across, can be grown in 5- to 7-gallon tubs. Plants a year or two old can be accommodated in a 3-gallon can. The dwarf miniatures can also serve as edgings, giving a welcome change from liriope as an edging in the South. The most rugged miniatures arc in the 12- to 18-inch height range, which makes them practical for edging taller daylilies or perennials.

As with all gardeners, I have my own set of preferences and biases. In daylilies, I like the bright or light colors that can be seen from a distance, rather than the darker hues that seem to disappear when the sun is low in the sky. I like a little frilling and waving on the petals but not so much doubling that the blossoms look clunky. Nothing pleases me so much, however, as a high flower bud count, which tells me I can expect fresh flowers to open every day for weeks. My great expectations for daylilies are seldom disappointed.

Roses

Charles and Lee Jeremias's life is filled with roses: growing, showing, and sharing them with others.

*D*eep within the subconscious of every man or woman is a rose. What else could trigger instantaneous comparisons between freighted stimuli: fragrances, textures, forms—and roses. Where would we be without the simile "like a rose"?

Man never was good at leaving well enough alone. Despite the beauty, fragrance, and ruggedness of wild roses, man began domesticating and improving them long before the dawn of systematic botany. Rose culture had to be the province of the wealthy or educated because common man was busy dawn to dusk, wresting a living from the soil or the sea. But we can believe that he, too, responded to the beauty of the roses of the field. Perhaps it was this common experience that planted an archetypal rose in the soul of each of us.

Long ago, rose culture expanded beyond the great gardens of the wealthy and the few public gardens, into the gardens of less-favored people. Along the way, roses collected champions: military, clerical, scholarly, and purely commercial. Collectively, these friends of the rose raised the level of awareness of their favorite and improved the genus *Rosa* tremendously. The name "rosarian" became attached to one who knew enough about roses to be regarded as an "authority" by his or her peers.

Over the centuries, rosarians have developed arbitrary divisions for the huge genus *Rosa*, dividing it more by form and function than by species. Without being divided into categories, the genus would be incomprehensible. Novices would be so bewildered by the thousands of cultivars in commerce that they would not know where or how to begin learning about roses.

Since the turn of the century, rosarians have evolved tight standards for naming, recording, showing, and judging roses. Gradually, they are resolving differences in international standards and are attempting to coordinate research to make rose growing easier and more gratifying for everyone. Progress has been rapid since World War II. Prior to that time, when German was the accepted scientific language, international communications were mostly limited to scientists and the few multilingual European nurserymen. With the coming of English as the major language of commerce, scientists, nurserymen, and amateur rose enthusiasts worldwide can work together more readily at international rose conferences.

Generally, the United States rose trade is a bit looser about divisions than the European. You will doubtless recognize some of the standard divisions that appear in American catalogs: hybrid teas, floribundas, grandifloras, climbers, miniatures, shrub roses, old garden roses, and polyanthas. (These are discussed in greater depth in the section "More about Roses" at the end of this chapter.) Of these divisions, "old garden roses" is the most heterogeneous. Any rose introduced before 1867 is automatically in this category.

Botanical historians have exhaustively studied geological and archaeological findings to trace when roses first appeared in fossils and artifacts. Fossils can validate origins that might otherwise be obscured by introduced plant material. Botanical artifacts—paintings, sculptures, medallions, carvings—can augment written records of man's wanderings, systematic exploration, war- or famine-induced migrations, or territorial expansion.

(Right) An artful arrangement of old roses by Lee Jeremias: (clockwise from bottom) 'Sombreuil', 'Belle de Crecy', R. rugosa 'Alba'. Top: 'Salet', 'Shailer's Provence'; center, 'Paquerette'.

Asia is believed to be the home of the greatest number of rose species of proven value. Reverence for roses was evident in early Chinese writings and, not much later, in poetry from India, Persia, and Southeast Asia. Always, roses were the stuff of romance, redemption, spirituality, grace, and surpassing beauty.

Rose species and "sports" (natural mutations) were collected, traded, bestowed as gifts, and transported over increasingly long distances as early centers of civilization expanded and coalesced. Long-distance transfers of plants were rare before the Crusades. Until that time, rose gardens were

filled with improved wild roses collected within the short range of trading ships, caravans, and limited military expeditions. Thus, each major center of civilization had its own set of rose species.

Roses, like tulips at a later date in Holland, were at times revered, exalted, and pursued to the point of irrationality. Blossoms, petals, oils, attars, and extracts were used prodigiously in festivals, anointments, funerals, and bacchanals. The numerous nurseries needed to produce fresh and dried rose blossoms for imperial Rome, at the expense of food production, were typical of the excesses and indulgences that toppled the empire.

The poignant effects of poverty, not only of the pocketbook but also of the mind, were typified in the decline and metamorphosis of rose culture during the Dark Ages. Cultivation persisted mostly around monasteries, where roses were grown more for medicinal uses than for landscaping or cut flowers. Commercial nurseries and royal gardens disappeared.

But, it would be a mistake to see the rose as a product of Christian endeavor. Islamic incursions into Europe—the Moors into North Africa and Spain, the sultans through the Balkans all the way to Austria—introduced Eastern species and highly refined landscape applications.

It was the spice trade that gave Renaissance scholars and gardeners access to the vast range of rose species from China, Southeast Asia, and, later, Japan. But it was not until the time of Josef Gottlieb Koelreuter in the mid-1700s that much progress was made in rose breeding. Well before Mendel, while working in the royal park at Karlsruhe, Germany, Koelreuter described the flower parts of roses and their functions.

Leadership in rose breeding moved around from France, Holland, and Germany to England and back, depending on the fortunes of royal or commercial underwriters of great gardens, and on freedom from the ravages of war. Competent and ethical nurseries developed to supply the demand for improved roses, including those from the Colonies.

The nineteenth century was the heyday of plant explorers from Europe and the United States. They descended on Afghanistan, China, Japan, India, Korea, and Burma. They were not always welcome and sometimes had to work through trusted, English-speaking native entrepreneurs. Some of the species roses in these areas are now threatened by agricultural expansion; these collectors may have saved certain wild roses from extinction.

North America is the home of several species of wild roses, but not until later years were these incorporated into the bloodlines used by plant breeders. For example, the first rose cultivar developed in the U.S.A. was produced from parental lines from Europe. This was 'Noisette', bred by John Champney of Charleston, South Carolina, in 1815.

Appreciation of roses in the United States is just as strong as in Europe. Roses are a bit more difficult to grow in many sections of the country, but easier in favored climates such as the West Coast. Some cultivars perform well in certain areas, but not in others. The trying winters across the North, and the heat and humidity of the South have necessitated the creation of American Rose Society Rose Testing Panels to evaluate the regional performance of new hybrids. Rose enthusiasts innovate new ways to grow, feed, water, prune, and spray roses to maximize performance under their particular conditions. While some cultural practices are common across the country, others vary widely.

The garden I visited is in South Carolina, on the northern edge of climate zone 7. It is large by any standard, with an old-fashioned, informal look. The dozens of beds are separated by broad turf paths. Neatly pruned modern and miniature roses are placed up front, with the huge, mounded plants of old-fashioned and shrub roses to the back and side of the property. Roses run up fences and over arches, mark boundary lines, and guide you from one section of the garden to another.

Mother's Day attracts visitors from all over the upstate of South Carolina to the rose garden of Charles and Lephon Jeremias in the historic town of Newberry. Families bring their mothers to see and smell the roses: some wear white roses to honor a mother who has passed on. Everybody calls Charles "Doctor" because he headed the chemistry department at Newberry College and holds a Ph.D. Lephon is known as "Lee," and hosts a local radio program, "Coffee with Lee," over station WKDK, Newberry.

The Jeremiases often grow old roses for identification. This tea rose grew from a cutting taken in an old cemetery; they are still trying to identify it.

*O*ne look at the rose garden of Charles and Lee Jeremias and you know it is a full-time activity. A closer look will reveal a few sensible concessions. When you learn the extent of the Jeremiases' involvement in the American Rose Society, rose shows, and community activities, you have to marvel at how they manage to keep their roses weeded, pruned, fed, and trained. Somehow they find time to care for nearly a thousand bushes, perhaps because they have sectioned off their garden and have planted each section with roses that require similar culture. Special areas are provided for old roses, miniatures, shrub roses, and modern hybrids such as grandifloras, multifloras, and hybrid teas. More than six hundred visitors showed up on Mother's Day the year the Jeremiases' garden was featured on *The Victory Garden*. Another six hundred or so trickle through the garden throughout the balance of the major bloom season, which, in an average year, can last into June. Every visitor is made welcome and headed out on a self-guided tour. Many visitors come especially to see the Jeremiases' collection of about six hundred old roses. Gradually, the Jeremiases are focusing on old roses because of their nostalgic charm and because the state of South Carolina has proved a good hunting ground for roses planted prior to the War Between the States.

It is obvious to visitors that Charles and Lee Jeremias are excellent rose growers and that they have an outstanding collection of old, modern, and miniature roses on their one-acre lot. What isn't obvious, and the Jeremiases aren't given to boasting, is the national standing of these two modest people. Charles was elected President of the 25,000-member American Rose Society in 1988, having worked up through ARS district and regional offices and a national vice-presidency. He is an ARS Life Judge of Long Standing and a Consulting Rosarian, often called on for advice in rose-growing.

Lee is a North Carolina farm girl by birth, an ARS Life Judge, and so knowledgeable about old roses that she took the first national trophy awarded to old garden roses in 1973.

The Jeremiases operate a small business, Bynum Manor Roses, chiefly as a vehicle for identifying, propagating, and preserving old roses that are adapted to the Southeast. The business was named for the Victorian home on the property, the townhouse of the original owners, the Bynum family. Charles and Lee do no plant breeding, other than watching for mutations that appear to have horticultural value. They sell a few old roses, which are difficult to obtain elsewhere, but the business is strictly secondary to their first love: growing and showing roses competitively. Their huge rose garden unquestionably helps them in exhibiting roses because of the choice it offers in varieties and blooms at various stages of maturity.

No quick answer comes when the Jeremiases are asked why roses mean so much to them. The answers may be rooted in their distinct personalities. Charles is a methodical man, analytical and precise, as one might expect in a chemist who holds important patents from his work in industry. His approach to taking up roses as a hobby in 1959 was typically objective. He cut out color pictures and descriptions of roses he liked, taped them on a board, studied them and rose gardening for a year, and finally bought seventeen plants for his first rose garden.

Lee is a natural gardener, strongly influenced by a dear and knowledgeable grandmother. She loves to recount how, as a wee girl, she grew curious about the progress of a rose cutting. Her grandmother was rooting it under a half-gallon Mason jar (which used to be the way most folks started rose bushes). Lee pulled up the plant to see if it was growing roots. Grandmother watched the tableau from the kitchen window, replanted the rose, and delivered a stern but loving lecture that cemented Lee's developing bond with gardening. Years later, when she was established as an authority on old roses, Lee returned to the old home place to help her grandmother identify an old rose that had been growing there for more than a hundred years. It turned out to be 'The Bishop', of the centifolia division.

Following a traditional education at Wake Forest, Lee worked in public relations for several years, then did something she really wanted to do. She took a two-year course in horticulture at Forsyth Tech. Along the way she began specializing in roses and winning top awards as an exhibitor. Judging followed, and she soon became respected for her fairness and helpfulness to exhibitors.

Both Charles and Lee were established rosarians when they married in 1981. They soon settled in at Bynum Manor, a rambling Victorian home surrounded by enormous sweet gum trees. They faced a full acre of neglected lawn, part of which had for years been under horse barns and corrals. Gradually, the side and back yards filled up with roses.

Even veteran rosarians such as Charles and Lee will, after some soul-searching, admit to having a favorite rose . . . or several. Lee likes 'Sombreuil', a fragrant white climbing tea. She calls it a "crowd pleaser." Then, 'Casino', a yellow pillar climber, and 'Dortmund' of the Kordesii class, red with a white eye. From the miniatures, she picks 'Jennie La-Joie', a climbing pink with tiny, exhibition-quality tea rose blooms.

Charles's first choice, "just for its marvelous fragrance," is the old 'American Beauty'. But to show his evenhandedness, he names a newer rose next, the yellow hybrid tea 'Sunbright'. For its historical significance he likes the first-ever polyantha rose, 'Paquerette', with clustered white blossoms brushed with pink. The colors of the tea rose 'Catherine Mermet' endear it to him . . . pink with overtones of lavender and white. From the miniatures he favors 'Rainbow's End', opening pure yellow and turning red.

Fragrance is high on the Jeremiases' reasons for preferring old roses. They recall with satisfaction the reaction of a blind and wheelchair-bound lady brought to the garden with a tour from the Council on Aging. Her attendant was fussing around wheeling her from place to place in the garden, when the blind lady stopped her. With her face wreathed in smiles she cried out, "Just leave me here, honey, I can smell every rose in the garden!" Such memorable experiences more than compensate Charles and Lee for the time they spend with visitors.

Charles has plenty of time for the garden, now that he is retired. Other than the period leading up to and during "Show Time!" at Mother's Day, he spends about sixteen hours weekly with the roses. Lee's job at the radio station leaves her only about half as much time. Visitors are amazed at the amount of work they do, and well, in such a few hours. Both are energetic and organized. Having done every task many times before, they whip through them quickly in order to have more time just to walk among and enjoy their roses.

It is frustrating to have the time and energy but not the space to grow more roses. The few trees on their property cast high afternoon shade, a desirable consideration for roses in the South (but not where summers are cooler). A deep edging each spring, with a sharp spade, cuts tree roots that would compete with the roses. All the incidental space is filled with containerized roses. Generous walkways have been provided to accommodate visitors, so they have no more lawn to convert to rose beds.

Charles and Lee are choosy about the roses they acquire, but they never discard any. A few plants were lost to the bitterly cold Christmas Eve freeze of 1985 when, following unseasonal weather in the 60s, the temperature plummeted to minus 3 degrees Fahrenheit. (Unaccountably, the old teas and hybrid perpetuals withstood the cold better than hybrid teas and floribundas.) A few more were lost to intensely hot and dry summers. The rugosa hybrids suffered most from the heat and dryness.

Chores around the rose garden are shared. "She does the buying, I do the planting," Charles jests. He does the weekly spraying, a necessary but tedious chore. Lee's legs are a bit younger, so she takes care of the miniatures to spare Charles the stooping. These two strong personalities do everything so well in rose-growing that they have found it works better if they labor separately in the garden rather than shoulder to shoulder. Yet, all the planning and preparation for shows is done together.

The Jeremiases have had to adapt traditional rose culture to their southeastern climate, soil, and unusual rose cultivars. Before planting a new acquisition, they research its origin for clues on how to grow and prune it.

New acquisitions usually arrive as small own-rooted or budded plants. Budding on a vigorous rootstock can mean better performance from a weak or disease-susceptible cultivar. However, many old roses are grown "own-rooted," which means not grafted. With the relatively mild winters at Newberry, own-rooted roses survive reliably.

New plants are potted up and grown on for a year, or until a place in the garden opens up. This gives the Jeremiases an opportunity to inspect the new plant for any sign of mosaic virus disease, and promptly pitch it if this transmittable systemic disease shows up.

Some of their roses are grown from cuttings given to them on visits to other growers of old roses, or from branches sent to them for identifica-

Charles introduces a young visitor, Cory Hamm, to the beauty of old roses.

tion. The cuttings are treated with Rootone rooting hormone and "stuck" in a propagating bed resembling a cold frame. The bed is filled with a mixture of equal parts of moistened peat moss, perlite, and white quartz sand. Softwood cuttings "take" quickly and form a good root system prior to winter.

The soil at Bynum Manor varies from heavy clay to sandy loam. Only the sandy spots dry out enough to require regular watering. Charles scrapes up basins around plants with a hoe and waters deeply, usually fertilizing at the same time.

The heavier soil has a high water table, and planting holes dug in the spring tend to fill with water. If they do, Charles dumps in a deep layer of gravel with a topping of soil, then positions the plant and backfills around it with native soil. He is careful to settle in the plant by flowing water around it to eliminate air pockets. Tramping down the heavy soil would compact it unnecessarily.

Own-rooted plants are set to a depth where the soil line in the container lines up with the surface of the garden soil. Grafted plants are set in with the bud union an inch or two below the soil line, to discourage sprouting by the understock. By northern standards, their roses, even the miniatures, are set far apart, because of the size to which rose plants develop in the Jeremiases' garden.

Upright rosebushes are grown without support. Climbers and large shrub roses are positioned around perimeter fences or at the back of the yard where wire trellises, resembling grape arbors, help in tying up plants and keeping them under control. The Jeremiases keep roses well away from walls because solid surfaces trap humidity and increase the incidence of foliar diseases.

Over the years, the Jeremiases have brought in so many leaves from neighboring yards that their soil is in excellent tilth. They compost the leaves in a pile so large that it would turn most gardeners green with envy. As the pile builds up, they scatter fertilizer and lime to speed the breakdown and to counteract the natural acidity. After the soil has warmed up in the spring, Charles and Lee dress the decomposing leaves around established rose plants. The mulch discourages weeds, conserves moisture, and prevents soil from splashing on the foliage. The continuing replenishment of organic matter in the soil also partly explains why their roses have never been damaged by nematodes, troublesome in some southern soils.

Charles's training as a chemist helps him select and use rose insecticides and fungicides efficiently. Summers in South Carolina are hot and humid. Without a regular preventative program, red spider mites, mildew, and blackspot would take over. For some time, Charles has alternated weekly sprayings with Orthene and Diazanon for insect and mite control. To prevent fungus diseases he uses Daconil 2787 and Triforene.

Sometimes, Actidione PM or Baleton is used, depending on the problem. All these are brand names for proprietary products.

Charles feels that waiting to spray until a problem is evident won't work in the South. "I don't believe in waiting until I see the whites of their eyes," he says. Yet, Charles and Lee are concerned about the amount of spray used, both from the standpoint of environmental responsibility and cost. They put away pump sprayers when they found that an electric Atomist unit did the job with only one-third as much active ingredient. Its only drawback is the long and heavy cord required to maintain the electric current while reaching all corners of the garden.

Recently, Charles began evaluating Safer Insecticidal Soap products for controlling insects, mites, and fungi. He hopes that these will reduce the amount of chemicals required to keep his roses clean, and the preliminary findings look good.

Their rose-feeding program is based on eight- to nine-month Osmocote Controlled Release Fertilizer and a potassium-magnesium source,

'Dortmund', a shrub rose of the Kordesii *class, flowers heavily.*

"K-Mag." Four ounces of each are top-dressed around established plants in the spring and covered with mulch. If growth appears to slow or if the foliage color goes off during the summer, Peters Plant Food, Schultz Instant Plant Food, or Ra-Pid-Gro is applied as a foliar spray and drench. Dolomitic limestone is worked into the soil as indicated by the soil tests, which Charles does himself.

The date and severity of pruning depends mostly on the habit of growth of the bush and whether the flower buds are formed on new or second-year growth. The Jeremiases handle the hybrid teas, floribundas, grandifloras, polyanthas, and hybrid perpetuals pretty much alike, pruning to four or five strong canes and shortening these to about two feet in length, somewhat longer than other rose specialists. They wait until January to begin, because such late (for zone 7) pruning causes new growth to come in in February and March, after the coldest weather is past. The new growth usually escapes frost damage because it has had time to harden off before late frosts come. January pruning is, of course, far too early for more northerly gardens.

The rather deep pruning of the exhibition roses concentrates the vigor of the bush into a few strong stems and generates larger blossoms for cutting and show. However, many of the old roses are grown more for landscape value than for exhibition. More often than not they are large, vigorous plants that can't be reduced to the size of modern roses without loss of color and plant vigor. And, some of them, mainly the climbers, bloom chiefly on second-year wood: deep spring pruning would reduce the number of blooms severely. Other old roses grow into shrub forms, some stiffly upright, and others arching and spreading.

The beautiful hybrid tea, 'Christopher Stone', circa 1935, is still found in some gardens.

Charles minimizes pruning on shrubby old rose varieties. Pruning of shrubby varieties consists mostly of tipping back unruly canes and removing weak or dead canes at the base. On those which are one-time bloomers, he delays pruning until after blossom drop. At that time he also removes weak canes flush with the crown. The plants bleed little because he paints the cut stems with a black material called "Tree-Cote," to prevent the cane borer fly from laying eggs.

On climbers, Charles first notes the stronger canes formed the previous year. They will be tipped back and saved because most of the blossoms will be formed on them. Then, he uses loppers to remove canes which are two years old, plus the weak year-old canes, by cutting them flush with the crown. Older stems are recognizable by their heavier bark and more knobby appearance.

Lee has found that little pruning is necessary on her miniature roses, other than occasional shaping and training, and removal of weak canes or those which are causing congestion in the center of the plant. Some of her miniatures grow three feet tall by the end of the season but are immediately recognizable from standard cultivars by their smaller blossoms.

For those interested in growing old roses, there are not many sources. Some of the best known have gone out of business, victims of catastrophic weather or of the difficulty of keeping the skilled labor required for propagation. Few people are qualified to operate old rose nurseries because of the encyclopedic knowledge of cultivars required and the extreme accuracy demanded to insure correct identification at every step in propagation and marketing.

Only one class of roses gives the Jeremiases difficulty in growing—the hybrid rugosas. They suffer more than other roses from hot weather and dry soil. Oddly, just one hundred miles north at Winston-Salem, the rugosas do pretty well. It may be that the slightly hotter, longer summers in South Carolina push the rugosas past their stress threshold.

Charles and Lee have some advice for beginners who are considering going into roses as a hobby. First, they advise, don't bite off more than you can chew. Start with no more than a dozen plants. Then, spend a few seasons gaining confidence in growing and in pest control. Before you get serious about showing, attend a few rose shows. Ask for copies of the schedules and read up on the various classes. Buttonhole one of the "helpers," the judges who are at shows to assist exhibitors. Ask them about points to look for or to avoid in showing. Generally, it isn't a good idea to bother exhibitors with questions when they are busy setting up or grooming. Some are so competitive and intent on what they are doing that they don't welcome questions.

Join your local Rose Society, they add, or, if you don't live in a city, sign up as a Member at Large. At Society meetings, rosarians are much more relaxed than at shows. They will cheerfully answer questions about stem length, cleaning foliage, grooming, and potential disqualifications. They can tell you how and when to disbud so that fresh scars won't disqualify your entry.

Most of all, keep a positive mental attitude. Be at shows when the doors open. Take one or two backup stems for each cultivar you intend to enter. Have your entry tags made out in advance. Enter the "Novice" class; some of the advanced exhibitors are so skilled that they could qualify as professionals. And, by all means, bring only as many roses as you have time to groom and set up; be selective in your entries.

On mental attitude, Lee Jeremias advises, "Don't take the decisions of judges personally. You may not win a ribbon your first time out. If you don't, ask a helper what specific shortcoming or disqualification you need to fix in your next rose show. Maybe it was nothing more serious than cutting your stems at the wrong time. We cut our old roses the evening prior to shows, and don't refrigerate them. Many exhibitors of modern roses do refrigerate them overnight. You have to know your cultivars to anticipate how far ahead of prime condition to cut, and how to transport them to shows."

You may not be as fortunate as Charles in his first garden and his first show. He grouped the first seventeen rosebushes he bought into a large raised bed. A lady saw them, stopped and identified herself as a local nursery owner, and complimented Charles's garden as the prettiest rose garden she'd ever seen. And, in his first show, he entered just one rose, a long-stemmed deep red 'Mr. Lincoln'. It took "King of the Show," second best among all entries. ("Queen of the Show" is tops.)

Lee grooms miniature rose blossoms for a show. She is brushing 'Pierrine'; 'Break O'Dawn' is in the white cup.

Your experience with roses will be more rewarding, the Jeremiases believe, if you collect a basic library of rose books. There is no single great American reference book on roses. Charles is a tireless researcher and has a large library, including many out-of-print books. Whenever he publishes papers or articles on old roses, he bibliographs to a depth and accuracy seldom encountered outside of universities.

Both Charles and Lee have a strong sense of public service. Their hobby gives them a means of serving others with garden tours while enjoying themselves. Yet it leaves time for Lee to work at a local radio station and for Charles to teach Sunday School and to lecture on roses. They haven't taken a conventional vacation since their marriage. Instead, they travel to ARS district and regional rose shows and to the two yearly meetings of the national.

Lee laughed when asked "What next?" in her career. She quipped, "I want to write a book entitled *Is There Life after Roses?*" Then she admitted she wants to exercise her gift for artistic arrangements—abstract and advanced compositions. Both she and Charles have enrolled as Apprentices in Artistic Arrangements with the ARS but Charles freely acknowledges Lee's advantage. She has an instinctive feel for it but his lifetime of disciplined effort may work against the spontaneity that inspires abstracts.

More about Roses

The best place to learn about roses is a rose garden, not a book. But it will help if you will take with you on your first visit to a rose garden, a list of the eight major rose divisions generally accepted by the American rose trade:

Hybrid Teas   At one time the best known of the divisions, the hybrid teas were created by crossing the old tea rose of China with selections from other species. The original tea roses were marginally winter hardy and lacked the colors deep yellow and dark red. For many decades, rose breeders concentrated on hybridizing to improve this division through greater winter hardiness, broader range of colors and bicolors, repeat blooming, and increased vigor. Unfortunately, the majority of hybrid teas produced in the first hundred years of modern rose breeding lacked strong fragrance; some lacked scent entirely.

Exquisite blossom form is probably the best-known attribute of hybrid teas—high-centered, tightly wrapped, symmetrical in the bud stage, long-stemmed, with few distracting leaves on the upper extension of the stem. Breeders look for other features as well: vigorous plants of medium height, blossoms with strong necks and good holding ability before and after cutting, resistance to major diseases, brilliant color, and a strong, pleasant fragrance, preferably fruity or spicy.

By the year 1940, more than six thousand hybrid tea cultivars had been introduced. Many did not last long in the marketplace and were displaced by superior cultivars. Unfortunately, short-sighted hybridization had introduced or overlooked some undesirable characteristics into hybrid teas: susceptibility to certain major rose diseases, or lack of fragrance. Breeders abandoned the trouble-making lines and have restored the image of hybrid teas to its former glory. However, in the interim, breeding emphasis began to shift to other divisions. If you like to display long-stemmed roses in vases, individually or in arrangements, you should have some hybrid teas in your garden. There are better landscape roses, but none can match the elegance of hybrid teas for cut roses.

Floribundas   A floribunda can be recognized at a glance from its medium- to large-sized blossoms borne in clusters. A quick guess can often be validated by a sniff: most floribundas are scentless.

Rose breeders listened to the buying public when they developed floribunda roses. All cultivars are in the short to medium height range preferred for landscaping. The plants are rugged, dark green, and vigorous, except for the yellow colors, which tend to look less robust.

Most floribundas are winter hardy except in the northern Great Plains and upper Great Lakes area, where winter protection is advised. Nearly every color known to the rose world has been incorporated into this division.

Some time ago, rose breeders began infusing more hybrid tea blood into the floribundas to produce larger blossoms with the depth of tea roses. That trend continues and is already blurring the distinction between floribundas and the newer grandifloras. Certain of the newer floribundas have loose clusters of medium-sized blossoms, with tight, high-centered, vase-shaped buds, much like down-scaled hybrid tea blooms.

Grandifloras   If you are just starting to buy roses, the place for the grandifloras is in ranks behind lower-growing floribundas and hybrid teas, or in tall flowering hedges.

This greater height, up to six or seven feet in warm climates, is only one of the hallmarks of the grandifloras. Additionally, they have large blossoms of the classic double tea rose conformation, borne in small clusters. Some of the first cultivars in this recently created division were not quite as hardy as contemporary floribundas, but the newer ones are. Some grandifloras lack scent and only a few have strong fragrance.

The distinctions between grandiflora, floribunda, and hybrid tea roses are wavering as breeders strive for repeat blooming, larger and better-formed blossoms, somewhat shorter plants, and intensified winter hardiness. Breeders are also working on strengthening disease resistance and incorporating fragrance in new releases.

Climbing Roses   "Climbing" roses are tall bushes with very long canes that can be espaliered, tied to trellises, or run over arbors. Some were developed from tall mutations from bush cultivars and bear names such as 'Climbing Peace'. Others have no bush rose counterparts. You may think of climbers as old-fashioned, more appropriate for the Victorian era when the tall vines could be trained up porch pillars and high walls. But, gardeners are discovering that contemporary landscapes can benefit from the addition of arbors, trellises, and pillars for training climbers. These vertical accents can add considerable interest to otherwise flat landscapes. The Rose Garden at the National Arboretum is an excellent example.

When you buy climbers you may find them divided into three groups:

Ramblers Perfect for draping over fences, the late-blooming, nonrepeating ramblers have long, limber stems and numerous clusters of small flowers. Most are winter hardy but, when espaliered against a wall, tend to get mildew disease from the still, moist air.

Some of the famous old ramblers such as 'Dorothy Perkins' have no scent; their appeal was in the tremendous show of color they put on at peak bloom season in early summer. They have largely been superseded by the large-flowered climbers that have heavier, less pliable canes, bloom over a longer span, and which are fragrant. Some of the ramblers can escape in mild climates and infest pastures. Their low, spreading growth and habit of rooting wherever they touch the ground make them extremely difficult to eradicate. (Except for kudzu, 'Dorothy Perkins' is the worst weed on my farm.)

Large-Flowered Climbers This group includes not only the popular climbing hybrid teas, but also the half-hardy *Bracteata* and *Gigantea* cultivars known mostly in California. The stems are longer and stiffer than the ramblers and tend to grow more erect.

Most cultivars are fragrant and the newer ones are repeat bloomers. Before you buy, ask about winter hardiness. Severe dieback or pruning can reduce bloom on marginally hardy climbers.

Pillar Roses These plants have shorter, sturdier canes that can be pulled together and tied up to a pillar, or trained up a tall cage. The flowers and foliage are altogether beautiful and the plants are hardier as a group than the large-flowered climbers.

Modern Shrub Roses You will be seeing more of these roses as tolerance to extreme cold, disease resistance, and repeat-blooming traits are strengthened. Four distinct types are currently in the forefront of shrub roses: they are hybrids incorporating the species *Rosa rugosa*, *R. rubiginosa*, *R. spinosissima*, and *R. moschata*.

Of these four, much of the recent North American work has centered on *R. rugosa* hybrids. The Canadian Department of Agriculture has recently released new *R. rugosa* hybrids with great cold tolerance, extended bloom, disease resistance, and large, colorful hips. These were developed for low-maintenance landscaping and as a source of winter food for birds.

While shrub roses vary considerably in appearance, you can, with a little practice, recognize them. As compared to the grandifloras, for example, *rugosa* hybrids usually have lower, denser, more solid looking bushes, some with rough-surfaced, ribbed leaves.

Rosa rubiginosa hybrids have dense, upright bushes, loads of medium-sized, fragrant, single blossoms, and apple-scented foliage. Traditionally, the *rubiginosa* hybrids have been more important in Europe than in the United States.

Rosa spinosissima is a name given to hardy cultivars developed from the wild species *R. pimpinellifolia*. Selections from the species were used as parents in *spinosissima* hybrids. Gardeners use these hybrids as background plants where their tall, open, lanky bushes can arch out to their heart's content. One of the first roses to bloom, the *spinosissima* hybrids are covered with large, fragrant, single or double blossoms.

One of the parents of modern hybrid musk shrub roses is *R. moschata*, the musk rose. It contributed a heavy but pleasant fragrance that characterizes the class, regardless of the modern rose used as the other parent. The vigorous plants grow five feet tall in most areas and up to eight feet high in the South and West. The clustered flowers are short-stemmed, medium in size, semidouble, and numerous, and come in red, pink, or creamy white and yellow shades. The plants bloom over a long period and bear attractive hips in the fall and winter.

Old Garden Roses   The name evokes images of quaint, charming rose gardens, but will your dream characters be dressed in medieval or Victorian costumes? Any date before 1867 will do. The American Rose Society chose this cutoff date; any garden rose introduced prior to 1867 will be entered in the Old Garden Rose division. This division is the largest, if not the most popular among all roses.

Most old garden roses are selections from wild species, but some are old natural or manmade hybrids, or mutations. The cultivars you are most likely to see in the gardens of old rose specialists are derived from:

Rosa alba, the white rose
R. burboniana, the Bourbon rose
R. centifolia, the cabbage or Provence rose
R. chinensis, the Chinese rose
R. damascena, the damask rose
R. gallica, the French rose
Hybrid perpetual or remontant rose
Portland rose
Tea rose

Miniature Roses   Tiny blossoms, but not necessarily tiny plants, distinguish miniature roses. Miniature roses, however, are not toys; they are sturdy, cold-hardy, reblooming garden and container flowers that are beginning to win high marks in the "Award of Excellence" competition established by the American Rose Society as well as All-America Rose Selections awards.

Some miniature roses grow only fourteen to eighteen inches high and spread out twice as wide; this type makes good container or hanging-basket roses. Others, under long-summer conditions, can reach thirty inches in height. However, if you look at the tiny individual blossoms or blossom clusters, you can immediately tell that they are miniatures, not low-growing, large-flowered standard roses.

It is significant that miniature roses boomed in popularity at about the time that soilless growing media became widely available, when fluorescent lights became the norm for indoor growing, and when controlled-release fertilizers proved their value for rose culture. All these advances made the growing of miniature roses in pots, larger containers, and hanging baskets easier and more reliable.

By the way, "minis" are not just for containers: they do well in outdoor plantings, excelling as edgings, bedding, or low background plants in well-drained soil and full sun. They combine beautifully with perennials, annual flowers, and seasonal bulbs.

Rose breeders have been able to transfer almost all desirable rose traits to miniatures, while retaining a height range of three to eighteen inches (under northern climates)—all colors, winter hardiness, disease resistance, and repeat blooming. Some of the cultivars are scentless. A few climbing miniatures have been introduced but are regarded by most rose enthusiasts as curiosities.

Polyantha Roses   You won't find many polyanthas in general nurseries in the U.S.A.; the division has been largely supplanted by the floribundas. This old division is not sufficiently venerable to fall under the Old Garden Rose division. It dates back to the bringing of a pink, semidouble form of *Rosa multiflora* to England. As a parent in crosses, it produced plants with numerous clusters of small flowers. Some polyantha cultivars are single-flowered; others are double.

Note: not to confuse you, but the American Rose Society recognizes many more categories of roses than these few divisions. They do it mostly so judges can compare "apples with apples" and "oranges with oranges" at rose shows. The additional categories include climbing cultivars of standard rose classes, greatly changed selections from species roses, and hybrids between species that don't fall into any of the major divisions. You can find these categories listed in the fine booklet updated annually by the American Rose Society, entitled *Handbook for Selecting Roses*.

Planting Bare-Root Roses

You can buy rosebushes as "dormant" or "containerized." Dormant bushes are dug from the growing fields after the leaves have dropped (or have been removed by a defoliant) and are cut back severely, graded, and often waxed to reduce evaporation from the stems. They are usually sold in illustrated bags enclosing shavings around the roots to keep them moist. Containerized roses are grown by potting up dormant roses in containers of 2- to 3-gallon size.

Dormant roses are usually planted in the fall in zone 5 and farther south, and in late spring where winters are extremely severe. In zones 5 and 6, fall-planted roses should be mulched after the surface of the soil freezes, to minimize heaving from freezing and thawing. Spring-planted roses bloom little the first season and should be watered faithfully during the early summer, when they are putting down roots.

Soak the roots of dormant roses in tepid water for a day before planting. Trim off frayed or broken roots and dig planting holes before bringing the plants out in the drying wind. Pour the holes full of water and let it soak in, but don't wet the soil to be used for backfilling. If your plants arrive during very cold weather, pot them up in containers of planter mix and let them develop a root system for a month before tapping them out and setting them in the ground.

Make planting holes for rose bushes 18 to 24 inches across and 12 inches deep. Allow 3 feet space on all sides of the bush, and 4 or 5 feet for climbers or large shrub roses. Mix moistened sphagnum peat moss or pulverized pine bark with the excavated soil, one part to three parts soil, and, if your soil is poor, mix in a cupful of superphosphate to encourage rooting. Shovel a cone-shaped pile of amended soil into the center of the hole, then spread out the roots and fit them over the cone. Lay a shovel handle across the hole and raise or lower the plant until the soil line on the central stem of the plant is about 1 inch below the shovel handle. This places the "bud union," the point where the desirable rose wood was grafted to the rootstock, about 1 inch beneath the surface of the soil.

Depth of planting is extremely important. Too-deep planting can cause roses to refuse to bloom properly or can bring on root rot in heavy soil. Yet, if you expose the bud union fully or partially by shallow planting, the understock may try to shoot up sprouts.

Some authorities recommend filling in 2 or 3 inches of soil around the roots, treading on it to firm it down, shoveling in another layer and treading on it, and so on until the hole is filled level with the surface of the soil around it. This works fine if you amend your soil with organic matter or if it is naturally sandy. However, if you are working with moist, heavy clay, treading on it will squeeze out the air spaces and make it so dense that it won't drain. It would work better if you trickled water in slowly as you shovel in layers, to make the clay flow among and around the roots. The idea is to firm the soil just enough to eliminate big pockets of air, which could dry out the roots.

On poorly drained, heavy clay soils in high rainfall areas, rose beds should be built up 3 or 4 inches above the surrounding soil. That guarantees that the bud union won't be submerged under standing water.

Containerized roses can be transplanted to the garden at almost any time, even when they are in bloom. Northern growers know to get their containerized roses in by late summer so they will have plenty of time to send down roots before the soil grows too cold for root proliferation. Some nurseries rush the sale of containerized roses, before a good root system has formed. You may want to slide a root ball out of a container and check it before purchasing; the root ball should not fall apart and it should not be matted and girdled with roots.

Planting Containerized Roses

When setting containerized roses in the garden, be aware that they are usually grown in artificial mixes containing principally organic matter and little or no soil. Roots may find it difficult to grow beyond the confines of the root ball if the texture of the surrounding soil is too different. Therefore, you should amend the backfilling soil with moist peat moss or pulverized pine or fir bark to raise its level of organic matter.

Gently clean the planter mix away from the central stem of the bush and check the depth of the bud union below the surface. It should be about 1 inch deep. If it is deeper, shave off the top of the planter mix until the union is at the right depth. Before setting the root ball in the hole, brush off any roots that are girdling the sides or the bottom. Firm the soil in the bottom of the hole so that it won't settle and position the plant so that the top surface of the root ball is level with the surrounding soil. Settle backfill soil around it layer by layer, by either treading on it or trickling water over the backfill.

Newly planted roses, dormant or containerized, should be watered every three or four days when the weather is dry. A square of the recently introduced spun-bonded synthetic landscape cloth, 2 feet on the side, can be laid over the soil around the plant. Weeds won't come through it. Cover the landscape cloth with hardwood mulch, pulverized pine or fir bark, freshly chipped wood or bark nuggets to keep the soil cool and to conserve moisture.

Antique Fruit Trees

Elwood Fisher, Virginia Renaissance man, "rescues the perishing" by finding and saving ancient fruit tree varieties for posterity.

The apricot cultivar HW 407 escaped spring frosts to fruit heavily at Harrisonburg, Virginia.

The "tree fruits" include all the species and cultivars of fruit borne on trees or large shrubs, but not the "small fruits" borne on bushes, canes, vines, or small herbaceous plants. The tree fruits predate most of man's other food plants because man did not have to cultivate them: he simply had to beat the animals to the ripening fruits, and reach or climb up and pick them. Later, man learned how to preserve fruit by drying, and it became one of his principal foods.

By the time the first "permanent" settlers sailed for North America, a huge pool of improved selections from fruit tree species had been developed in Europe. Previously, traders and warriors as far back as Alexander the Great had brought seeds and cuttings to Europe from all over the known world. Significantly, one of the most important items brought to North

America with colonists were fruit tree seeds and cuttings. Parts of the New World proved very favorable to tree fruit culture, but some areas were disappointing. Colonists discovered a number of new fruits in North America, including native plums and beach plums, papaws, persimmons, and the red mulberry, *Morus rubra*. They were also mystified to find peach trees, not realizing that Indian tribes, on their journeys to Florida, had brought back and planted peach pits from old Spanish settlements.

The few colonists who were farmers understood how particular tree fruits can be about site, soil, exposure, and length and dependability of season. It was difficult to transpose European experience to this vast continent, with its wild swings in temperature, extremes of weather, and hungry wildlife. Yet, within a few years, colonists had begun to stake out sloping land near bodies of water or hilly table land shielded by mountains.

Later, as successful home growers expanded and began to sell their fruits and fruit products, locations near navigable waterways became a consideration. Fresh fruit and cider were too fragile or heavy for oxcart transportation over rough roads. Dried fruit and cider became important export items in the colonial economy and, when faster sailing ships were developed, fresh fruit joined the list. Settlements in the West Indies were especially good markets because pome and stone fruits grow poorly in the tropics.

Looking back on the statistics for fruit production in colonial days, it is unbelievable how much fruit and cider were produced by small farmers for home consumption and sale. Fruit was prepared in so many ways: it was dried, made into fruit leathers, boiled down into syrups to use as a sugar substitute, preserved as fruit butters in crocks, but, above all, expressed for fermentation into cider. Colonial cider was strong stuff, running 12 to 15 percent alcohol, yet was the most popular beverage excepting (arguably) water. Northern farmers soon learned how to concentrate cider even further by letting barrels of cider freeze and drawing off the concentrated hard cider liquid.

One reason cider was so important was that European varieties of grapes could not be grown successfully in our climates, despite many attempts. Wine had to be imported. Stills for making liquor from grains were yet to come.

A wide selection of fruits was grown by the home gardeners and farmers for the next three centuries. Apples were the shoo-in favorite, followed by pears, peaches, plums, cherries, apricots, nectarines, quince, figs, and medlars. The old trees planted around settlers' homes languished as towns grew up around them and city people began buying rather than growing fruits and vegetables. A few trees, however, lived to great ages, two hundred years for apple trees in favorable climates.

The concentration of people in cities led to the development of commercial tree fruit orchards in favorable climates, near rail transportation or

Elwood propagated this ancient pear by grafting a cutting to a seedling pear understock.

navigable rivers. Apples, pears, and cherries, which are not notably resistant to summer heat or extremely cold winters, were grown in cool, upland areas. Early-blooming peach and cherry orchards were located where bodies of water and sloping land protected them against loss of blossoms or young fruit to late freezes. The mid-Atlantic and southern colonies offered many good peach and fig sites. Among the peach sites were a few especially favored locations where the more demanding apricots and nectarines could be successfully grown. Plums are very adaptable, especially the native species, but have never been as popular as the leading tree fruits.

Until this era, tree fruit cultivars were selected for flavor, juice content for cider making, season of maturity, winter hardiness of the rootstock and scion, season of bloom, self-fertility, and production. Farmers had long since mastered the principles of grafting: in fact, they were as good or better at it than we are now. They had little or no means of insect or disease control, but their tolerance for blemishes on fruit was greater, and they could always consign wormy apples or bruised pears to the cider press or vinegar vats.

Then, as shippers began to control the fruit market, and the equipment and chemicals for pest control became available, specialists in fruit trees emerged. They began to tinker with the dwarfing rootstocks from Europe, to give farmers smaller trees, handier for picking, pruning, and pest control. The thickness of skin, color, size, and holding quality in cold storage became important considerations. Many fine-tasting old fruit cultivars brought from Europe were discarded because of the small or soft fruits of indifferent color, too-dry or too-juicy flesh. Even some of the selections made in North America, early in the life of the Colonies, such as 'Rhode Island Greening', became obsolete.

Tree fruit nurseries geared up to meet the demand for the new cultivars, customized for commercial production. This marketing shift decided the cultivars which would be principally available to home gardeners until a revival of interest in the delicious old varieties occurred. Brief but significant booms in fruit tree growing occurred during the Liberty or War Garden days of World War I and the Victory Garden days of World War II.

All the while, with every passing year, antique tree fruit cultivars were disappearing. Once gone, fruit tree cultivars cannot be retrieved. For a long time, virtually no one seemed to care that this irreplaceable genetic treasure was being allowed to slip away. We are all beneficiaries of the foresight of the few people who did care, and did what they could to save what was still left. Their concern has grown into a worldwide movement with networking and exchanges to lessen the chance of losing rare cultivars, some of which were literally down to only one tree in all the world.

Elwood shows me that fruit size decreases when the trees are not thinned.

At his home in Harrisonburg, Virginia, Elwood Fisher maintains one of the finest collections of antique varieties of fruit trees, grapevines, and berry bushes in North America. His orchard and vineyard cover more than half an acre of his back yard and adjacent property leased from a neighbor. And while other fruit tree hobbyists might grow trees for fun or profit, Elwood grows principally because he is concerned about the loss of germ plasm when antique cultivars of fruits and berries die out. His hobby has gained him international notice.

Friends marvel at how much Elwood accomplishes in the time remaining from his teaching position at James Madison University. He leads wildflower tours deep into the mountains of his native West Virginia, teaches courses on identifying and using wild foods, including mushrooms, leads birding expeditions, and is a consulting parasitologist. That's just what he does away from home!

Inside and all around the Fishers' home are signs of his skill as a craftsman. Beginning twenty-one years ago, he and his wife, Madge, took a roughed-in house and gradually converted it into a beautiful home. Outside, hundreds of feet of precisely laid stone walls, more than head-high in places, are his handiwork. Each chunk of broken limestone is fitted with a flat surface out, and the mortar joints are raked and brushed out to a uniform 1-inch depth. The walls break his steeply sloping lot into terraces; they required heavy poured footings and extensive drainage to prevent buckling under hydraulic pressure.

Before we toured their beautiful home and gardens, Madge served us a generous piece of marvelous apple pie. We talked about what led up to Elwood's strong sense of commitment and his well-developed skills as a plantsman, artist, and craftsman.

Fortified with apple pie, Elwood and I meandered around the house and adjacent gardens, with many stops to admire unusual plant material and constructs. The front entrance and heavily used areas inside the home are floored with serpentine, but the construction that really catches your eye is a wall-to-wall fireplace made of strips of serpentine.

Stonework is Elwood's thing; for several years, dynamic Madge busied herself hanging the wall and roof insulation and doing much of the fine finishing inside the house while Elwood was wheelbarrowing seventeen tons of stone through their front door.

More stonework lies outside. All around the house are sculptures made from the stone excavated from the home site and, in the back lawn, you can see the flat tops of huge limestone boulders left in place rather than blasted out. Madge and Elwood chipped out cavities to use as bird feeders and they work beautifully. Inside the home are several of Elwood's whimsical wood or stone sculptures, sleek and functional or slyly amusing.

Alongside the house is an exquisite Japanese garden, actually a deep grotto with walls made of water-worn limestone. Some of the pieces are of awesome size. Elwood described, with understandable pride, how he singlehandedly maneuvered each piece into place using a simple iron pipe tripod to lift, and the power of his International Harvester Scout to skid stones into place. Then, he used hydraulic jacks to tilt and rotate rocks so that they fitted the design in his mind's eye. You can walk across the grotto on thick cylinders of limestone standing on end. (They are actually 16-inch-thick cores from holes drilled on a nearby building site, to accommodate the hydraulic equipment of an elevator.)

Elwood realizes that the time has come to begin winding down some of his more physical projects. Although still in good condition, he is of World War II vintage and has to pace himself on heavy jobs. Reminders of the long hours he works around the house and yard are everywhere but none more telling than the tall poles for streetlights that enable him to work in the yard at night.

Searching out and saving ancient fruit trees, berry and grape varieties, south to Georgia and the Carolinas and north through New York State, has taken much of Elwood's spare time and energy for twenty-odd years. The expense in time and travel has been considerable. He continues his crusade largely because he is uniquely qualified to find and preserve old fruit tree cultivars.

The area of West Virginia where he was raised was settled in the 1700s largely by German immigrants. These good farmers brought cuttings (scions) of fruit trees, berry bushes, and grapevines over with them, often keeping cuttings alive by sticking the cut ends in potatoes. Over the mountains to the east, major landholders of English stock, including Thomas Jefferson, imported starts of apple trees of varieties they or their forebears knew and grew in the old country.

Early on, Elwood was marked for growing fruit trees. His grandfather Shuman, on his farm near Clarksburg, had eighty-four varieties of apples, pears, peaches, plums, gooseberries, and currants. By the time Elwood was seven years of age, his grandfather had him grafting fruit trees. As the two of them traveled around the coves and ridgeland, his grandfather would point out old trees and have Elwood memorize their

A bird's-eye view of Elwood's orchard shows the density of planting and the size of the trees, all of which have multiple grafts.

variety names. Elwood told me, with mixed pride and regret, "I have found every apple cultivar that Grandfather Shuman grew except the one named 'Seedless' (without pips). It was developed in Vermont in 1869."

His grandmother Fisher figured equally in teaching mountain skills to Elwood. While Grandfather Fisher ran a country store, Grandmother served as the local folk authority on herbal medicine; she diagnosed by looking at patients . . . the color of their eyes, skin, and nails, condition of their hair, and other signs that old-time general practitioners knew to watch for. Customers got "doctored" while they were shopping for supplies and clothing.

Elwood tagged along behind his grandmother while she collected native plants, and cultivated vegetables and herbs for poultices, potions, antiseptics, emetics, and expectorants. She knew not only where to find the plants she wanted, but when to harvest them and how to store them for maximum potency. Twenty years later, when Elwood went on his first field trip with a botany class, he amazed the professor by identifying every plant and giving its medicinal use.

Elwood remembers his grandmother collecting yellow root, ginseng, black cohosh, golden ragwort, may apple roots, and dozens of other species for medicine, and how his grandfather sold smokeless sumac wood to moonshiners. At night, his grandmother practiced the traditional German "fractur" art of embellishing marriage licenses, certificates, and homilies with traditional German art.

Elwood was only seventeen when, late in World War II, he volunteered for the U.S. Navy. Seeing the world convinced Elwood that he didn't wish to follow the strict Dunkard upbringing of his childhood, but a driving curiosity about other religions and cultures led him into divinity school, and later into studies of art and history and, finally, botany. School followed a hiatus of several years after he came home, during which he worked as a lineman for a power company and as a welder on a pipeline.

Elwood and Madge met when she was teaching home economics in Ohio and he was teaching high-school biology, history, and art. Later, he completed work on his masters in zoology at Miami University. Madge also helped while he went on to get his doctorate in biology at Virginia Polytechnic Institute in Blacksburg. Since he "owed her one," Elwood helped her become certified in library sciences, once he joined the staff at James Madison University. Madge is now a librarian at an elementary school in Rockingham County.

Elwood wasn't thinking about fruit trees during their first years in Harrisonburg; he was busy teaching medical entomology, parasitology, ornithology (Grandma taught him birds, too), zoology, and history of botany. Then, three developments conspired to shape his future for him. First, he watched with concern as southern corn blight disease threatened to decimate the corn crop because geneticists had allowed the gene pool of maize to shrink. Next, the Seed Savers' Exchange asked him to collect seeds of old varieties to assist them in preserving germ plasm. But the turning point came when someone asked him if he knew where to find the old apple variety 'Winter Banana' that had originated in Indiana. Yes, he knew just where to find 'Winter Banana' . . . on Grandfather Shuman's farm, where he had seen it as a lad. But, when he got there, he found that a landslide had hit the orchard, burying two trees. Those two were the only 'Winter Banana' trees on the place and they were dead as a doornail!

That incident started Elwood thinking, and he realized that he was one of the few people in the entire country who knew many old fruit varieties on sight, and where to find them. Coincidentally, he and Madge had moved to their present home and had a large lot for planting trees, berries, and vines.

So began Elwood's quest to find and save old varieties, and he admits that he had no idea, then, how involved and all-consuming it was to become. He used many ingenious methods to find old trees. "I would come into a little town," he recalls, "and ask who around those parts grafts trees for home orchards. Usually, I would start at the town filling station, and would get my answer right there. Professional fruit tree grafters were always local men and were always willing to cooperate when I explained what I was after. Of course, it helped that I grew up in the mountains and could still talk like one of them!

"Circuit-riding ministers are getting hard to find now," he said, "but there were quite a few around when I first began searching for old trees. They rode horseback in the roughest parts of the mountains and, since they were put up and fed by local families, they knew who served the best apple pies. I've had them lead me straight to long-abandoned farmsteads where they had enjoyed apples years before. We found many long-dead trees, but also a few old survivors.

"It took me five years of searching to find 'Winter Banana', and even longer to find the 'Leathercoat' russeted apple mentioned by William Shakespeare. I am still looking for the 'Wasp' apple, also called 'Birdstow Wasp', and Thomas Jefferson's favorite cider apple, 'Talliaferro'. I keep hearing about an apple with the local name of 'Chuke', known in Great Britain as 'Chuket' or 'Teuchat Egg', but have yet to find a tree by that name. It was recorded in Scotland in 1768.

"The luckiest find in all my searching," Elwood said, "was a man who had served for many years as a judge at county fairs. He would ask entrants for cuttings of varieties that placed well in fruit exhibitions. He was ninety-six years of age when I ran across him, and still had twenty-two great old apple varieties, some of which I have found no place else.

"One of my other hobbies, bird watching, ties in beautifully with my searching for old fruit trees. I visit several areas in the mountains during the spring and fall to count or study migrating birds. While driving, I keep one eye peeled for fruit trees, or remnants of old homesteads. Whenever I spot something promising, I will mark it on a map for a visit on the way back home.

"For several reasons, I am having better luck in finding old apple varieties than other fruits," Elwood explained. "First, hundreds of apple varieties were planted in the Colonies; the settlers apparently learned from seamen that stored apples and cabbages could help prevent scurvy during the winter when greens were not available. Also, apple trees can survive longer than most other fruit tree species . . . sometimes more than two hundred years.

"Pear trees usually don't last as long as apples. They need good soil, and tend to be shorter-lived where soils are thin or infertile. Fire blight tends to debilitate and eventually kill trees, especially where bees can bring the bacterium in from other fruits," Elwood continued. "For that reason, the old varieties of pears I have obtained have usually gone through several cycles of renewal by rooted cuttings or grafts. Like apples, pears tend not to come true when grown from seeds. Apparently, their genetic makeup is so complicated from eons of hybridizing, that tremendous variation occurs among seedlings.

"Among the stone fruits, cherries are fairly long-lived," he said. "I've found some trees that must have been sixty to seventy years old. Up in the mountains where it is cool, they can grow the large sweet cherries as well as sour or pie cherries. Growers treasure them so much that they will graft desirable scions onto seedlings to keep the variety going.

"On the other hand," Elwood said, "the relatively short-lived stone fruits such as peaches, plums, apricots, and almonds usually produce pretty good trees when grown from seeds, and they resemble the parent tree fairly closely. The American Indians fell in love with the first peaches introduced by settlers, carried seeds with them all over the mountains, and planted patches which still survive. The red-fleshed 'Blood' or 'Indian' peach was one of their favorites."

Elwood caught my doubting look when he was describing the true-breeding character of peaches and plums grown from seeds. "Oh, yes!" he reassured me. "I've seen some seedlings from old greengage and French prune plums that were superior to the original." He showed me one of his selections, grown from a seed and code-numbered "EF-33-74." It certainly bore out his contention.

"American Indians and settlers alike," he said, "used fruits in a way not generally known today. They fed them to livestock. Lacking any means of preserving the stone fruits other than drying, they fed surplus peaches, plums, and apricots to pigs and cattle. Apples and, to a lesser extent, pears, were stored in caves, cellars, and straw-lined pits."

I asked Elwood about gooseberries and currants, of which he had several attractive varieties. "One of the great gardening disasters, in my opinion," he said, "was the misdirected eradication program against gooseberries and currants during the 1930s. I can recall crews of WPA men combing the hills, valleys, and home gardens to find and burn gooseberry and currant bushes because they were felt to be alternate carriers of white pine blister rust disease, which endangered this valuable timber tree.

"Our old German families were law-abiding, but not inclined to go along with edicts that didn't make sense to them. Consequently, they tended to dig up and store plants of currants and gooseberries and replant them after the eradication crews had moved on. Thanks to them, I have been able to find quite a few of the really old garden favorites. I expect to see more gooseberries and currants planted in gardens as people learn what delicious pies and preserves can be made from them."

1)

2)

3)

4)

5)

Antique Fruit Varieties

Searching out and saving antique fruit trees, berry and grape varieties have taken much of Elwood's spare time and energy for more than twenty years. He continues his crusade largely because he is uniquely qualified to find and preserve old fruit cultivars such as those shown here: a seedling from an unnamed antique nectarine (1); 'General Hand' plum (2); 'Perfection' red currant (3); 'Medlar of Nottingham' (4); an antique crab apple grown for preserves (5); 'St. Edmund's Pippin' apple (6).

6)

As Elwood's collection of fruit trees expanded, it became apparent that he would soon run out of room. His half-acre lot would hold only seventy-five or so mature fruit trees of standard size. Then, he made a decision that multiplied the capacity of his orchard severalfold. He began grafting several kinds of apples and other species on each of his existing trees, always tagging the grafted scion by cultivar name. He also began cordoning trees by the Belgian system to allow much greater planting density. Some trees were espaliered up walls or trained flat against trellises made by lacing and tying together canes of local bamboo. His trees are crowded, by any standard, and berry canes and bush fruits are chinked in wherever he can find a sunny spot. It isn't the optimum arrangement for growing fruit trees but it has enabled him to save countless cultivars that otherwise might have been lost.

Here and there among Elwood's collection of conventional fruits are oddities such as medlars, figs, almonds, nectarines, quince, and jujube (which grows into a good-sized tree at Victory Garden South). Someday, you might see jujubes on the gourmet produce counters; they are delicious little fruits the size and shape of a large date, apple flavored but rather dry in texture, tan to brown when ripe. Medlars will probably remain obscure; they look a bit like the fruit of quince but smaller. You have to develop a taste for them. Madge made a face when Elwood mentioned medlars. "The nearest next-to-nothing fruit I ever tasted!" she exclaimed. "You have to pick and store them until the pulp ferments before they are worth eating. When they are ready, you have to really work at it to get more than a taste of fruit." (Well, that pretty much explains why more people don't plant medlars.)

Elwood asked me to help him diagnose what was wrong with a medlar tree he had espaliered, for protection, in a corner between a brick wall and a chimney. The margins of the leaves were bleached almost white. I hipshot and guessed at overly high soil pH, which would tie up iron and perhaps other trace elements. This condition frequently occurs where lime from concrete foundations and walls gets into the root zone of nearby plants. Elwood agreed to apply a blend of chelated micronutrients in the fall to see if it restores the desired color to next year's foliage.

What really impressed me about Elwood's orchard was the extraordinary range of flavors in the old apples. Mind you, these were rather small fruits, some no larger than the crab apples you see pickled and colored red. We ate them warm, out of hand, peeling and all. I detected flavors I never knew came with apples: cinnamon, licorice, nutmeg, banana, pineapple (and, once or twice, worm). Elwood explained that certain tart varieties are preferred for cider-making, others for pie-making, still others for drying. You can use antique cultivars for other than their primary uses, but some of the fun in growing them is using them as their developers intended. Truly, gardeners are missing something good by settling for just the few modern cultivars that are sold for home orchards today, a sentiment to which Elwood added a heartfelt "Amen!"

"All told, I have nearly eleven hundred varieties of apples here," said Elwood, "plus three hundred pears, nineteen grapes, some fifty-seven cherries, twelve apricots, twenty-nine plums, several figs (including the hardy Siberian and one which is claimed to be seedless), and some thirty varieties of red, white, or black currants and gooseberries. I have several kinds of brambles but they tend to get out of hand. I don't know how much longer I can continue to grow them.

"I feed the whole neighborhood with fruits," he said, "but a lot of it goes to waste. I have to overpower my instinct to provide food, by reminding myself that my most important goal is to preserve the plants and not to save the fruit crop. But, at the same time, I feel I should learn how to thin, prune, and spray all the kinds I grow, in order to advise people on the best regimen for fruit production. I have an obligation to my neighbors to keep the place clean and not to have my orchard harbor insects or plant diseases that could spread."

We talked for a long time about ways he might reduce the dreadful number of hours he has to spend in the orchard spraying, often in the hot sun. Elwood is a highly conscientious man about protecting the environment but is reluctantly convinced, as am I, that a certain minimum of

Antique apple varieties are espaliered Belgian fashion atop a terrace formed by one of Elwood's stone walls.

Madge and El-wood Fisher gather apricots in a Welsh trug.

spraying is required to keep damage from insects and diseases at an acceptable level. Being a scientist, Elwood is extremely careful about spraying, and wears the full recommended regalia of rubber clothing and gloves, goggles, and respirator.

Madge is concerned about the effect on her husband of the heat and hard physical labor of spraying. Elwood uses a gasoline-powered "Solo Port 423" backpack mist blower, which is a great sprayer, but heavy to lug around. He is going to look at the electric-powered Atomist as a lighter, less noisy alternative, which uses less actual chemicals because it micronizes the spray.

Elwood's spraying program begins in the fall, after leaf drop, when he drenches all the trees with a dormant spray of Ferbam and dormant oil. This is his first line of defense against overwintering insects and the bacterial disease peach leaf curl. To control plum curculio and codling moth on plums and apples, he sprays with malathion at blossom drop and again later when the insects begin to emerge.

He sprays at full flower to prevent fire blight, which is destructive in Harrisonburg. He uses Agrimycin or a 4 percent solution of Chlorox. Later in the season, he "target sprays" spot outbreaks of such diseases as quince rust. The fungicide Polyram works well for him against scab, cedar-apple rust, fly speck, and sooty blotch. He also uses benomyl (Benlate) to control powdery mildew on apples, but only when necessary.

He advises using common sense in reducing brown rot damage by concentrating on early varieties of peaches, plums, apricots, and nectarines. Elwood has observed that the disease is much worse on later varieties that mature during hot, humid weather. On the few occasions when warm, humid weather has come at ripening time, he has used Benlate and Funginex to control brown rot on peaches and other stone fruits. "But, I have gone back to using old-fashioned Bordeaux mix on stone fruits and grapes we plan to eat," he said. "I feel it is safer. At times I have used Carbaryl to control Japanese beetles on grapes and roses."

Elwood realizes that thinning fruits, particularly peaches, apricots, and nectarines, would reduce the incidence and severity of brown rot. However, thinning an orchard the size of his is physically impossible for one person, part-time. He has to prop up many overloaded branches to keep them from breaking under the weight of fruit.

"One of my best weapons against the spread of diseases and insects, and the effect of drought," Elwood said, "is mulching between the rows of trees in my orchard. I have all my neighbors save leaves and lawn clippings and I sheet-compost them. I know that the trees are withstanding the drought better. Believe it or not, I didn't water once during our long drought, except when I transplanted new trees. I think that, being healthier, my trees suffer fewer disease and insect problems, perhaps because more predators can live in the mulch than in clean-tilled soil. I frequently bring in 'helpers': toads, salamanders, lizards, and their skink cousins."

Elwood explained "summer pruning" of apple trees to me. It must have seemed to him that I had been living on another planet because, literally, I had never heard of it, nor seen it done. He showed me how, come June 15, he cuts back each shoot with fifteen or more leaves on it. He takes off two-thirds of each shoot, being careful to disinfect his shears between trees or after pruning in an area that appears diseased. Then, in late July, he cuts back to two leaves, the growth put on since the first pruning. Finally, in late August, he repeats the procedure used for the second pruning. The technique, he explained, forces more fruit to form the next year, instead of excessive vegetative growth, and may prevent the tree from getting into the cycle of "biennial cropping," setting a heavy crop every second year.

Elwood is especially skilled at grafting. April is the time for cleft, bark, and whip grafting of scions collected during the winter. Then, from June through August, he does budding, or chip, grafting of both pome and stone fruits.

Cleft grafting is used mostly when topworking existing trees to replace all or part of the smaller limb structure with a more desirable cultivar. He cuts off limbs up to a size of about 1 inch in diameter, splits the ends, and inserts one or two short pieces of scion wood so that cambium meets cambium, and wraps the union and all the exposed cut with a rubber grafting band.

Bark budding is used mostly to start a new branch growing when a tree is lopsided, or to replace a broken branch. You have to wait until new growth is pushing out and make a tee-shaped slice in the bark. Insert a short piece of scion wood with the end trimmed into a "vee," and dab the exposed surface with grafting wax to prevent drying out.

Whip grafting is used to join a piece of scion wood to a slender branch of equal diameter. You can cut both pieces on a slant and join them so that cambium meets cambium or, if you are dexterous, you can match two sawtoothed cuts so that the graft won't slip. Wrap the whip graft with a rubber grafting band and tie snugly.

Budding is used to graft desirable scion wood to young seedlings with strong root systems, and is done by inserting a chip of scion containing a bud, into a cross or tee-shaped cut through the tender bark. Whip a wide rubber band around the graft and tie it snugly. Elwood prefers to do most of his grafting by the chip-bud method because buds done at the right time "take" almost 100 percent. Yet at the many grafting workshops he conducts, he demonstrates every known method because of the special situations which call for specific grafts. He isn't doing much grafting now, because he is concentrating on keeping his present inventory alive and healthy, rather than adding to it.

Although Elwood is an ace at pruning, he balks at trying to describe it, or how to graft, to anyone, other than at workshops where he can also demonstrate the procedures. "I've been pruning so long," he says, "that I do it automatically, like riding a bicycle or laying stone. Every tree of every variety of every kind calls for different pruning. It is an art that has to be explained to a person as you show him or her how to do it, just as my grandfather taught me."

Elwood smiled as he recalled three rigid rules of pruning given to him by Granddad Shuman all those years ago:

1. There are only fifty-two days of the year when you should not prune fruit trees . . . Sundays! (Grandfather Shuman was of the strict Dunkard faith.)
2. Never leave one limb superimposed over another; the bottom limb will be too shaded.
3. Open a tree enough that a bird can fly through it.

Elwood starts his pruning in the winter, right after Christmas, and continues through February. He prunes the older trees first, but waits until February to prune trees that are three years of age or younger. (These require minimal pruning.) Then he moves on to grape pruning and the special pruning required for cordoning and espaliering trees.

I asked Elwood how he felt about disinfecting shears and painting wounds on trees. He grinned and said that professional pomologists, Extension Service personnel, and he agree on disinfecting with Clorox or Lysol spray but disagree on wound paints. They maintain that paint is more cosmetic than effective, but Elwood says he suspects that decay organisms can enter wood at unprotected cuts, especially if the wound is large enough for the wood to crack. He applies a homemade mix of asphaltum diluted with xylene solvent or, in a pinch, a shot of cheap latex paint from a spray can.

Elwood glossed over his feeding program because, in his rich Shenandoah Valley soil, not much is needed. "Oh, I will scatter a little 19-19-19 corn fertilizer under a tree in late summer if it looks a little puny but, truly, I rely on the decaying mulch to supply most of the needs for nutrients. Too much vegetative growth results in poor production . . . the energy goes to shoots, not fruits."

Since Elwood and I are within a year of each other's age, we couldn't avoid the subject of what happens as he loses some of his stamina and when he is finally called to that great orchard in the sky.

"Madge and I have thought about selling this place and moving to a farm after retirement. It would take me about three years and a great deal of work to move all two thousand or so plants I have on this property. I would be willing to do it, if a way could be worked out for a

1)

2)

3)

4)

Grafting Fruit Trees

Elwood demonstrates his proficiency at grafting fruit trees. He prefers the chip-bud method because such grafts done at the right time "take" almost every time. He cuts a chip bud from scion wood (1). Then the chip is fitted to match a chip taken out of the understock branch (2). The bud graft is wrapped with flexible "parafilm" (3) to protect it, then labeled with the date and names of the scion and the understock (4). When slender branches are splice grafted (5), the cut surfaces of scion and understock must match perfectly. Whip the two pieces together with parafilm or a broad rubber band to secure and protect the splice.

5)

foundation to take over my collection for posterity. There isn't any point in moving it if it can't be carried on. I think it is crucial that this country protect the gene pool of its major food crops in the event the standard commercial varieties are attacked by a plague of insects or diseases, or unforeseen events such as destruction of ozone burn or acid rain . . . both of which are already real threats.

"A few others have collections of old fruit trees, grapes, and berries, including individuals such as myself, the restored garden and orchard at Monticello, the Luther Burbank Garden, the Colonial Williamsburg Foundation, and the American Museum of Frontier Culture at Staunton, Virginia. There are a few germ-plasm banks in Europe but they have had to turn to us for new starts on old varieties that have disappeared there.

"Cornell University has over thirteen hundred old apple varieties at their Geneva, New York station. I send them scions of the rediscoveries I have made, and I send scions to several collectors and breeders to reduce the risk of loss. Cornell is undertaking a valuable program of heat-treating and tissue-culturing old apple varieties to rid them of disease-causing viruses carried in their tissue."

I did convince Madge and Elwood to divulge the names of some of their favorite fruit varieties. Elwood winced when Madge chose the modern Japanese apple variety 'Mustu', a cross between 'Golden Delicious' and 'Indo'. Both like 'Tabarza' plum from Iran. Elwood likes the gooseberry 'Kathleen Olenberg' with large, red fruit, and the pearl-like white currant, 'White Imperial'. "My taste buds would soon tire of just one variety of a given fruit," Elwood commented.

After extracting my promise to return someday soon, the Fishers took me over to their regional airport. On the way, Elwood asked a favor. "Have anyone contact me," he said, "if they know anything about the history of the old apple variety named 'Walla Walla'. It has been grown in these parts since 1919 but no one has a record of it anywhere else. What's an apple named 'Walla Walla' doing in the Shenandoah Valley?"

More about Antique Fruit Varieties

You will seldom find antique varieties at retail stores. When you do, they might be labeled incorrectly, because synonyms are rampant among antique varieties. This is not due to deceptive trade practices but, rather, to the fact that original names of some varieties were lost years ago and local names assigned.

"Some of the supposedly 'lost' varieties have been rediscovered under synonyms," says Elwood Fisher. "For example, I have found very old English varieties, which have been lost over there, under different names in this country." Elwood is a bear on keeping fruit tree names straight and kindly gave me the names of reference books on antique fruit trees.

"These old books, plus some twenty others of the nineteenth century, help me key out unknown varieties. For example, the books describe the shape of the fruit: flat, conical, elongate, round, quadrate, etc. Then, I look up its color: red, yellow, green, blush, striped, spotted, solid, russeted, or smooth. If still in doubt, I can split a fruit and look at the core and the shape and color of the seeds. Even the calyxes, straight, reflexed, or absent due to aborting, can settle difficult identification questions. The season of ripening is also significant, though it varies, of course, from North to South."

Elwood is outspokenly critical of the books written for the general public on the subject of growing fruit trees. When I asked him to name good books on fruit culture he replied, "There aren't any!" Then, he went on to explain that fruits and berries are so regional in their adaptation and demanding in their requirements that no one has written a book which could apply to all climates. "It would take three or four volumes and several years of work to do it thoroughly," he said. "I think that gardeners would be further ahead relying on variety recommendations and pruning and spraying information from their State Cooperative Extension Service.

Terminology

A relatively modern innovation may complicate your ordering of antique fruit trees. Some nurseries, as a nod to the smaller gardens of today, graft antique scions onto dwarfing rootstocks. For your guidance, here are the terms used to describe the mature height of grafted and own-rooted trees, both antique and modern:

- *Dwarf:* 4 to 8 feet at maturity. (While most trees in this class will grow to 6 feet in height, the M-27 rootstock can produce 4-foot-high trees when grafted to certain scions.)

- *Semidwarf:* 8 to 12 feet.

- *Semistandard:* 12 to 20 feet.

- *Standard:* 20 feet or more at maturity.

The tree size should be listed as a part of the description of a fruit variety in catalogs or on tags. If not, don't buy the tree; you may be getting a full-sized tree when you have room only for a dwarf.

Dwarf Fruit Trees

A continuing decrease in the size of home gardens and yards has created a new demand for dwarf fruit trees. From the home gardener's viewpoint, the little fully dwarfed apple and pear trees may seem the most attractive, but the semidwarfs usually give greater satisfaction and can be controlled to some extent by pruning. In addition to the obvious advantage of being able to pick fruit from the ground or a short stepladder, you can also reach all parts of small trees with an ordinary pump-type sprayer. You are less apt to crowd small trees together, and the incidence of foliage and fruit diseases is lessened by the improved circulation of air. You can easily reach all parts of the tree for pruning, thinning, and summer tipping-back, which can prove especially important in years of heavy bearing. Without thinning and summer pruning, a feast could be followed by a famine. Finally, with a soft landing pad of a mulch under the foliage canopy, you will lose fewer fallen fruits to bruising. As with a child learning to walk, they don't have far to fall.

Peaches grow very fast, and are usually sold as standards, assuming that you will replace them when they overgrow or succumb to borer damage. Yet, certain plum tree stocks, when spliced in between the rootstock and the scion, can restrict top growth.

Cherries are also usually sold as standards although they can be dwarfed on G-9 rootstock. Of all fruit trees, cherries often suffer the worst from bird damage, and dwarfed trees can be reached for covering with bird mesh.

Plums are also susceptible to bird damage, and can be dwarfed with the 'Pixie' rootstock. Neither 'Pixie' nor G-9 are widely available, but are increasing in popularity. They are grown by a nursery called Oregon Rootstocks.

If you can't find dwarfed peaches, cherries, or plums, you can prune these trees relatively severely after two or three years of growth. You may suffer remorse after pruning, asking yourself, "What have I done!," but the tree will form more fruiting spurs and reward you for keeping it within bounds.

Care and Training

The care and training of young fruit trees soon after planting has changed drastically in recent years, due to new discoveries and new products. No longer do the experts advise gardeners to prune new trees severely at planting time. In fact, they advise minimizing pruning for the first two or three years after planting, except for training to a low head, because pruning very young trees can stunt a tree. By preserving the maximum amount of limbs, twigs, and foliage, you can increase photosynthesis and promote a stronger root system. Once the tree is settled in and growing strongly, you can begin a program of "tipping-back," or shortening limbs, as Elwood Fisher does with his summer pruning.

"Crop props" support heavily laden apricot branches and prevent breakage.

You can trick apple and pear trees into producing more fruit by a branch-training technique, discovered years ago. The procedure works better on young trees, especially apples, which tend to head lower. It doesn't take much time and needn't be done precisely. Drive a number of pegs around the dripline and tie stout strings to them. Loop the strings over outer branches and pull them down as far as you can without breaking. Or, you can tie a cinder block to a rope and loop it over a heavier branch to persuade it to bend down. You will see that the outer section of the limb, which is below a horizontal line, will bear more heavily. This works because sugars are partially trapped in a downwardly arched limb, and a high suger level in tissues can cause more fruit buds to form. With each succeeding year, training branches downward will become easier.

Home gardeners in the northern tier of states and at high altitudes have difficulty getting apple trees to survive. But they can copy a technique perfected in Siberia (apples in Siberia?) which results in a bizarre-looking but hardy tree. There, orchardists head the trees quite low and train the branches low to the ground and horizontally, supporting them with pegs and posts. As the tree grows, they train the limbs into a pattern like a four-leaf clover, so they can get into the center without stepping over branches. The trees survive extreme winters and bear good crops because the bulk of their top growth is down near the warming effect of the earth. Snow covers the branches and protects them from drying out and destruction from freezing and thawing.

Mulching

Landscape cloth, one of the new weed barriers developed for agriculture and home gardeners, and mulches of various kinds of organic matter combine to save labor and help trees grow and produce to their full potential. Commercial growers have long known that grass and weeds growing under fruit trees can compete for food and water, slowing growth and reducing yields. They are also aware of the damage done by cultivation, either to feeder roots near the surface, or accidentally to tree trunks. One of the saddest sights I know of is a poor little fruit tree with lawn grass growing right up to the trunk, whipped and nearly girdled by a string trimmer.

Commercial growers also know that mulches under the foliage canopy of fruit trees help growth and production in many ways: by keeping down weeds, reducing evaporation, and decomposing into humus while nurturing beneficial soil organisms. There is a downside to mulches such as hay or straw; they offer protection to meadow voles and pine voles as well as to rabbits, all serious pests in the eastern U.S. You need to protect the trunks of trees mulched with hay, straw, chipped wood, pine or fir bark, with a loose wrapping of half-inch-mesh hardware cloth. Commercial growers often protect trunks but don't mulch, mostly because of the cost of labor.

The ultimate mulch combines organic matter with an underlayment of landscape cloth under the entire area beneath the foliage canopy. The fabric looks like a thin blanket. No weeds can penetrate it except nutgrass, which is one of the sedges, and certain aggressive grasses. You could eradicate such ugly customers with a herbicide such as Roundup before planting. Here's the sequence for planting new trees and mulching:

Planting

After killing out aggressive perennial grasses and weeds, work lime and fertilizer into the soil according to soil test results.

Plant and water the new tree and wrap the trunk loosely with hardware cloth to protect against mechanical injury and chewing of bark by rodents. Tie the wire on with cotton string so, if you forget to loosen it later, the string will decay and prevent the wire from girdling the tree.

Spray the trunk and inner parts of lower limbs with cheap latex flat white paint. Technically, this isn't necessary except where sunscald or winter burn is a problem. But, why take chances? It won't hurt and, at the least, will keep the trunk from splitting on that warm day in midwinter when the sunny side expands rapidly while the shady side is still frozen.

Cut a square of landscape cloth and make a slit halfway into it. Slip it around the tree as a collar. Overlap strips of the fiber to enlarge the covered area. You can enlarge the mulched area as the tree grows.

Scatter a cup of vegetable garden fertilizer or organic equivalent over the landscape cloth and spread mulch 3 to 4 inches deep. The mulch will protect the fiber from ultraviolet ray deterioration. Don't draw the mulch up close to the trunk. Use pine or fir bark, hardwood mulch, or chipped wood, preferably precomposted. Let me caution citrus belt gardeners not to mulch around their citrus trees with organic mulch; it can encourage serious root and crown diseases.

The fertilizer should prevent nitrogen drawdown. However, if yellowing foliage makes you suspect a nitrogen shortage, drench the mulched area with manure tea or a liquid fertilizer. Don't fertilize late in the growing season; it can tenderize the young tree. Subsequent applications of fertilizer can be made as drenches or broadcast over the mulch and raked in. If you top-dress stable litter or manure over the mulch, you may introduce weed seeds and defeat the major purpose of the mulch.

As the tree increases in size, the layer of mulch can be made deeper to keep aggressive weeds under control by shading or smothering them out.

Buying

The selection of modern fruit trees for your home garden is more complicated than simply deciding which sorts you like to eat, and planting trees. You can start by visiting your Cooperative Extension Service office and picking up bulletins on adapted fruit tree varieties and their culture in your climate. Often, the value of Extension Service literature depends on the importance of commercial orchards in your state, and their recommendations will be tilted toward varieties grown commercially. For a balanced perspective, send for catalogs from fruit tree growers in your region, or one of the national suppliers. Here are a few of the things you will learn:

Fruit trees are indexed by the number of "chilling hours" (less than 40 degrees F.) required for blooming. Some with a high number of chilling hours will not bloom or bear fruit in warm climates with mild winters. Most catalogs cover this requirement by listing adaptation to the various climate zones on the U.S. hardiness zone map. The most reputable nurseries will not ship unadapted varieties, even if you ask for them.

While many tree fruit cultivars are moderately self-fertile, production can often be increased by the presence of another tree, of a kind known for good pollination and for flowering at the same time as your chosen cultivar.

Some kinds of fruit trees, notably cherries and Japanese plums, require "two to tango." If a neighbor happens to have a recommended pollinator in his yard, bees will probably carry the pollen to your tree. Or you can graft a piece of the recommended pollinator on the fruit-bearing tree. If fruit set is poor after planting two trees known to pair well for pollination, suspect lack of bees, due to indiscriminate spraying nearby, or rainy or cold weather when blossoms are open to pollen transfer.

Very early blooming cultivars should be avoided in areas prone to late frosts, as this can result in poor or no production.

Certain areas are "frost traps," where frost will occur even though surrounding areas are frost free. These can be basins caused by the topography, or traps caused by obstructions such as buildings, fences, or evergreen trees. Before planting, look all around and try to choose a spot where cold air will drain away rather than be trapped.

Each kind of fruit has distinct soil preferences. While all will grow well on deep, fertile soil, peaches and plums do better on comparatively poor sandy or gravelly soil. Of the tree fruits, pears show the strongest preference for fertile soil. Yet, on fertile soil, especially if forced with fertilizers, pears will produce soft, lush growth that may develop fire blight, if the disease is entrenched in that neighborhood. Few of the tree fruits, except certain plum cultivars, will tolerate poor drainage and, on dense clay soils, will do better if planted on low, wide mounds.

Care and Feeding

All new trees, and especially those of standard size, need a number of years to set the first significant fruit crop. You have to regard the care they need during those years as you would the feeding and training of a child. If you are faithful in your obligation, both tree and child should reach a healthy, productive maturity. Although early-bearing differs by cultivar, peaches, apricots, nectarines, and plums are generally the most precocious, followed by cherries, pears, and apples. Some apple cultivars don't hit their stride for six to seven years, and a few even longer. Elwood Fisher's experience with 'Northern Spy', for example, is that dwarfed trees should produce in seven to nine years, but standard trees not until fourteen years! I think that the definition of an optimist would be an eighty-year-old gardener planting standard trees of 'Northern Spy'.

All fruit trees need fairly frequent watering the first summer after planting and, later, generous watering when setting fruit. You can taper off for a short time, but resume watering again when trees are forming fruit buds for the next season. Water by flooding around the tree, rather than by a sprinkler.

All fruit trees benefit from yearly feeding at rates per square foot of soil comparable to those of large, greedy vegetables. From 2 to 3 pounds per 100 square feet of soil beneath the foliage canopy should be sufficient. Scatter the fertilizer around the dripline and slightly outside it, where the greatest concentration of feeder roots can be found. Spring feeding is preferred because late summer or fall feeding can tenderize the tree.

Pests and Diseases

The testimonials from gardeners who grow fruit without chemical sprays or dusts often neglect to mention the amount of fruit spoiled by insects or diseases, or damage to trees by borers. Even the most dedicated organic gardener will search out effective botanical and biological controls and acceptable mineral sprays such as Bordeaux mix and dormant oils. The amount of insect and disease controls you need is dependent on how much damage to trees and how much blemished or spoiled fruit you are willing to accept.

Insects such as borers, codling moths, plum curculios, and the various scales can weaken trees and damage fruit. Diseases such as brown rot, scab, rust, and bacterial leaf curl can have the same effect. If you are dead set against the use of proprietary insecticides or fungicides, ask around for the best organic fruit growers in your area and inquire how they manage it. Start with your local Master Gardeners Association. If you can accept the small amount of environmental impact caused by spraying a home orchard, ask your Cooperative Extension Service for a preventive spray program, scheduled for your area.

A growing trend, particularly at the universities, however, is the inclusion of nontoxic controls in "Integrated Pest Management" programs, which rely on a balance of predatory insects and biological controls. In the South and West, where nematodes are a problem on fruit trees, universities are researching green manure crops which either repel nematodes or will not harbor them.

If you'd like to try antique varieties of fruit trees in your garden, remember that they will grow into standard, full-sized trees. The options are to order antique varieties grafted to dwarfing rootstocks, or to graft scions of antique varieties onto existing trees of the same species. Any way you do it, the result will fully justify the effort.

Herbal Arts

Her love of growing and drying herbs for seasoning and crafts draws Maureen Ruettgers's family and friends into her hobby.

(Left) Drying herbs and everlasting flowers fill Maureen Ruettgers's antique barn.

*H*erbal arts is a new name for a very old pastime. To sit and weave wreaths from herbs or to dry and toss petals and flower heads into fragrant, colorful mixtures links you with a chain of humankind all over the world, back to the dawn of civilization. We have the leisure time now to practice herbal arts, which relieve stresses and satisfy our creative instincts by busying our hands and stimulating our senses. Ancient Greeks and Romans, Chinese philosophers, and medieval ladies might not have described their motives and gratifications in the same way but they, too, hung herbs and flowers to dry, wove them together with thread, and scented closed spaces with what we now call potpourris, and sprays of lavender, sage, and rosemary.

The herbal arts have advanced on the wave of interest in herbs for culinary, landscaping, and medicinal purposes. As gardeners experimented with herbs for seasoning foods, added silvery or gray-foliaged herbs to landscapes, and soothed upset stomachs with mint teas, they discovered that their attractive and durable flowers or seed heads could be dried for winter arrangements. And, as they grew in gardening, they evaluated garden flowers and wild species for drying and ranged out over the landscape to find natural materials to add variety to their dried creations. The result has been a vigorous revival of the ancient art of decorating with dried plant materials, only more eclectic and considerably faster, thanks to glue guns, monofilament line, desiccants, Styrofoam forms, and floral essences not available to previous generations.

The growing interest in country living and our colonial heritage has spawned research into the part played by herbal arts in the lifestyles of earlier days. Restored settlements such as Colonial Williamsburg, Old Sturbridge, Old Salem, and Plimoth Plantation reproduce the dried arrangements, swags, and fragrant mélanges of dried petals settlers made from the herbs and flowers of their day. All of this has raised our awareness of growing and utilizing herbs as a rewarding hobby, steeped in tradition and lore. Few other hobbies can call forth such strong images of families, on long winter evenings, clustered around lamps or hearths for light, busy with herbal crafts or capturing the images of flowers in needlework or quilts.

Always, there have been lively cottage industries associated with herbal arts. When practitioners reach a certain level of proficiency, and people begin to admire their handiwork, some decide to sell what they make. Today, herbal arts are often displayed at crafts fairs and harvest festivals. Thus it was, too, at medieval fairs and festivals. Lacking tools and the money to buy them, peasants made and marketed what they could from materials they could gather from gardens, fields, and hedgerows. Even the most highborn shopper must have reacted favorably to the cunning combinations of homegrown or found materials.

At herbal arts displays today, many of the hobbyist-exhibitors are well educated; some are trained in fine arts. But many are plain, everyday people with extraordinary talents in growing and utilizing herbs and flowers artfully.

Most of these hobbyists are good gardeners. They grow their own herbs and flowers for drying, and combine them with seed pods, vines, and flowers gathered from the wild. Some buy dried material and floral scents from florists and specialty suppliers at trade fairs or through the mail. They feel their way into the hobby, enticed by the beautiful creations they see at craft fairs and garden club flower shows. They ask questions, attend workshops and seminars, study how-to books, and practice with simple creations. All the while, the people who are good gardeners expand into

Maureen created this wreath from artemisia decorated with gomphrena and statice.

growing species and cultivars known to be useful in making wreaths, dried arrangements, bunched mixed herbs for hanging, collages, and potpourris. The more adventurous scout roadsides, stream banks, fencerows, botanical gardens, and vacant lots for weeds and wildflowers, vines, trees, and shrubs with decorative flowers or seed pods.

The typical herbal arts hobbyist does not have the dark, drafty barn so often featured in articles about drying herbs and flowers. Well-ventilated, dark barns are great for hanging hundreds of bunches of garden flowers or herbs for drying. Good ventilation reduces the incidence of molding, and gradual drying in the dark reduces fading and loss of natural fragrance. But, favorable drying conditions can also be created by darkening a room, opening a window from the top, and running an electric fan to keep the air moving.

The majority of herb hobbyists dry their herbs and flowers in darkened rooms, garages, or sheds, often with help from a small heater and a fan. Their gardens produce too much raw material for drying with silica gel, except for particularly fragile blossoms. Hobbyists use cookstove ovens set on the lowest heat, commercial dehydrators, and microwave ovens for drying during rainy weather or to speed up the process to meet show deadlines.

I know many gardeners who are deeply involved in herbal arts. Their hobby involves them year-round, yet accommodates time needed for work, family, or social obligations. Herbs and flowers for drying are easy to grow and don't demand harvesting within a tight time frame. Harvesting and preparing flowers for drying is especially enjoyable, and putting them together artfully can wait until you have spare time and feel creative. I know of no other hobby that has so many dimensions or that involves more sensory stimulation. The fragrances transport you to the garden or fields where you harvested the plants; the bristly textures and muted colors remind you of the fullness and brilliance of the fresh flowers and leaves.

A few miles out from Boston, in the countryside that sent militia for the first battles of the Revolution, and in a home occupied by three generations before the call went out from Lexington and Concord, lives the Ruettgers family. Without a doubt, families who tilled this farm in past years and gardened near the old white frame home grew herbs and flowers for drying, and used them artistically.

Perhaps emanations from generations past guided Maureen Ruettgers into herbal arts, or it could have been a near and dear role model, or an inborn and carefully nurtured artistic talent. Whatever the source, it has produced a good gardener with a gift for landscaping with herbs and flowers useful for drying, and for employing them in highly creative ways.

Maureen shows me how she selects materials for wreathmaking.

Maureen Ruettgers is living proof that a young woman can have a satisfying plant hobby while raising a family and doing community work. She and her husband, Michael, have gradually converted the grounds of an historic home into a large, beautiful, and functional garden for herbs and flowers for drying. The old barn that came with the place proved to be a perfect site for drying and storing herbs and dried flowers. Their three children grew up in the garden and at the feet of their mother as she worked away at herb crafts. They took to it naturally, much to the delight of their mother and father.

Michael shares Maureen's love for growing things but he describes himself as "more of an inside man." He loves to cook and preserve the vegetables and grapes he and their son Chris grow. Michael learned gardening from his father at their homes in England and, later, in San Diego.

Maureen is among the many herb growers who are enlarging the scope of the hobby to include herbs for seasoning, for medicinal purposes, and for inexpensive, fragrant decorations for the home. Although she considers herself an herb enthusiast, Maureen grows many annual and perennial flowers, and some wildflowers, for decorative flowers and seed heads. She uses them to enrich her materials for dried herb crafts: wreaths, swags, bunches, sachets, potpourris, and so forth. This infusion of nonherb plants adds color and texture to her garden, which, for much of the growing season, would otherwise show mostly the muted green, gray, and silver colors of her herbs. Maureen grows several of the healing herbs in her garden, not for medicinal use but because they look good in landscapes or can be used in herbal arts.

A tour of the Ruettgerses' garden is a learning experience because of the many uses to which Maureen puts her plants. We began our tour just outside their back door, in view of the kitchen windows:

"The first garden we built here was a 'ladder garden,'" Maureen recalled. "We laid an old ladder on prepared ground and planted in between the rungs with herb plants. We used it to teach visiting schoolchildren how to garden in small spaces: they loved to sample the herbs. The kinds of herbs vary from year to year but are basically the

The "ladder garden" makes a pretty display for French tarragon, center; 'Spicy Globe' basil, foreground; and chives and parsley in the background.

edible herbs that can be bought anywhere as plants . . . sweet basil, parsley, dill, spearmint, thyme, sage, rosemary, and chives. I was trained as an elementary school teacher and it did my heart good to see the difference that old ladder made in getting the story over. We still use the ladder garden with visiting school groups.

"Gradually, we expanded the herb garden to its present size of a quarter of an acre and added beds for perennials, mostly those with interesting flowers for drying, seed pods, or shade-tolerant cultivars. It is hard to find shade-tolerant plants with useful seed pods. I use pods of hosta, one of the best shade plants. Alchemilla, or lady's mantle, one of my favorites, withstands moderate shade and stands up well to wind and rain. It has greenish yellow blossoms that dry well, and the cupped leaves collect large, glistening drops of dew or rain. The drops slide over the leaves like quicksilver. I like to plant lady's mantle in drifts. Out in the sunny areas of the perennial beds, we grow the eryngiums, baptisias, verbascums, horehound, and butterfly weed for decorative seed pods which we combine with dried pods of annuals such as *Nigella damascena, Scabiosa stellata,* and Shirley poppy.

"There really is a fine line of distinction between what nurseries call 'perennials' and the perennial herbs. I suppose that what qualifies a plant as an 'herb' is its usefulness in flavoring, medicines, or scenting. Many herbs have decorative uses as well, and I will confess a fondness for them, but when it comes to choosing flowers for drying or for decorative seed pods I'm not so much of a purist that I discriminate against annual or perennial flowers. I need a wide variety of blossoms, seed pods, and dried foliage for my creations, as well as fragrant herbs.

Tall artemisia 'Silver King' stands guard for Maureen's drying barn in the background.

"Next to lady's mantle, cinnamon basil is my favorite plant in the garden. It is easy to grow in full sun, and quickly develops a mounded shape. The tip growth of each branch is purple green and the blossom scales are deep purple. The blossom spikes retain their color when dried and, being short, mix neatly in potpourris. The fragrance is intense and clovelike, fresh or dried."

Maureen has found it helpful and pleasing to the eye to divide her garden into two parts: one half, dubbed by the children "The Magic Garden," is planted with pastel colors of flowers for drying, and mostly silvery or gray herbs. The other half, "The Kitchen Garden," is reserved for brighter colored flowers, mostly grown for potpourris, and herbs that are blended in their manufacture. The garden is made up of raised beds separated by mulched walks; the perennial border is elevated two feet and surrounded by a wall of gray fieldstone.

Near the house is a forty-foot-long arbor for grapes, very ornamental and painted white. Maureen's father built it; he is a master woodworker and was restless in retirement. Michael's wine and jelly grape varieties are beginning to climb up and over it. The arbor is a work of art; it looks much like the one at the Victory Garden in Lexington, Massachusetts.

Maureen and her daughters, Polly and Abigail, and I had a great time touring the herb garden. Of all the plant classes, I suppose I know the herbs best, having grown the culinary herbs commercially for several years. Nevertheless, the Ruettgerses were growing several I'd never seen before. Their cooler climate and emphasis on decorative herbs has allowed them to collect and propagate some kinds you won't find outside of the catalogs of herb specialists. Odd species of salvia, thyme, artemisia, and mint kept me guessing, and rarely successfully. Maureen swapped what she knew about unusual herbs for what I knew about container growing, pest control without chemicals, and plant nutrition, in relation to herb growing. The children didn't say much but I could tell they were absorbing the conversation.

In the Ruettgers garden, the plant that impressed me most was the ambrosia, *Chenopodium botrytis*, also called feather geranium or Jerusalem oak. I know it can become a weed in some gardens, but growing it in the hot, dry soil of the South where I live is anything but easy. Maureen's garden was well stocked with ambrosia; she told me she has to thin out and discard surplus volunteer plants every year.

I was particularly interested in her collections of salvias for drying, including *Salvia hordeum* and *S. leucantha*, and numerous artemisias (wormwood). Unusual alliums were blooming all over the place; August is the time for these onion family relatives to shine. I saw yellow, white, pink, and purple varieties from 8 inches to 24 inches in height.

Here and there, around the garden, were herbs growing in containers. I asked Maureen which herbs, in her experience, do best in containers. "The shorter ones," she replied, "especially herbs that trail over the sides of containers; lemon thyme, oregano, and creeping rosemary are good. You need some erect plants of the shorter varieties for vertical accents and foliage or flower color: chives, lavender, or sage, for example. The gross feeders such as basil need larger containers, as does mint."

I was curious to learn if Maureen left any of her containerized perennial herbs out of doors during the winter. "No," she said, "not only because they would die from freezing, but also because the containers would break up from the pressure of expanding ice." Maureen uses terra-cotta containers to blend with her old-fashioned garden. She knocks the plants out of containers in the fall, heels them in for winter protection, and repots in the spring. She takes plants of the tender herbs indoors: bay, lemon verbena, rosemary, and such.

Maureen and I agreed on the difficulty of growing herbs on windowsills during the winter, despite the bland assurances in some books that it is easy. As you travel north, winter days grow progressively shorter and often more cloudy. Herbs have a hard time existing, let alone producing enough new growth for cutting. The overly warm, bone-dry winter atmosphere of many homes also works against plants. You can get around the problems by installing fluorescent lights in a cool room and enclosing the plant growing area with clear plastic sheeting. Under lights is a great place for starting seeds and saving plants and starts of your prized tender perennials.

Maureen's raised beds for herbs enjoy many of the advantages of containers, without the need for frequent watering. She fills them with moderately fast draining soil that holds moisture well, yet never becomes waterlogged. The porous soil is easy to cultivate and to keep free of weeds. Her raised beds reminded me of a similar arrangement for herbs at the Birmingham, Alabama, Botanical Garden. Volunteer herb enthusiasts had converted a steep slope into an outstanding herb garden by using weathered railroad ties to break the slope into level terraces. *The Victory Garden* taped the Birmingham "Herb Army" at work weeding and grooming their wide selection of improved cultivars.

Maureen gets her information on esoteric herbs from a large home library and from her association with the oldest group within The Herb Society, the Massachusetts chapter. "An office I held in the chapter proved invaluable to me," Maureen said. "I was elected librarian. That gave me access to 700 volumes on herbs, some very old and valuable." At one time, The Herb Society's national garden was nearby, at the Arnold Arboretum. It was a valued resource that assisted Maureen in learning the many genera and species that are called "herbs." Now, it has been moved to Holden Arboretum in Mentor, Ohio, near Cleveland.

At chapter meetings, Maureen has met many notables in herb growing: Madeline Hill, Joy Martin of Logee's Greenhouses, and Cyrus Hyde of Well Sweep Farm, to name a few. Some have visited her garden and have shared information and plants. I reminded Maureen of the several *Victory Garden* programs which have featured herbs, among them being visits to Caprilands in Connecticut, to the Denver Botanic Garden, and a wreath-making workshop at Callaway Gardens.

At the time I visited the Ruettgerses, they had just returned from a trip to Europe, and Maureen's daughter Polly was preparing to leave on another trip. Nevertheless, she took the time to show me the flowers and herbs she likes to grow, and how she makes potpourri by mixing dried herbs and flowers from the garden. She and her mother are keeping notes to establish the best stages of maturity for harvesting herbs and flowers for the best color, fragrance, and keeping quality.

I asked Maureen about sources for seeds, plants, and supplies for herb crafts. "You can avoid a lot of trial and error," she said, "by asking a member to recommend you for membership in a local chapter of The Herb Society. If there is no chapter nearby, you can network with other herb enthusiasts in horticultural societies, or within the Master Gardener organization; many of their members grow herbs along with vegetables.

"Some herb enthusiasts bring back seeds from foreign countries, of species not known in this country. Bringing in seeds is permitted, but importation of plants is so complicated that usually only botanical gardens are willing to make the effort. Once in this country, it is a slow process introducing a new species until one of the major herb seed and plant marketers gets behind it. Conversely, greatly improved cultivars can catch on rather quickly, as did 'Dark Opal' and 'Spicy Globe' basils. Also, the seed and plant companies seem to be making an effort to locate and market more flower varieties with potential for drying."

(Left) Polly gathers roses for potpourri while Abigail holds an armful. (Right) Abigail and Polly mix dried herbs to make potpourri.

We spent some time in the fragrant drying shed, already filling up with bouquets, swags, wreaths, and the makings of potpourri. "In about two weeks," Maureen said, "every tray in the big dryer will be covered with herbs and flowers, and every hook on the wall will be loaded with wreaths." She emphasized the necessity of darkening all the windows and maintaining good air circulation in the drying room, to retain color and fragrance. Slow microwaving or drying in ovens is being used by

1) 2) 3)

4) 5) 6)

Herbs and Flowers for Drying

A basic selection of herbs and everlasting flowers for drying includes florist's statice, Limonium statice (1); teasel, which is widely naturalized (2); matricaria or feverfew (3); *Gomphrena* 'Strawberry Fields' (4); *Salvia farinacea* 'Victoria' (5); yarrow, *Achillea filipendulina* 'Moonshine' (in the foreground); and ambrosia (6). All have versatile colors and textures that hold up well in dried arrangements. A variety of techniques, from air-drying to microwaving, are used by hobbyists. Experimentation will show you which method is most effective for you.

other enthusiasts for preserving herbs and flowers, but the Ruettgerses' production would overwhelm home units.

Maureen and Polly use silica gel to dry certain delicate flowers, and most species with blue or purple flowers, which tend to fade in air-drying. The silica gel helps to retain natural colors. Silica gel is a powdery substance. When flowers are imbedded in it, and the powder dusted in among the petals, the silica gel draws the moisture out of the tissues. It has to be shaken off the dried flowers, and can be reclaimed by heating to drive off the absorbed moisture. "We found that we could air-dry the blue flowers of 'Hidcote' lavender so perfectly that they could hardly be distinguished from the fresh. We can't grow and dry enough lavender to meet the demand at our annual sale," said Maureen.

"Members of the Massachusetts chapter come out and help us dig and pot up plants for the sale. We have many other herb enthusiasts in the area; they bring friends to see the dried materials and crafts and to pick up ideas. They especially like our wreaths and necklaces made of spices and can't seem to get enough of Polly's potpourri. We are very choosy about the essential oils we use to reinforce fragrance: some of the commercially available stuff is cloyingly sweet or offensively oily smelling. You can buy essential oils extracted from all the major herbs and fragrant flowers. They add life to potpourris; just stir the contents of the jar gently and the fragrance will come to life again and again.

"In wet years, we have had to cancel the sale. Continuing rains and damp weather can make drying of herbs and flowers difficult for everybody. What a difference a dry summer can make! In just two or three days, herbs can dry sufficiently to keep. Wet seasons have convinced me to install a warm air drying system in the barn similar to the one used here years ago to dry digitalis grown on the farm for pharmaceutical use. Also, the heat would let us work later in the winter here in the barn; without heat, it gets too cold by January.

"One little extra that makes our sales so successful is that we serve an herb lunch, along with herb teas. That alone has persuaded many customers to take up herb growing. It helps that we offer books on growing and using herbs. Books on birds and butterflies also sell well because they naturally go with herbs.

"Above all, I want to do everything I can to lead, but not push, our children into gardening with herbs and flowers. It has meant so much in my life and I hope it will in theirs. We were so proud of Polly for two term papers she did; they were on medieval gardening and heart drugs. She did all the research, including tracing how Mr. James Patch grew digitalis on our land years ago."

That her large garden is both beautiful and functional is a tribute to Maureen's dedication to the aesthetic values and country traditions that the herbal arts represent.

More about Herbal Arts

Herbal arts, the "craft" side of herbs, is one of many specialties open to the hobby herb grower. It attracts nearly as many herb growers as producing herbs for gourmet cooking. Both of these specialties lead medicinal herbs in popularity, but such has not always been the case. Mankind was using medicinal herbs when diagnoses were by supposition and treatment by trial and error. Scenting herbs were used not only for such civilized purposes as imparting a sweet smell to linens and clothing, but also for masking unpleasant odors and repelling insects. Herb uses are described at length in the writings of early physicians and philosophers, from Europe east through China. Some herbs were gathered from the wild but, as trade and commerce grew, seeds and plants helped gardeners everywhere to grow a broad range of herbs. Improvement by selection began more than two thousand years ago.

Now, gardeners can buy seeds or plants of herb varieties developed especially for drying. These hold their flower colors with little fading, and resist shattering during handling. For instance, the common purple-flowered oregano, *Origanum vulgare*, is no great shakes for flavor, but has superb color, holding power, and stem length for drying. Cinnamon basil, one of the recently rediscovered "rare basils," is perfect for potpourris, where its bronzy purple color and strong, clove-like scent will hold for several months.

The cultural methods for growing herbs for culinary uses are not always compatible with those for herbs to be dried. Herb cookery calls for tender vegetative tips. To produce new vegetative growth, you need to trim off the very flower heads and seed pods that are useful in herbal arts. For this reason, the herb specialist usually grows culinary herbs in the vegetable garden or dooryard plot, and isolates the herbs for drying in a special herb garden. This arrangement also makes best use of the landscaping value of the gray and silver herbs which are so important in herbal arts.

Most gardeners hate to waste the beautiful flowers and seed heads on their herb plants but, every year, many do. They might be pleasantly surprised at how easy and satisfying it is to work with dried materials, and at the extent of their own creativity. Herbal arts is not gender-oriented; many men are quite good at it. Their dried herb and flower creations tend to be large and robust and to include wild materials such as cattails, which can be collected only by slogging through marshes, and teasel weed and rabbit tobacco from the roughest terrain.

Starting Right It is possible to throw yourself wholeheartedly into herbal arts—simultaneously to begin growing special herbs and flowers for drying, all the while scouting for wild seed pods and flower heads. I would counsel moderation. If you are already growing herbs, start evaluating a few new herbs every growing season; learn how to grow and when to harvest them for drying. Experiment with blending them with herbs you already know. Discard the varieties you don't like or which don't hold well when dried and move on to others.

Once you become proficient in herb growing, study the catalogs of seed companies and specialists in flowers for cutting. Select a few varieties which are adapted to your climate and which are specifically recommended for air-drying.

Watch this last point carefully; some suppliers recommend varieties which are so fragile that careful and tedious drying with silica gel is required. Grow a short row of a few new varieties each year, in your food garden, where cutting arm-loads of flowers won't disrupt the landscape. Anticipate that the colors, even after careful drying, will be subdued when compared to fresh flowers. Of all the colors, blue is the most elusive in drying and the yellows and oranges the least likely to fade. Good clear whites are rare; most dry to cream or dingy shades.

Drying Herbs
People who love to tinker can find plenty of room for their talents in techniques for drying herbs and flowers. First place in drying techniques is held by uncomplicated air-drying, using a dark area ventilated by fans. But, air-drying is speeded up considerably by drying for two or three days in a refrigerator, then hanging bunches in the dark to complete drying. Hanging lets stems and leaves assume a more or less natural stance, while laying them to dry on racks or layers of paper towels flattens them like herbarium specimens. Microwaving at low settings can preserve colors at exceptional levels of brilliance, but some flowers tend to collapse and lose their shape. You will have to experiment with settings and duration of microwave drying; it varies from oven to oven. Very slow drying in an electric oven with the door cracked works well; sometimes the oven pilot light alone will do the job in a gas oven. Commercial or home-made dehydrators are good for drying petals for potpourri and seed pods with short stems, but usually lack the capacity to handle long-stemmed flowers.

One of the best rigs for drying is a home greenhouse. Gardeners drape the houses with black plastic to exclude light, hang their harvests of herb and flower stems in bunches, crack the vents to let out moisture-laden air, turn on the fans, and, in less than a week, their plant materials are dried just right, pliable but not

These wooden drying trays were made by Maureen's father.

brittle and prone to shatter. Almost as good are large cold frames covered with black plastic, cracked for ventilation, and fitted with a fan in one corner to force out moist air. Such units can dry small wreaths made up from fresh vines, branches, and flowers, but the monofilament thread or thin copper wire used to hold them together should be tightened after drying.

Making Wreaths

Wreaths are probably the most popular herbal art. Most are made on Styrofoam or straw forms purchased at florist shops or specialists in flower-arranging supplies. Or, you can weave your own forms from kudzu, honeysuckle, and wild grape vines, or prunings from vineyards. Where I garden in the South, tall silver artemisia, lemon verbena, and anise-scented (licorice) basil grow so large that the limber branches can be half-dried, woven into wreaths, then completely dried before adding decorations.

There is an art to making wreaths perfectly round and symmetrical, or to other special shapes such as ovals and hearts. The professionals use jigs fitted with slots through which the monofilament, thread or wire can be passed for wrapping. But, the real art starts with the decoration; a well-made wreath is solidly covered with a mixture of dried flower and herb heads, frothy dried foliage, tiny conifer cones, seed pods in scale with the size of the wreath, and ribbons to suit your taste. It should be so securely wrapped with monofilament thread in a muted shade of gray, or fine wire, that it will stand up to handling. All decorations should be either firmly threaded into the base or stuck on with a glue gun so that they won't shake loose in handling.

Wreathmaking

Maureen demonstrates the art of wreathmaking, using artemisia, sage, and oregano. Using blue-gray thread, she ties the fresh artemisia to a wire ring (1). The real artistry begins with the decoration. Over the artemisia, Maureen arranges sprays of sage leaves with oregano flowers, and ties them securely to the wreath (2). Lamb's ear, gomphrena flowers, sage flowers, and gray santolina add their decorative effects (3). When the wreath is completely assembled, Maureen hangs it to dry.

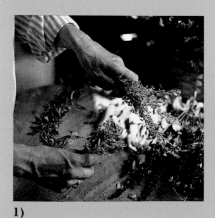

1)

2)

3)

Making Potpourris	Potpourris also make excellent gifts when packed in the special decorative large-mouthed jars on sale at pottery outlets. Some gardeners use so many petals that they arrange with local greenhouses and public parks to deadhead their geraniums and roses. Not all dried flowers used in potpourris are fragrant; some are added for color and bulk. Herbal arts specialists are divided on the issue of using floral essences to enhance the fragrance and carrying power of petal and flower blends. Some use none at all. Some load their potpourris with perfume. Others compromise by using only highly refined natural floral fragrances discreetly, along with orris root as a stabilizer and extender.

Bunches of dried herbs are rather plain and simple, but are appropriate for hanging in kitchens. They look at home in kitchens with a colonial or country design but are not out of place with any decor. Sage, rosemary, common oregano, and English thyme cut at first flower stage look good and hold well. There is no denying how attractive mint looks when the stems are cut at the ground and dried when the first flowers are opening, but it tends to shatter, as does basil. Sweet marjoram can be cut when the little seed balls are still green. Common chives and garlic chives should be cut at full flower; garlic chive seed heads are also quite decorative. Ordinary garlic flower heads dry beautifully and don't smell rank. If you consider the many other alliums to be herbs, you add many excellent colors and blossom forms to your flowery workbasket.

Landscaping with Herbs	Some of the decorative herbs have potential as landscape subjects, as do some of the species grown mostly for medicinal purposes. Landscape architects have begun to appreciate certain of the herb species for their foliage, flowers, and fragrance. Some of the interest is due to the imaginative plantings in the National Herb Garden within the United States National Arboretum at Washington, D.C. Also, designers have seen how Europeans use herbs in conjunction with perennials, groundcovers, and shrubs, often to get special textural effects and silvery colors. Greenhouse growers who produce herb plants for sale often install demonstration gardens to show visitors how herbs will look at maturity in various landscaping situations. As yet, most full-service nurseries market herbs as a class and don't separate the species with special potential for herbal arts or landscaping. That day will come.

Once you get started in herbal arts, you may wish to attend one of the national seminars and trade shows for hobby and commercial herb growers and herb craft specialists. The Cooperative Extension Service at Purdue University and the International Herb Marketers Association sponsor yearly conferences. The lectures are superb and the trade fair attracts all kinds of suppliers and products for herb specialists. Your Cooperative Extension Service office will have dates and locations. Until and if the time comes when you head for the national herb meeting, there is plenty at home to feed your curiosity about herbal arts. Every town of any size has a hobbyist so good at herbal arts that they lecture and give demonstrations. Books on drying flowers and herbs are plentiful and well illustrated. Yet, the best way to learn is by growing and drying your own, and experimenting to make herbal creations that please you. You will seldom go wrong and, when you do, you simply take your less-than-a-masterpiece apart and do it better.

Dwarf Conifers

Ed Rezek gains international notice for his Long Island collection of dwarf conifers, miniature jewels of the evergreen world.

This corner of Ed's back yard displays his exotic-looking collection in an artful landscape.

Dwarf conifers are not a modern discovery. Interest in these slow-growing, miniature forms of standard plants goes back centuries. They are found in all the forms of standard conifers—ground-hugging, spreading, mounded, ball-like, vase-shaped, columnar, and conical erect plants, and special forms such as weeping and contorted—and in a wide range of colors including blue, variegations of silver, white, or cream-yellow, as well as every shade of green. Such myriad variations make the plants eminently collectible.

The early collectors of dwarf conifers were noblemen or traders with the time and money to devote to scholarly pursuits, including collecting plants from afar and learning how to identify and grow them. The first collectors were probably wealthy Chinese and Japanese hobbyists who, hundreds of years ago, gathered dwarf conifers from the wild to include in their bonsai collections. Though many of their bonsais, then as now, were normal plants artificially dwarfed by severe pruning and root restriction, these collectors sought out and cultivated true miniature conifers as well.

Interest in collecting dwarf and unusual forms peaked during the mid-nineteenth century as wealthy gentry in Great Britain and on the Continent vied with one another for exotic garden specimens. Sheltered courtyards, old walls, granite troughs, rock gardens, and alpine screes accommodated dwarf conifer collections naturally. When wars and hard times took their tolls on the estates, interest in dwarf conifers went into decline, but they were protected at botanical gardens and smaller private collections.

Today, as gardens become smaller in scale and gardeners become more discerning, dwarf conifers are increasingly prized for their beauty and longevity as well as for their compact size and slow growth habit in the landscape. The distinctive forms invite close inspection and contemplation, for many are best appreciated at close range. Landscapers think of them as "designer plants" because, as in designer clothing, their style, uniqueness, and finish are immediately apparent.

The term "dwarf" is a relative one and therefore somewhat misleading. A dwarfed forest tree might grow ten times as large as a dwarfed shrub. However, all dwarfed plants mature at smaller sizes than are normal or typical for the species. At maturity, dwarf plants can range from one-half to only one-twentieth the size of normal plants. Furthermore, dwarf plants grow very slowly, from less than one inch to five inches a year.

Some dwarf and unusual conifers come about as chance seedlings. Others are propagated by cuttings taken from a dwarfed branch of an otherwise normal plant. No one knows all the causes of spontaneous dwarfism in plants, but it may be due to air pollution, radiation, or viruses. Dwarfing anomalies may show up as:

Juvenile fixation. Ordinarily, the foliage of juvenile conifers differs from that of adult plants in form and color. Some plants never "shift gears"; they retain their juvenile characteristics at an advanced age. *Thuja occidentalis* 'Rhineglow' is an example. Others, such as *Chamaecyparis thyoidies* 'Andelyensis', may exhibit fixation, but become unstable later on and revert partially or fully to normal performance.

Witches' brooms. No causal organisms have been found to create these profusely branched and often low-growing malformations on conifers and deciduous plants. As the name suggests, they are congested and resemble brooms. You can reproduce them by cuttings or grafting, and they will often grow into dwarfed or unusual plants. Witches' brooms or grafted

cuttings made from them rarely set seeds but, when they do, mutations can occur at a higher rate than with normal plants.

Grafting cuttings from witches' brooms to normal rootstock is one way to propagate these curiosities, but the plants sometimes suffer from incompatible grafts, due to different rates of growth of the scion and understock. The rate of growth of grafted specimens (dwarf scions grafted on normal rootstock) can depend on the vigor of the rootstock. Strong rootstocks can sometimes force dwarf conifers to grow too large. Grafts are unavoidable, because certain forms of dwarf conifers don't set good root systems when you try to make cuttings and root them.

Dwarfed or stunted alpine forms. Most of these will start to grow normally when planted in regular garden soil at low elevations. They can, with difficulty, be maintained as dwarfs by growing them as severely pruned bonsai. A good example is *Abies lasiocarpa* 'Sub-alpina' from the timberline in the Northwest.

Fastigiate (narrow, flattened, upright) forms of conventional conifers.
These generally come about as chance seedlings and are identifiable at an
early age. The flattening effect is most noticeable in the tips of the twigs,
but can also show up as kinked branches.

Side shoots from erect conifers. If you have ever tried to root and grow
a cutting from the tip of a side branch of a conifer, you doubtless found it
to be stubbornly geotropic. They usually produce prostrate or descending
forms that will not turn upright. However, if you injure one of these forms
by severe pruning or mechanical damage, or if they are injured by freezing,
they can revert to upright growth, resulting in a freakish-looking plant.

Many dwarf conifer specimens are not perfect miniatures of the standard
version, but show the effects of the various conditions that dwarfed them.
Early attempts at identification left a confusing legacy of mixed-up Latin
and variety names. Now, a botanist or knowledgeable amateur can, after
a brief inspection, identify each by its genus and species and make an
educated guess as to its cultivar name. The shape and arrangement of the
leaves, and, if available, cones and seeds provide the botanical "finger-
prints."

What is it about these miniature plants that exerts such fascination?
Aside from smallness, collectors look for forms that differ from the norm

for the species. Whereas a normal tree might be conical in form, a dwarf offspring might grow into a weeping shape, or globose, drum-shaped, creeping, or spreading. Collectors look as well for color variations or variegations: a yellow-foliaged plant from a green parent, a silvery-blue plant from a green parent, a green and white or green and gold variegation from a solid green species. They look for curiously contorted plants resulting from the genetic aberration called "fasciation" or flattening of stems and terminal growth, for thread-leaved foliage where flattened foliage would be normal, and for mimicry of other species in leaves or needles.

Not content with variations from the norm, some advanced dwarf conifer specialists experiment with topiary effects, grafting ball-like or weeping forms onto tall, single trunks to get tree forms, and splicing variegated foliage among solid-colored growth. They prune larger specimens to imaginative designs: spirals, poodle puffs, mushroom shapes, tall columns, Medusa-like branching, and pearls-on-a-string fantasies. They interplant their dwarf conifers with choice small deciduous trees and perennials. They want to do more than simply charm visitors with their collections; they want to overwhelm them with effects not seen since royal gardeners sought to please their lords and ladies.

In the landscape, dwarf conifers are often combined with young specimens of Japanese maples, alpine plants, dwarf perennial flowers, and small-leaved groundcovers. With more commercial nurseries offering a wider selection, home gardeners can choose superior dwarf conifers to replace overgrown or overused shrubs. These plants hold great potential as container-grown specimens for decks, patios, and terraces, where space is valuable and every plant must have year-round impact. Both the visual effects and the maintenance are enhanced by grouping dwarf plants together.

Part of the challenge of growing dwarf conifers is in keeping the surroundings and accessories in scale with the plants, to emphasize their beauty and not purely their oddness. Skillful collectors, like Ed Rezek of Long Island, New York, can work magic in creating miniature landscapes that display their plants to perfection.

Ed created this spiral topiary form by clipping a Chamaecyparis pisifera *'Squarrosa Intermedia'.*

*E*d Rezek of Malverne, Long Island, typifies the new breed of dwarf conifer collectors. Enthusiasts such as Ed can't stop with simply collecting new specimens: their love for their specialty plants compels them to master the art of displaying dwarf conifers. And it is an art, the art of illusion. When the *Victory Garden* crew arrived at Ed Rezek's home, they couldn't resist rubbernecking around the front, side, and back yards. I think it is safe to say that, in the many years of the show's existence, we have never seen such an extraordinary garden!

On a tour of the garden, my eyes told me I was looking at very young evergreens, but Ed told me they were up to forty years old! Tiny ball-like *Chamaecyparis*, wee spruces growing like hand-high Christmas trees, and sculpted miniature topiaries made a bewitching sight.

Ed's yard is the centerpiece of the neighborhood, immaculately kept, rising up in tiers from street level. The back yard is short from front to back but, by designing a peninsula to jut out from the side and past the center of the yard, Ed manages to convey an anticipation of what lies beyond. A tastefully constructed waterfall and pool catch your eye as you round the tip of the peninsula. By stair-stepping deep beds of plants down from slow-growing deciduous trees in the back, to waist-high dwarf conifers in the center and, finally, to very short dwarf conifers in the front, he creates a harmonious and totally artistic effect. The illusion is one of looking at a much larger landscape compressed to miniature scale.

Ed Rezek could sell the plants in his back, front, and side yards for several thousand dollars. But he won't—not the whole collection, not even a single plant. Monetary return never has been a consideration in his hobby of growing dwarf conifers. Ed is not a wealthy man; comfortably situated, yes, but living on retirement income. His wife of more than forty years, Maureen, plans to work a year or two longer before retirement. She is an excellent typist and helps Ed with his many compilations and reports.

"The day I start expecting money or recognition for my dwarf conifers is the day I begin losing the fun of it," Ed says emphatically.

Ed is an agile, energetic man, yet infinitely patient. His is a class of plants that you have to get on your knees to appreciate fully, and that require a full measure of faith from the grower. You'll never hear a dwarf conifer grower boast, "You can almost see my plants grow!" These diminutive plants grow so slowly that, years after the passing of the hobbyist, most will still be wee, little things as compared to the original, standard-sized species. Ed is so advanced in his hobby that the tinier and more difficult the plant, the more he likes it. He showed me a couple of seedling plants that, although several months old, had grown into little knots of foliage no larger than a pea seed.

His production of dwarf conifers, choice variegated conifers, and deciduous trees and shrubs could rival that of a commercial nursery. He grows from seeds and cuttings. Hundreds of plants, started in his ten-by-twenty Everlite greenhouse in pots, fill every spare inch of space in his yard. Prior to joining the International Plant Propagators Society, he learned to root cuttings and germinate seeds of dwarf conifers by trial and error. Now, he has excellent success, using sterile rooting media, mist propagation, and bottom heat in his greenhouse.

Some of his benches hold propagating boxes, filled with perlite and watered with an overhead mist system. At the time of my visit, they were full of recently stuck cuttings, stripped of lower leaves, dipped in rooting hormone, and plunged deep into the rooting medium. Other benches were covered with trays filled with deep pots of potting soil. He uses these to put a compact root system on the cuttings rooted in perlite. His greenhouse space is so valuable that, after a few weeks, he moves the tray of potted plants to a lath-covered holding area wedged in between the garage and the greenhouse.

"You might think I'd want to move to a home with a larger lot to hold all the dwarf conifers and special grafted plants I produce," he said. "But no, my neighbors have helped to keep me here. They have let me help renovate their landscapes with choice evergreens and dwarf conifers that have overgrown my space. I bet I've placed a thousand plants in good homes!"

You can see what Ed means when you drive down his quiet side street. Several of his neighbors have the most distinctive landscapes you ever saw, each bearing Ed's signature—multiple colors or forms of the same species grafted on one plant, elaborately trimmed topiaries, imaginatively trained creeping or prostrate plants, and, more than anything else, dozens of dwarf conifers that would make a retail nurseryman's mouth water.

Ed says, "I got hooked on dwarf conifers shortly after I moved into this house. The guy that built it hauled off the topsoil and sold it: I had to have thirty truckloads hauled in to raise the level of the ground in my side yard and to build up raised beds to hide the high walls of the base-

ment. I had the usual 'quick and dirty' landscaping done: I didn't have the money to buy choice plants. So, I ended up tearing it all out about two years later.

"What happened is that I met Joe Reis at the printshop where I worked as an electrotyper. Joe was a true pioneer in dwarf conifers: he ate and slept dwarf conifers. He found out that, while stationed with the Marines in Peking in 1945, I had seen the 'Forbidden City' and had vivid memories of its old and fantastically trained bonsais. Joe showed me how to prune and train dwarf conifers to start bonsais and gave me starter plants for a new landscape." (Ed paused a minute to show me two dwarf Alberta spruces from Joe's original gift: they are now ten feet tall. Then he had to explain to me that some dwarf conifers grow rather large after several years, yet not near as big as the standard species.)

Ed continued his story . . . "Joe Reis was a scrounger. He had to be. The nurseries on the Island didn't handle dwarf conifers, except maybe a few Alberta spruces and other semidwarf cultivars. We'd get the bums' rush when we asked too many questions or wanted the nurseryman to order special stuff for us. One nurseryman said to us, 'This is the stuff

I've got to sell. If you want it, buy it. If you don't, I've got other customers to wait on!'

"So, Joe and I began sniffing out the few collectors on the East Coast and swapping what we had for what they had. We visited the Arnold Arboretum in Boston and Longwood Gardens in Kennett Square, near Philadelphia. Those were exciting days, not only discovering fascinating new plant materials but finding other specialists who were just as crazy about dwarf conifers as we were. When I look back on the dwarf conifers we perceived as outstanding in those days, I have to admit that, today, they'd be rated as rather ordinary 'Old Standards.'

"Other collectors and I had what amounted to a 'dwarf conifer underground' out here on the Island because, with our mild climate, we could grow plant material that would succumb to weather stresses on the mainland. And most variegated conifers won't sunburn or fade here. By word of mouth, we found several other private and commercial growers near enough to us to get together every now and then. All were knowledgeable about dwarf conifers: what one didn't know, another did. We had a ball, exchanging plant material, going plant hunting and bringing back cuttings in Wardian cases like those Darwin took with him."

Ed mused, "Some of the collectors in those days were secretive about their sources. I expect it was because they wanted first crack at anything new their sources might come up with. Other collectors would not sell starts of their plants to a plant propagator, protecting, I assume, their potential for profit. Other collectors, and they were in the majority, shared freely.

"Personally," Ed continued, "I think it is foolish to have a dog-in-the-manger attitude about a plant which you alone have. You could lose it and it could never be duplicated. Whenever I grow or discover a plant that seems to have potential, I propagate it and give a plant or two either to the National Arboretum in Washington, D.C., to the Planting Fields here on Long Island, to the Arnold Arboretum in Boston, or to close friends who are collectors. Should something happen to my original plant, it is not lost, never again to be cultivated. When I share with other collectors or arboreta, I often get something in return that I may prize. It is a two-way street.

"I also send rooted cuttings or scions to friends who operate large wholesale nurseries in Oregon; they specialize in dwarf and unusual conifers. One has a color picture of my garden in their catalog, and another grows many of my developments for retail nurseries." Ed showed me an inventory list from the commercial propagator: an outstanding number of dwarf cultivar names were followed by an I.D. for the source . . . "Rezek."

"It has taken all these years for dwarf conifers to be available in local nurseries on the Island, and I know that only a few old standard dwarfs are available in even the best retail nurseries in other states, except on the West Coast. Dwarf conifers haven't quite 'arrived' in much of this country. But, they'll become well known, just as they have in Europe."

Often, dwarf conifer enthusiasts also grow unusual forms of conifers, not dwarf, but standard-sized shrubs and trees with novel color forms, weeping or creeping habit, unusual leaf or needle formations, attractive bark, or with the potential for shaping into topiary forms. Ed's garden includes multiple-graft trees in various colors or growth habits of the same species and "multigeneric" plants with two or three plants of different kinds twisted and bound together so the trunks would apparently (but not actually) fuse. There are trees with kinks in their trunks, shrubs espaliered up trellises, and hundreds of offspring of dwarf conifers which Ed shared with commercial nurserymen years ago.

Nurserymen in the area regard Ed as some sort of phenomenon because he knows so much about his subject. He knows where and how to look up information on plants and propagation. Early on, he was accepted into the International Plant Propagators Society and attends their meetings in North America and abroad. He was a founding member of the American Conifer Society, and has served on its board since its inception in 1980.

Wherever he travels, Ed watches for aberrations in plants. A trip into a nearby town can turn into a collecting expedition. He is very good at spotting anomalies: color mutations, witches' brooms for dwarfing, growth habit mutations, anything that sets a conifer off from the "type" or standard for the cultivar. He soon discards any plants that lack grace or beauty. However, a sugar maple, *Acer saccharum* 'Monumentale', which grows in his side yard, is more startling than graceful. It is thirty feet tall and twenty inches wide, like a telephone pole with leaves. Ed loves to tell visiting kids that it is "Jack's Beanstalk." They believe it; so do I!

I was curious about how Ed has discovered so many oddities in his small back yard. It has partly to do with the fact that he is working with genetically unstable plants, but more to do with his daily prowling of a relatively small garden: weeding, clipping, and thinning. Nothing escapes his notice and he is out there every day during the growing season.

Right before our eyes, he pointed out a silver-fringed branch on an all-green dwarf conifer, a tightly clustered witches' broom on a tiny juniper, and a ground-hugging seedling grown from seeds harvested from an upright conifer. Later, we discovered that such mutations are more prevalent in urban areas, perhaps due to air quality.

Some of Ed's most productive seed parents are old dwarf hinoki cypress growing around the neighborhood, many from his collection. He gathers and plants the seeds, and watches for variations from the norm. The seeds have grown into many useful and beautiful variations on the

Two old specimens of Ccdrus Atlantic *'Glauca Pendula', weeping blue Atlantic cedar, are trained on supports around three sides of Ed's house. Posts hold the limber branches clear of the path.*

original . . . the not-so-beautiful-nor-useful were discarded. Apparently, these old hinokis have an involved genetic makeup, which accounts for the wide segregation in offspring from seeds. Ed doesn't do any hybridizing, but relies on genetic anomalies to get new material from seed propagation.

Now that Ed has virtually no room to grow new plants, he is concentrating on making his old plants look better. Out front, he trimmed and trained two old and overgrown bird's nest spruces, *Picea abies* 'Nidiformis', into flat-topped pom-poms. From the street you can see the character of the old and twisted stems with their attractive mature bark.

Ed is changing the top growth of some old but not particularly valuable plants by grafting on new scions from desirable cultivars within the same species. Not content with that, he is tying knots in whippy *Chamaecyparis* suckers, plaiting trunks into incredible forms, and training procumbent plants like Atlantic cedar thirty feet around the sides of his house, where the twigs hang like green icicles.

Now that Ed is so sure of what he can do with plants he seems to be playing with them to amuse himself, his family, and neighbors. But, whatever he conceives has to look graceful, not grotesque, or he will prune it off and start all over. Harkening back to the plants he saw at the Imperial Palace in Peking, Ed grows bonsai and sets the containers wherever there is a little space in his crowded garden. Come winter, he sinks the containers in the ground and the warmth keeps the tiny, artistically trained plants from freezing. He has some bonsai that could grace any collection, including one cork-bark pine with an exquisite line, and a forest of Norway spruce seedlings.

Ed freely admits that three things have helped him to succeed in his specialty of dwarf conifers: an understanding and supportive wife, a job with regular hours (he worked for twenty years as a postman in Valley Stream after leaving the printing industry), and growing up in a family that loved gardening. He credits his automatic watering system for helping preserve domestic harmony: he and Maureen never feel trapped by their garden. They just set the automatic timers on the sprinkling system and the mist emitters and ventilators in the greenhouse and take off!

Ed is a natural teacher, gifted with enthusiasm and quick, sure hands. He taught a neighbor, Regina Scimeca, to graft trees. She showed me her Japanese maple with twelve grafts on it, all taking! Such multigraft trees, after you get over the shock of seeing several foliage and color forms on one tree, can be beautiful. More important, they give gardeners with small yards a way to enjoy several kinds of trees in a small area.

Always teaching, Ed showed me how to wait until axillary buds show on Japanese maples before taking cuttings, and to trim off all the leaves from the scion (the piece to be grafted on the understock, which is the bottom, or rooted, part).

Quick as a wink, Ed stripped the scion, carved the ends into a long "vee" shape, cut a cleft into the bark of the understock, inserted the graft, and whipped it into place with a wide rubber band. "New growth should start in two to three weeks inside this protective baggie," he said; "it maintains high humidity around the graft."

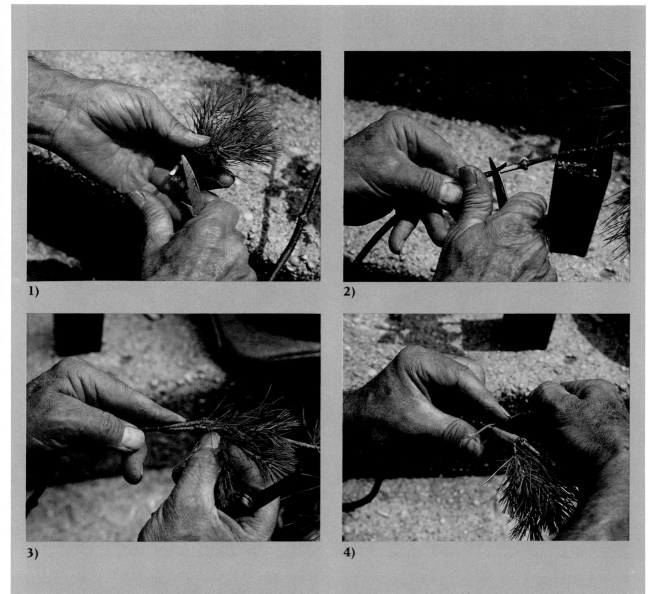

1)

2)

3)

4)

Grafting Dwarf Conifers

Ed explains the process of grafting dwarf conifers. He begins by trimming the tip of a scion branch into a vee shape (1). He cuts a matching slit through the bark of the understock (2) and slips the scion into the slit so that cambium meets cambium (3). A good bond will start the sap flowing from the understock to the scion right away. Finally he wraps a wide rubber band snugly around the graft and ties it tight (4). To maintain high humidity around the graft, Ed slips a protective plastic bag over it. New growth will begin in two to three weeks.

Ed matches the diameter of the scion to the diameter of the under-stock when cleft grafting, so that the connective tissue (the cambium) matches up. A good cambium-to-cambium bond will start the sap flow-ing right away from the understock into the scion, so it won't wilt. He prefers to work with small-diameter branches, less than ¼ inch in diam-eter. On deciduous trees, he uses new-growth wood from near the tips of branches.

The top growth of a sapling tree can be entirely changed by grafting a desirable scion on the stem of a vigorous but common seedling of the same species. That's the quick way to convert a cheap garden-variety tree into a choice specimen. Ed calls these "high grafts" and often uses them to replace the top growth of common green Japanese maple, *Acer palma-tum*, with scion wood from a more valuable crimson or cutleaf cultivar. The branches of choice Japanese maples descend from the main trunk to form a flattened, pagodalike canopy that looks very good in the company of dwarf conifers, and which becomes picturesque with age.

I asked Ed to recommend a starter collection of dwarf conifers and choice, compatible Japanese maples for gardeners just entering the hobby. His list includes many colors, forms, habits of growth that lead to distinctive shapes, and novel foliage characteristics. These cultivars lend themselves to an infinite number of landscape situations:

- *Abies balsamea* 'Nana': Dwarf, globose, dark green, with stomatic lines on undersides of needles.
- *Chamaecyparis obtusa* 'Gracilis Nana' (Japanese hinoki cypress): Pyra-midal, medium to dark green, obtuse leaf shapes.

- *Chamaecyparis obtusa* 'Lutea Nana': Dwarf, broadly pyramidal, bright gold, cup-shaped leaves.
- *Chamaecyparis pisifera* 'Golden Mop': Dwarf, mound-forming, with bright gold, threadlike foliage.
- *Chamaecyparis thyoidies* 'Little Jamie': Dwarf, dense, columnar, rock garden plant, purple cast in winter.
- *Juniperus chinensis* 'Procumbens Nana': Low-growing, groundcover-type juniper, ideal for overhanging walls.
- *Juniperus communis* 'Berkshire': Very dwarf, broadly globose, dark green, blue-striated foliage.
- *Juniperus communis* 'Compressa': Very dwarf, spirelike cultivar. Excellent for use in small-space gardens.
- *Juniperus scopulorum* 'Table Top Blue': Silver-blue foliage grows like a table top.
- *Juniperus squamata* 'Blue Star': Dwarf, mounding, with star-shaped, steel blue foliage, a recent introduction from Holland.
- *Picea abies* 'Little Gem': Very dwarf, dense, bun-form plant; diminutive, excellent for the rock garden.
- *Picea pungens* 'Globosa Glauca Nana': Dwarf, globose, dense shrub, with good blue coloration.
- *Picea pungens* 'St. Mary's Broom': Diminutive, mounding blue spruce with conspicuous buds; a real "mini-gem."
- *Picea sitchensis* 'Papoose': Dwarf, compact, broadly conical bush; fine needles with blue striation beneath.
- *Pinus parviflora* (Japanese black pine) 'Adcock's Dwarf': Diminutive, slow-growing, congested bun; a jewel for a rock garden or small area.
- *Pinus strobus* 'Nana': Dwarf, compact, spreading mound; long, soft, dense bluish-green needles.
- *Pinus sylvestris* 'Repens': Rich green, compact ground-hugger.
- *Tsuga canadensis* (hemlock) 'Cole's Prostrate': Dwarf, slowly creeping, well-branched mound; center wood is exposed; partial shade is best.

As taller companion plants for dwarf conifers, Ed suggests "high grafts" or four Japanese maple cultivars: 'Garnet', 'Crimson Queen', 'Ever-Red', and 'Filigree Lace'.

- *Acer palmatum* 'Garnet': Coarse, dissected, gem-red foliage on a broad, compact mound.
- *Acer palmatum* (Japanese maple) Dissectum 'Crimson Queen': Mounding, cascading form; deep red, finely dissected foliage and branches.
- *Acer palmatum* Dissectum 'Ever-Red': Leaves emerge with fine silvery hairs; retains good red color in hot weather.
- *Acer palmatum* 'Red Filigree Lace': Fine, threadlike, deep red foliage: the finest cutleaf red in existence.

A cork bark black pine, Pinus thunbergiana *'Corticosa Nishiki', has been trained into bonsai form.*

As companion perennials to cover the soil between dwarf conifers, Ed suggests: the compact sedums and sempervivums; *Lamium* 'Beacon Silver', and dwarf *Thymus* (thyme) cultivars. These are smaller than the culinary thyme cultivars. Miniature hostas and dwarf iris such as *Iris verna* and *I. cristata* are quite appropriate for interplanting among dwarf conifers.

As annuals for color spots among the dwarf conifers, he uses (discreetly): tuberous-rooted begonias, New Guinea impatiens, and wax begonias. When they grow so large that they begin to look out of scale, Ed pulls them out and replants with younger plants of annuals.

In his rich topsoil, Ed never feeds his dwarf conifers. His object is neither to starve his plants to retard growth nor to stimulate them into growing rapidly. Rather, he wants them to grow slowly but steadily and retain good foliage color. He has applied a light mulch of pine bark for several years and feels that the nutrients released during its decomposition are sufficient to nourish the slow-growing evergreens. They certainly looked well fed to me!

Red spider mites are a major problem on conifers everywhere; they can be troublesome in hot, dry weather. Ed is planning to use insecticidal soap to increase the effectiveness of his spray program. He is watching with considerable alarm a serious pest on other parts of the Island, the Adelgid hemlock scale. These armor-plated insects are difficult to control, except at the crawling stage. Then, insecticides mixed with spreader-sticker agents will penetrate and kill them.

Slugs are a minor problem, mostly on the hostas Ed uses in shaded areas. Squirrels try, and sometimes succeed, in digging up his precious plants. Ed captures them in a humane trap and carts them off to a large park some distance away.

In Ed Rezek's garden, it is easy to see why dwarf conifers are the designer plants of tomorrow. Experts like Dr. Henry Marc Cathey of the National Arboretum predict that the new American landscape will be composed of smaller, slow-growing, choice plant material, sited with care for maximum impact. Anyone looking for a prototype garden will find it in Malverne, New York.

More about Dwarf Conifers

Dwarf conifers have been selected from a number of genera. Most of these species are native to temperate climates and prefer rather moist soil conditions. With the growing interest in water conservation and xeriscaping, we may see more interest in selecting dwarfs from warm climates, plants which can tolerate dry soils:

Abies (fir)
Cedrus (true cedar)
Cephalotaxus (plum yew)
Chamaecyparis (false cypress)
Cryptomeria (Japanese cedar)
Juniperus (southern red cedar)
Picea (spruce)

Pinus (pine)
Podocarpus (southern or Japanese yew)
Pseudotsuga (Douglas fir)
Taxus (yew)
Thuja (arborvitae)
Tsuga (hemlock)

Dwarf conifers can be grouped into three divisions by size:

● *Pigmy:* Only one-twentieth the size of normal plants of the species at maturity, the specimens can be quite expensive because they grow so slowly.

● *Dwarf:* One-twentieth to one-quarter the size of normal plants of the species at maturity, these are usually easier to grow than the pygmy types, because of their vigor.

● *Compact:* One-third to one-half the normal size of the species when mature, these should not be confused with young plants of standard-sized shrubs, trees, and groundcovers, which grow considerably faster and up to three times as large.

Rate of Growth   The rate of growth of dwarf conifers depends not only on the length and warmth of the growing season but also on precipitation, irrigation, exposure to wind, nutrition programs, and underlying soil. Hobby growers make their soil well drained, and keep it on the poor side, although well fortified with organic matter for water retention and biological activity. Maintaining an organic mulch by adding to it each year or two is standard practice in most dwarf conifer gardens.

Rate of growth can also depend on the interaction of the scion and the understock of dwarfs grafted on normal rootstocks. Grafting is the only practical way to increase certain desirable specimens that may be difficult to root as cuttings, or don't set seeds. Much trial and error has gone into matching scions to understocks that won't force them to grow overly large and that weld into strong unions.

Buying Dwarf Conifers   Accumulating a dwarf conifer collection is usually a long-term proposition because of the care needed in acquiring compatible specimens adapted to one's climate. You often see rock garden enthusiasts evolving into dwarf conifer enthusiasts as well, for they already have the site and a feeling for working with small plants.

Use caution when planting balled and burlapped plants. Most sources offer dwarf conifers as balled and burlapped plants or containerized specimens. Generally, the slower-growing the plant, the costlier, because of the time it has to spend in the nursery growing large enough to be sold. Rezek told me that plants can be grown in fields with soils that are too sandy to retain a good, solid root ball, or sold before a new network of roots has proliferated inside the burlap. If the nurseryman knocks these around with careless handling, or if you rush the planting, you can end up with a bare-root plant that may not survive. Ed always leaves the burlap in place, but unties and folds back the top after he has pulled the backfill soil up and around the root ball. He firms the backfill thoroughly to eliminate air pockets that could let roots dry out. I might add that you should avoid plants that are balled in woven plastic; you must completely remove this stuff. Roots won't grow through it.

Ed uses a lath cover over plants in his holding area for winter protection and for summer shade.

Prepare the soil for dwarf conifers by thoroughly mixing in a 2-inch layer of moistened peat moss or finely ground composted pine or fir bark to spade depth. If your soil is heavy clay, also mix in 2 inches of sand. This will raise the level of the dwarf conifer bed 3 to 4 inches above the surrounding soil for good drainage. Raised beds give no particular advantage on deep, sandy soils.

Landscaping

Effective arrangements can be as simple as a small, uncomplicated combination of shape and colors for an intimate corner, a little colony of various shapes and colors among a cluster of large rocks, one or two in a stone trough interplanted with alpines, or on a gritty, gravelly, scree sloping down from a scattering of rocks that appear to have been deposited by a retreating glacier.

Group pygmy plants fairly closely: individual specimens tend to fade into the wallpaper. However, space dwarf and compact types far enough apart so that they do not become crowded with age. Leave generous spaces between groups of dwarf conifers and fill them with choice groundcovers and spring bulbs.

Between groups of dwarf conifers, establish mats of low-growing, nonaggressive groundcovers. You will have to hunt up suppliers of choice groundcovers to get cultivars to set off the color and texture of your dwarf conifers.

Care

You can keep the interiors of large plants free of accumulations of dead needles by shaking them and, if you can reach the interior, raking and disposing of needles. A few dead needles do no harm, but a deep layer can be unsightly, can shed water, and can actually become a fire hazard around smokers.

Some authorities recommend that you syringe plants with a fine spray of water frequently during warm weather. But Ed Rezek cautions you not to do it on new growth, not until after it has hardened. Water on tender young needles or leaves, followed by hot sun, can cook them. Some of the dwarf hemlocks are particularly susceptible.

Sharp, fine sprays of water can discourage spider mites. One of the best ways to do this is to use a backpack sprayer with plain water or insecticidal soap. Maximum pressure will blast many of the red spiders off, if directed up toward the undersides of leaves. It is difficult to get a sufficiently fine spray with a water hose without so much pressure that needles or leaves are damaged.

Propagation

Once you have developed the touch for siting and growing these fascinating plants, you may be inspired to try growing them from seeds, collecting them from abnormal growths such as witches' brooms, and propagating them by cuttings or grafting. Growing and propagating dwarf conifers from seeds or cuttings taken from growth anomalies is not really difficult, but it does require more attention and concentration than most other plant specialties.

You really need to see pygmy, dwarf, and compact conifers to appreciate their uniqueness and to get ideas on where and how to use them. Don't be overwhelmed by the complex plantings displayed at public gardens. Start with a small grouping of plants that please your sense of color and balance, and let your collection evolve from there. If you plan to grow your dwarf conifers in containers, select cultivars that are hardy in the next zone to the north to assure their overwintering reliably.

Peonies

With a good eye, a green thumb, and a little bit of luck, Wisconsin's Roger Anderson makes a breakthrough in peony breeding.

(Left) 'First Arrival' was Roger Anderson's first introduction from his efforts to cross tree peonies with herbaceous cultivars.

*P*eonies are legendary for their opulent, often fragrant flowers in luminous shades, from pastels to deep reds and creamy whites. The vivid hues of the emerging spring growth and flower buds provide color impact long before the blossoms open. After bloom, the foliage is clean and glossy, a handsome foil for later-blooming perennials. Peonies deliver an end-of-season gift; seed pods on long stems can be dried for arrangements. Peonies are long-lived, too; a mature plant can eventually spread to four feet, a commanding spectacle in the perennial border.

The range of peony flower forms include *single*, with the flower's center composed of stamens and pistils, and a single, daisylike layer of ray petals; *semidouble*, with two or more layers of petals in open blossoms, and with the stamens and pistils clearly visible at the center; *double*, or *"fully double,"* nearly ball-like, with many layers of petals concealing the stamens and pistils; and *"Japanese type,"* in which the single or semidouble blossoms have a distinctive crested, petaloid or staminoid "boss" in the center.

Most gardeners are familiar with herbaceous peonies, cultivars which freeze to the ground during the winter and regrow each spring from strong, deep rootstocks. All require a long winter dormancy and do not perform well south of zone 7B. Long-stemmed and fragrant, herbaceous peonies are one of the most desirable flowers for cutting. Though the double cultivars that look so spectacular in the garden can overpower arrangements, the single or crested anemone types combine well with other blooms. Early, midseason, or late-blooming cultivars provide an extended flowering season.

The relatively rare early-blooming herbaceous rock garden peonies, *Paeonia tenuifolia*, are very hardy. They average twelve to eighteen inches in height, with fernlike, deeply cut leaves. Some of the cultivars in this class have a blossom form not found in other classes, single with tufted centers.

More unusual are tree peonies, which actually resemble shrubs rather than trees and develop woody, persistent top growth reaching two to four feet or more in height. Their bloom period begins with the late herbaceous types, and extends two or three weeks thereafter. The flowers have distinctive frilled petals with dark "flares" at the base; in some cultivars, the petals are fringed with contrasting colors. In many parts of the United States, tree peonies are more difficult to grow than herbaceous types. The West Coast, Northwest, and protected East Coast sites provide the requisite mild winters and cool summers to produce the classic large, shrubby tree peony forms so coveted as landscape specimens. Where they can be grown, the dramatic size, fragrance, attractive foliage, and characteristic form of the blossoms rank tree peonies with rhododendrons and roses for sheer beauty.

A class recently expanded by breeders in the United States is one that crosses herbaceous peonies with tree peonies. These crosses resemble either true herbaceous or tree peonies, depending on the percentage of traits inherited from a particular parent. Their bloom period corresponds to that of tree peonies.

As a genus, the peonies number about thirty species, some of which are no longer found in the wild. Of these, six or eight have been extensively improved for garden use or incorporated into hybrids. Originally, peonies were brought to Europe from the Caucasus in the sixteenth century, and a different group of species from China and Siberia in the eighteenth century. The first mention of peonies in the United States was a listing of five varieties in M'Mahon's catalog in 1806.

American peony breeding was inspired by the progress made in Europe, notably by Lemoine in France, and by the English nurseryman James Kelway. Lemoine succeeded in crossing the Chinese peony with *P. Witt-*

manniana. The Chinese peony, *P. lactiflora*, is the ancestor of most herbaceous peonies and has long been cultivated in the Orient. Lemoine broke with the long-standing infatuation of European breeders with the indigenous *P. officinalis*. Lemoine's crosses became known as "European Hybrids." Kelway focused on selecting from the Chinese peony.

During the prosperous years of westward expansion following the War Between the States, keen American gardeners discovered how well the hardy herbaceous peonies grew in our northern climates. European travel grew, and gadabout gardeners saw and ordered the latest European peony hybrids. Interest peaked in the days of Queen Victoria, when spacious homes and yards provided room to grow large perennials and abundant domestic help freed genteel ladies to exercise their talents in making florid arrangements for their homes and churches.

'Coral Charm', an early, semidouble herbaceous peony, won a gold medal from the American Peony Society.

By 1903, interest in peonies was very high, and the first annual meeting of the American Peony Society commissioned Professor John Craig of Cornell University to plant and observe and standardize the many named varieties of peonies for sale in the United States and Europe. In addition, the Society had Craig rate peonies on a scale of 1 to 10 and recommended that the trade drop all varieties scoring less than 7.5.

During the 1930s, the foremost pioneer American breeder of peonies, Dr. A. P. Saunders of New York State, succeeded in crossing several species and made many desirable selections from the progeny. He also refined certain species imported directly from their native countries. Today, more than half a century later, eight of his herbaceous peonies, twenty-three of his tree peonies, and two of his rock garden cultivars are still being offered.

Between the two world wars peonies suffered a lag in popularity. In part this was due to certain limitations of the plants themselves. The blossoms of some of the older varieties are so large that they fill with water and tip face down during spring rains. The mature plants of some cultivars are simply too large for compact modern gardens, a far cry from Victorian times when tall peonies with blossoms as large as cabbages were in scale with homes. Moreover, the palette of traditional peony colors—shades of rose, magenta, lavender, and dark reds—has been subject to the whims of fashion trends.

Sluggishness among commercial producers contributed to public indifference. For various reasons, many commercial peony growers' offerings failed to keep pace with changing tastes. As their huge inventories of old favorites waned in popularity, these growers were slow to replace them with improved varieties, which tended to circulate within a small group of amateur breeders. Increasing stocks of new peony varieties is slow and expensive; it can be five years or longer between the evaluation of a deserving new hybrid and the production of an inventory sufficient for introduction. Good peony varieties are not cheap. Older varieties average ten to twenty-five dollars apiece, but new introductions, especially those which have received an award from the American Peony Society, can bring two hundred fifty dollars or more.

Even the way in which peonies are sold has held back their progress. Producers ship herbaceous peonies mostly in the late summer and fall, the traditional planting time. Yet, spring is the time when the mass of gardeners wish to buy plants. The peony plants offered for sale in the spring are mostly dormant root divisions, usually boxed in illustrated waxed-paper cartons and kept moist with shavings. If these are not sold within a few weeks, the warmth of the display area will wake them up and sprouting will commence. It is most difficult to transplant a sprouted peony root, with 3 or 4 inches of succulent growth, without its suffering considerable shock.

Several developments have pulled peonies out of their sales slump. Most important, devoted amateur breeders have risen to the challenge to improve the genus; their greatly improved cultivars and hybrids are becoming more widely available. The leading commercial growers of peony plants are now quick to react when an amateur hybridist develops a promising new seedling, by arranging for marketing rights. Some are also funding research and breeding programs of their own. Propagation by tissue culture promises to speed up the initial increase of these new varieties, and nurseries are beginning to grow and sell improved peonies in containers to make planting possible at any time during the growing season.

Yet, hobby peony breeders outnumber the professional plant breeders and, in the foreseeable future, will be having the greatest impact on improving the genus. One successful amateur breeder, Roger Anderson, feels there is plenty of room for more hobby breeders. His story will show you one way to get started in this fulfilling hobby.

Roger stands before the impressive array of his peony evaluation trials.

Each spring, the spacious, sloping front lawn of a farm home near Fort Atkinson, Wisconsin, undergoes a transformation. During the winter, little can be seen except long rows of tilled soil crossing the lawn on contour, and the glint of sun reflecting from plant tags. Then, with the melting of snow and warming of soil, strong spears, like bronzy-green asparagus, begin pushing up through the mulch. By late May, cars will be stopping on the farm-to-market road in front of the house to admire the rows and rows of flowers, breathtaking in their color. Roger and Sandra Anderson's peonies are doing their thing again, all twelve hundred plants, tall and short, single and double flowered, ruby-red or green leaved, moving with the slightest breeze, and, later, perfuming the air and exciting the senses.

The star of the peony show is a hybrid produced by Roger, a cross between an herbaceous cultivar and a hybrid with a tree peony as one of its parents. He named his hybrid 'Bartzella'. The plants are semiherbaceous in response to winter, yet the large, citrus-scented blossoms are like tree peonies, a lovely lemon yellow and fully double, with frilly-edged petals. Individual established plants of 'Bartzella' have produced more than sixty blooms each, up to six inches in diameter. The foliage resembles, at first glance, that of an herbaceous peony. A closer look reveals similarities with tree peony foliage. A cross between two species is difficult and unpredictable; that an amateur was able to accomplish it speaks well of Roger's self-taught skills.

The dense, compact plants of 'Bartzella' grow to a height of twenty-four to thirty inches and the sturdy stems won't gooseneck when weighted by rain. The petals have more substance than tree peonies. Plants have survived temperatures of 30 degrees below zero F. They froze back to about three inches above the ground but regrew strongly.

Roger didn't become a peony enthusiast and hybridizer overnight. His was a long and involved hegira, filled with summer romances with other plants, specialties which he explored then set aside to move onward. His journey began at Whitewater, Wisconsin, his boyhood home. All his people farmed, raised purebred Holstein cattle, and grew vegetable and berry crops to feed their families and to sell. His pragmatic father liked to kid

Roger about his fondness for flowers. His favorite line was, "When are they going to be ready to eat?"

It was Roger's grandfather who encouraged his involvement in flowers. Noticing the sturdily built toddler sniffing the gladiolus he raised for cutting, his grandfather nicknamed Roger "Ferdinand" after the famous bull in a children's story. Roger can still remember helping his grandfather harvest long gladiolus stems and seeing, around his yard, plants of old 'Festiva Maxima' peony.

After high school, Roger served a hitch in the military, then returned to truck gardening for several years, to supplement income from an eight-to-five job. They were good but hard years, with Roger and Sandra growing and selling many kinds of vegetables, fruits, and flowers for extra income. His interest in flowers led Roger to Bill Himmler, a local amateur plant breeder, who taught him how to hybridize gladiolus and grow them from seeds. Under Bill's tutelage, Roger learned how to evaluate new breeding lines critically. After taking a long, hard look at the limited market for new and improved gladiolus hybrids and the numerous breeders competing for the business, Roger went into other hobbies. He bred and sold black Labrador dogs, Golden-laced Wyandotte poultry, and Roller pigeons. A dog lover myself, I asked Roger why he moved from dogs to flowers. He answered "Well, I made money breeding Labs, but they tended to wander. I always knew where the flowers were at night!"

Along the way, Roger and Sandra were raising a family of four and making plans for their present hilltop home on ten acres just south of Fort Atkinson. To meet the needs of his growing family, Roger went to work as a purchasing agent for a local meat packing plant and, later, as a machinist . . . his present occupation. He still takes contracts for house painting. "Lets me make money to support my hobby," he says with a smile. (I know what he means.)

About fifteen years ago, Roger was introduced to peonies by his friend Carroll Spangler, who showed him photos of one of the first Itoh hybrid peonies from Japan. It was love at first sight! Roger scraped up forty dollars and sent to Gilbert H. Wild's nursery for plants to use for seed production. Roger told me that at the time, the forty dollars was his life's savings and he really felt guilty about spending the money on flowers. I'm sure that a lot of older gardeners who grew up during the Great Depression can relate to that feeling.

Roger had to wait several years for his small Itoh hybrid plants to produce flowers. They made such an impression that he has purchased more peony cultivars every succeeding year. His collection grew, and provided a large and diverse gene pool among his twelve hundred plants. As he mastered his specialty, Roger refined his objectives in peony breeding, foremost of which was the introduction of the yellow color into hardy herbaceous peonies. The way he got the female parent for the cross that produced his first breakthrough was serendipity itself.

One day, when Roger was visiting Carroll Spangler, he noticed a chance seedling peony in bloom. It was a plant Carroll had found years earlier, growing in an asparagus patch, apparently from a seed dropped there. Carroll took pity on the little plant and moved it to a peony bed where, at first, it produced double blooms. Thereafter, it always produced single blooms.

Roger looked beyond the rather homely single blossoms and saw possibilities for the plant as a parent in hybrids. It was vigorous, produced an abundance of pollen, and set loads of large, fat seed pods. Carroll saw no value in the blossoms for shows and was about to discard the plant when Roger intervened and asked to move it to his garden. He divided the crown of that vigorous seedling into three sections. Strangely, while one grew into a single flowered plant, two produced double pink flowers! Roger used the single-flowered plant not only as a female parent in crosses but also as a pollen donor. Roger has been very thorough about early removal of all anthers on female parents, and is positive that the resulting seeds from crosses with tree peonies have produced true hybrids and not "selfs."

Roger is not the first hybridizer to cross herbaceous and tree peonies. About forty years ago a Japanese (they are mad about tree peonies) named T. Itoh succeeded in crossing the herbaceous peony 'Kakodin' and a hybrid out of *P. lutea*, named 'Alice Harding'. Out of twelve hundred crosses he got nine plants: the offspring of four of these made it to the United States where they became known as the Itoh hybrids. As yet, they are curiosities to most gardeners except peony fanciers.

The Itoh hybrids are proving more valuable to gardeners than either of their parents, and should continue to attract interest for years to come. They are quite winter hardy, and resistant to wind and rain damage. To date, no problems with diseases have been noted. With their ease of growth and low maintenance requirements, they should be a landscaper's dream. Early in the season the bushes take on a symmetrical globe shape, which holds until late in the fall. The plants color up nicely after a light frost.

Actually, Mr. Itoh was only one of a line of peony breeders who sensed the commercial possibilities of transferring the yellow color of *P. lutea* to other peony species. The French breeder Lemoine and, later, A. P. Saunders crossed the Japanese tree peony with *P. lutea* to produce what became known as the Lutea hybrids.

Roger Anderson saw the Itoh hybrids as a means to an end. He felt that he could transfer their yellow, golden, and softer colors to herbaceous peonies, *P. lactiflora*, and retain the best qualities of the three contributing species. It took a few years, but he did it! A few other American

'Cora Louise', which Roger named for his grandmother, was his second tree x herbaceous peony hybrid.

hybridizers have succeeded with similar crosses: two named cultivars have come out of their efforts.

Rather than clutter the nomenclature, the American Peony Society has decided to list all Roger Anderson's cultivars and genetically comparable strains from other breeders with the Itoh hybrids. Roger commented, "I should have enough of my hybrids increased to begin selling small quantities on a first-come, first-served basis in 1992. Prices will be rather high, due to the limited number of plants available." Roger and Sandra have named their budding commercial peony plant enterprise "Callie's Beaux Jardin." Says Roger, "Out here in Holstein country that French name

These two un-named seedling tree x herbaceous peony hybrids are under evaluation. Hybrid 81-08, left, and 81-18 are from crosses Roger made in 1981.

ought to be an attention-getter!" Visitors are welcome at Callie's Beaux Jardin during bloom season, by advance arrangement.

As we talked peonies, it began to emerge how Roger and Sandra have accomplished so much, with both working full-time jobs. An energetic and physically powerful man, with shoulders an ax handle wide, Roger has worked his way through several hobby plants and up through the ranks to the inner circle of peony breeders. (He would modestly decline the latter distinction, but I feel he deserves it.) Roger is a study in goal-oriented self-discipline.

His wife, Sandra, would like to see the day arrive when Roger will feel comfortable leaning on a hoe handle and admiring the fruits of their labors, rather than working harder every year. Much of her spare time has been spent in the garden with Roger, planting, weeding, labeling, and assisting him in evaluating experimental hybrids. "There are many days," Roger said, "when Sandra spends more time in the yard than I do, patrolling the peony beds, pulling and spraying weeds." But now, with an empty nest, Sandra is going back to school to get her degree in nursing, which has sent Roger scurrying to find herbicides to reduce the weeding problem.

Roger is a likable man but very serious about his work with peonies . . . so serious that he doesn't realize that he can now let up and take the time to extract more joy from every minute of his hobby. I think he realizes that he may be quite close to making his mark in the peony world and doesn't want to risk letting the opportunity slip from his grasp.

Sandra and Roger work together to grow peony seedlings from his precious hybrid seeds. After putting so much work and so many hopes into producing a few hybrid seeds, Roger wants as many as possible to grow and produce plants. Peony seeds germinate slowly, over a period of several months, and should be planted within two months after the pod turns color and before the seed coat dries hard.

Roger and Sandra pick off individual seed pods just before they become fully mature, shell out and label the seeds. He puts the fresh seeds in a plastic bag of moist sphagnum moss, in a warm corner near the furnace. This treatment produces roots on the viable seeds, but no shoots for a while.

As the roots show, Roger places the seeds in a refrigerator for two to three months, or until a growing point emerges. This satisfies their dormancy requirement. Then the seeds are potted in individual pots. When the shoot breaks through the surface of the soil, he sets the pots under fluorescent lights to hasten growth and development.

Their light fixtures can accommodate only about one hundred seedlings, so the Andersons hold back the remainder by sowing the seeds in boxes of growing medium made by mixing sphagnum peat moss with potting soil. In midwinter, they move the boxes to an unheated but sunny garage. Little happens until spring, when the seeds resume growing. By that time, Roger will have moved the indoor-grown plants to the outside to harden off, making room under the lights for additional seedlings. Seeds that germinate even later are potted up and grown outdoors.

The Andersons have almost an ideal situation for growing and evaluating peonies. Their house sits on a high hill, with their two-acre front lawn sloping down to a country highway. The land was once a dairy farm and the only trees are close to the house. The display beds, two to three hundred feet in length, run across the slope to minimize erosion.

The plants are in bloom from mid-May through late June, and attract visitors from all over the Midwest. When I phoned Roger during a dry September to check on how his plants were surviving, he told me, "Hey, don't worry, once peonies are well rooted, they are very drought resistant. And, Jim, I wish you could have been here in late August. My line of Itoh hybrids bloomed again, that late in the season! It was weird seeing peonies repeat!" he said. "I've never seen anything like it before . . . maybe the dry soil set up the situation."

The Andersons have very few problems with their peonies. Their rich, black soil seldom needs fertilizer or lime, and the carpenter bees which tunnel into peony stems elsewhere haven't yet reached Wisconsin. They spray occasionally during damp spring weather to control botrytis and other blights, with either captan or Bordeaux mixture, made by dissolving copper sulphate and hydrated lime in water: about a quarter pound of each in three gallons of water.

1)

2)

3)

4)

5)

6)

Hybridizing Peonies

Roger demonstrates his procedure for hybridizing peonies. He begins by removing the petals from the bud of the female parent's unopened flower (1). Then he emasculates the female parent by removing the anthers (2). With his finger, he dabs pollen on the receptive stigma (3). Good record-keeping is essential. Colored tape records the details of the cross for posterity (4). Covering with a paper envelope prevents contamination by pollen from other blossoms, carried by bees and other insects (5). Individual blossoms of the female parent peony, 'Martha W.', have been crossed with various pollen parents (6). Roger harvests the individual seed pods just before they are fully mature. The seeds are shelled out and labeled. Peonies germinate slowly, and the Andersons are careful to plant their precious hybrid seeds within two months after the pod turns color, before the seed coat dries hard.

Even though the peony beds are fully open to cold, drying winter winds, the Andersons never lose peonies to freezing. In severe winters, tree peonies freeze back nearly to the ground, but send up new wood from underground buds. These produce large, late blooms.

Roger feels that the good survival is due mostly to good drainage combined with very deep topsoil. He could use Snow Cones to protect flower buds, but doesn't because they would interfere with his getting a true measure of winter hardiness.

We talked for some time about why peonies had not taken off in demand like daylilies and hosta. Considering their beauty, adaptability, longevity, and freedom from problems, they should be ranked with the leaders. "Four things are holding them back," he said: "the slowness of propagation, unpredictable performance from the one-year-old grafted plants sold at retail stores, lack of promotion, and, more than anything else, lack of advanced, committed hobbyist hybridizers. I feel we are on the verge of breakthroughs in peonies that should make them the new frontier in perennial plants!

"We badly need to learn how to increase valuable new hybrids by tissue culture and to accelerate production. To my knowledge no one has succeeded at tissue-culturing peonies in quantities. Vegetative propagation is so slow that desirable new hybrids remain expensive for several years, and are known only to the fanciers who are accustomed to paying fifty to two hundred fifty dollars for a single plant. The cost of patenting a new peony is high; therefore, most new ones go unprotected. The breeder is lucky to recover his development costs.

"This situation produces no funds for promotion of peonies. Consequently, the growth of interest in peonies has been the result of one-on-one missionary work by the enthusiastic members of the American Peony Society, plus the exposure in a few national and regional mail-order catalogs.

"I think the situation is about to change," he continued. "Many other hobbyists such as myself have invested substantially in peonies. To date, it has been a labor of love for me, but my investment in plants is approaching ten thousand dollars. Some of us, myself included, will want to convert our hobby into retirement income and will go commercial.

"One promotion that is attracting attention from other gardeners are the flower shows put on by the American Peony Society. When we get together for annual meetings at various midwestern and Canadian cities, we hold shows in shopping malls, botanical gardens, and the like. We have a number of hobby growers of peonies in southern Wisconsin and hosted the 1989 annual meeting of the American Peony Society at Janesville."

I asked Roger what he had up his sleeve to follow his beautiful 'Bartzella'. "In 1988," he said, "I got my first look at a new batch of hybrids

between herbaceous and tree peonies. Two of them looked mighty good . . . doubles, with yellow blossoms, tinged coppery gold. They'll be increased, and evaluated elsewhere as well as in Wisconsin.

"Also," he said, "I'm trying to introduce the orange color into herbaceous peonies. I now have seven plants produced by crossing pollen from *P. lactiflora* (herbaceous) onto an orangeish Lutea hybrid tree peony. They are young now but should bloom in two years. I think I have something good, but time will tell. David Reath, over in Vulcan, Michigan, is on a similar breeding track.

"I continue to try crossing the various species to increase my peony gene pool. Sometimes it works, sometimes not. I tried *P. delavayi* but none of my crosses took. However, I did have success with using *P. Potanini* in a cross: it is a tall, shrublike peony with small yellow flowers.

One cross took: the female parent was *P. lactiflora*. The resulting hybrid was a fooler: the first-year plant produced small, dark pink, incomplete flowers. But, on the second year, it grew into a very nice plant, covered with bright red flowers. It could be the start of a new breeding line.

"And, I'm shooting for a true dwarf peony that can be containerized in an eight-inch pot and sold fully grown at four years of age. To get it, I'm using a double-flowered mutation from the fern-leaved rock garden peony *P. tenuifolia* and a dwarf *P. lobata* seedling which grows to a height of only seven to eleven inches. That's a tall order, and I probably won't succeed without several hundred experimental crosses. I won't quit until I get a dwarf with blossoms as large as teacups, even though I may have to wait from four to ten years to see the first flower on a hybrid seedling." (Note, some authorities question the existence of a distinct *P. lobata* species, but Roger and other peony hybridists will use the name to identify a generally recognized breeding line until the taxonomists agree on what it really is.)

"You can find dwarf herbaceous peonies listed now. They grow no higher than eleven to twelve inches and have blossoms about two inches across. But I want to improve on them."

As "starter" varieties for beginners, Roger recommends:

- 'Msr. Jules Elie': A double pink with good plant habit; very fragrant.
- 'Lord Calvin': Double, creamy white, accented with red candy stripes; fragrant.
- 'Wilford Johnson': Large, fragrant, dark pink.
- 'Karl Rosenfield': Double red.
- 'Paul M. Wild': Large, dark pink double; great for shows.
- 'Norma Volz': Large double, blush pink.
- 'Virginia Dare': Arrangers like it for its small white single blossoms.
- 'America': Dark crimson-red single hybrid.
- 'Sparkling Star': Pink single; looks good in flower shows.
- 'Sky Pilot': Pink, tall plants, up to 34 inches when well grown.
- 'Paula Faye': Semidouble, glowing pink; outstanding garden performer.
- 'Cytherea': Coral, cup-shaped.
- 'Eastern Star': White double.
- 'Shawnee Chief': For its red fall foliage color.

In addition, any of the 'Estate' cultivars, developed and introduced by the Klehm family, would be good prospects.

Looking forward to his retirement in a few years, Roger has already started hybridizing other garden plants, such as bearded iris, daylilies, and flowering crab apples. And, he has begun an ambitious program for renewing the landscaping around his house with choice trees and shrubs. Roger has completed putting in a water garden and will landscape it with peonies and amenable perennials.

I aked Roger what makes him so fond of hybridizing. "I guess I can't leave well enough alone," he said. "I love trying to do what no one has done before, or doing it better." You can't beat that for an attitude!

More about Peonies

I plant peonies partly because I remember the plants in my mother's garden in Memphis and in the cemeteries we visited on Confederate Memorial Day, and on Decoration Day. That's what we called the Memorial Day that everyone celebrates. The connection between peonies and Memorial Day is universal: before the days of plastic containers and plastic flowers, people used to cut armloads of peonies and stick them in half-gallon fruit jars of water to decorate the graves of their war dead.

One of our old family varieties, I believe, was 'Festiva Maxima', a fragrant white peony with crimson flecks. It was introduced in 1851!

People everywhere respond to the powerful nostalgic pull of peonies, to their bountiful beauty, their fragrance and long life as a cut flower. But some gardeners have given up after a brief fling with peonies because they don't understand that how you grow them depends largely on your climate.

Herbaceous peonies require a winter dormancy to rebuild the food reserves necessary to renew plants year after year. Therefore, they will not live for more than a year or two in mild-winter areas. There is no sharp line of demarcation, but the area where herbaceous peonies are difficult to grow corresponds roughly with hardiness zones 8 and 9. It starts at about Virginia Beach, North Carolina, and takes in the low country of the Carolinas and Georgia, including all of Florida, a strip about two hundred miles wide around the Gulf Coast, and all low-elevation areas in Arizona and California. Surprisingly, however, herbaceous peonies can survive for years in certain parts of northern California, perhaps because the summer dryness forces the plants into a pseudo-dormancy.

Planting

I asked Roger Anderson what advice he could give to beginners on growing peonies. "If possible," Roger said, "plant herbaceous peonies in the fall. If you have to start in the spring or summer, buy potted plants that can be set in the garden with minimum disturbance to the roots. Good-sized potted plants, when planted in early spring, will probably bloom the first year.

"The more advanced nurseries grow and ship tree peonies in containers from early spring through fall. The plants can be set in place in the garden at any time during the growing season but spring or fall planting, when it is cool and rainy, creates less stress on the plants.

"Peonies like loose, airy soil, with plenty of organic matter such as peat moss, rotted leaves, or pasteurized manure worked into the soil before planting, because the peonies are going to be there a long time," Roger said. "I don't like to use sawdust as a soil conditioner or mulch because it continues to cause nitrogen deficiencies in the soil.

"Planting depth is critical to the success of peonies. When planting herbaceous peonies in the northern states, locate the 'eyes,' which are the buds that produce the shoots for the coming year. Look for the tallest ones. These should not be positioned more than two inches below the surface of the surrounding soil, and preferably a bit less. If you plant the crowns deeper, chances are the plants will not bloom. Conversely, if you position the eyes level with the surface of the soil, they could freeze or dry out during a severe winter.

"However, in the South and West where winter temperatures don't drop much below 20 degrees F., plant herbaceous peony crowns so that the eyes are about level with the surface of the soil or slightly above. The shallower planting exposes the eyes to colder temperatures and helps to satisfy the requirement for winter dormancy. "Fall is the best planting time for herbaceous peonies because strong plants may bloom the following spring. However, many herbaceous peonies are sold bare-root in early spring for planting as soon as the soil can be worked. They may produce only vegetative growth the first season.

"I plant tree peonies deeper than herbaceous hybrids, and position the 'union' (where the rootstock joins the scion) 5 to 6 inches below the ground level. Where rainfall is heavy and soils are tight clay, be sure to raise the beds for tree peonies and modify the soil with organic matter.

"Plant bare-root tree peonies in the fall, between September and the end of November, or until the soil freezes. You can plant containerized tree peonies from early spring through fall. Here in Wisconsin the dates are April through November. I mulch fall-planted peonies to keep them from heaving out of the ground due to freezing and thawing.

"With herbaceous or tree peonies, the depth of planting is the same for both bare-root and containerized plants. You can't always go by the depth of the soil in the container. The sure way is to gently feel your way in from the side and brush away enough soil to see the eyes. Once you know where they are, you can position the new plant at just the right level.

"When planting any new peony, don't let the roots dry out while digging the hole, and settle it in with plenty of water. If there is no rain, give it water two or three times weekly. Spring-planted crowns will need watering several times during the first season, but fall-planted peonies develop a strong root system during early spring months to support the plants from then on.

Mulching and Fertilizing

"I use little or no fertilizer when planting because, for two or three weeks after planting, the roots can't take up fertilizer," Roger said. "The fleshy roots are busy sending out a new network of fibrous feeder roots to absorb water. At this stage they are very sensitive to excesses of fertilizer. In my rich soil, I work in a handful or two of bonemeal around each plant, about two weeks after blooming, or in the fall. On less fertile soil, I would recommend a standard commercial fertilizer of a low-nitrogen analysis, drilled in a circle around the dripline of the plant in the early spring, per manufacturer's directions. It has been my experience that feeding late in the spring, when plants are making new growth, can disturb flowering, and should be avoided.

"Wisconsin winters are severe, so I mulch new plants to prevent the soil around them from heaving due to freezing and thawing. Heaving can uproot plants and expose the roots to drying. Composted chipped wood from tree trimmings is good for mulching: it won't blow away like straw or settle into a dense layer like leaves. Piling the fresh-chipped tree trimmings with a little nitrogen and occasional sprinkling will start the decomposition process and prevent nitrogen drawdown. The pile should be started in the spring or summer and turned once or twice to prevent fermentation due to lack of oxygen.

"If you live where winters are severe, pull two or three inches of mulch right over the crowns after the ground starts to freeze and mice have found a home elsewhere. Remove the mulch in the spring when the worst of the cold weather is past but before sprouts show. If you forget and fail to pull the mulch away from the tops of crowns, the plants could suffer from excessive moisture and perhaps contract diseases. I like to use pine boughs for mulching; they stay put and are easy to remove. But, I don't always have them available.

Pests and Diseases

Roger told me: "In the North, the major pests of tree peonies are carpenter bees, deer, and rodents. I protect against deer, rabbits, and mice by surrounding plants with fine mesh wire. Carpenter bees are not as easy to control. They enter peony plants through the scar left from cutting stems, and the young burrow down to the roots, killing the plant. You can prevent their entry by sealing cut places with soft wax or tape.

"Ants are often perceived as pests of peonies, when actually they do no harm. I can recall telling this to an older lady who, while an excellent gardener, was convinced that ants had to be on peony flower buds before they would open. Perhaps I was a bit less than tactful in telling her that it was 'nonsense and an old wives' tale,' because she took it personally and gave me a severe tongue-lashing.

"Maybe someone can suggest how to convince people that the ants aren't eating the peonies. If they'd just take a good look, they would see that the ants are merely tending aphids like we tend milk cows. They want the sticky honeydew the aphids excrete, or the droplets of sweet sap on the flower buds.

Care

"Peonies prefer full sun, except in the middle South and the West. My peony-growing friends there tell me that afternoon shade on peonies lessens the stress from intense heat and dryness. Also, tree peony blossoms hold up longer when they are protected from hot afternoon sun.

"There is little need to 'deadhead' spent blossoms except for cosmetic purposes," Roger continued. "I've seen plants grow to a great age with no one removing spent blooms. Flower arrangers would be happy to take all your long-stemmed seed pods. The pods split open when dry and are great for winter arrangements. However, you do need to remove the top growth from herbaceous peonies when it freezes back in the fall, to lessen problems with foliage diseases. The frost-killed tops twist off easily. Leave the tops on tree peonies or Itoh hybrids. After the new growth has started, you can trim the tops to about three-quarters of an inch above the topmost bud on each shoot, to tidy up the plants.

"Notice that I haven't talked about dividing peonies? You shouldn't do it unless a clump needs to be moved. New divisions can take two or three years to hit their stride. I've seen fifty-year-old clumps that have never been divided, still blooming vigorously."

Regional Differences

Let me add that peony culture in the South differs slightly from northern practices. Growing up in climatic zones 6 and 7, I saw my parents apply rotted manure two to three inches deep as a mulch on herbaceous peony beds after the tops had frozen. They were careful not to cover the crowns with it. The mulch seemed to slow the emergence of spring shoots by a week or so, just enough to keep the buds from being frozen during late cold snaps. Every two or three years they would apply a top-dressing of lime before mulching with manure, to keep the soil from becoming too acid.

Like Roger Anderson, we had few insect and disease problems with peonies. However, this was before Japanese beetles began invading the upper South. Unfortunately, the late-blooming peonies can still be in flower when the first of the Japanese beetles arrive. Now, we hang beetle traps 100 yards upwind from our peony and rose plants to trap as many as possible on the wing. We also patrol the garden mornings and evenings during the worst of the beetle season to handpick the critters. We drop them into a can of kerosene. Thankfully, the beetle season lasts only a month or so where we live.

Unlike Roger Anderson's rich, deep, black soil, southern soils are generally poor. To grow good peonies, you need to fortify the soil with organic matter to improve nutrient holding capacity and drainage. We feed peonies with a balanced garden fertilizer once, in late summer. Our soils are so low in nitrogen that a low-nitrogen fertilizer can't supply enough nitrogen to meet the needs of peonies. Deep, fast-draining, sandy soils have little capacity for nutrient storage and call for an additional feeding right after blooming is completed. We mulch peonies as Roger does, using compost or hardwood bark mulch.

If you like the idea of growing peonies and want to start out right, the catalogs of peony specialists would be a good place to get a feel for the cultivars, their classes, sizes, colors, advantages, and limitations. In surveying the catalogs, you may be attracted to the old standbys because of their modest price. Let me recommend that you consider buying fewer, but better, cultivars. The newer introductions are so dramatically improved, and peony plants last so long, that the additional cost for modern cultivars is an investment which will repay you many times over.

Wildflowers

It took thirty years of study and work, but now Weesie Smith's woods teem with choice southeastern native plants.

(Left) A trail mulched with wood chips leads from the forest and up stone steps to the Smith home.

Great expanses of wildflowers in full bloom can knock your socks off with their vivid colors, movement in the wind, and the extra added attractions of butterflies, skippers, moths, and other colorful insects. These native or domestic stands of plantings are what "hook" many gardeners on wildflowers. But what keeps them involved has to do with the need to live closer to nature: if you can't go out into the woods and fields as often as you like, bring small reminders of the great outdoors into your garden.

Unlike garden flowers, wildflower plantings in full sun depend on a succession of bloom, one species overgrowing and following another, all season long, rather than a few kinds of highly selected flowers remaining in color for extended periods. Dominant species come and go, with pinks and blues much in evidence in the spring, followed by earthy yellows, reds, and mahoganies; and white, purple, and gold in the fall. Almost always, the annual grasses are very much a part of the scene; you learn to view them not as weeds but as a foil for the flowers.

The past two decades have seen an enormous growth of interest in native stands of wildflowers and in bringing wildflowers into home gardens. The crossing over of many gardeners into conservation and restoration of wildflower sites has swelled the ranks of wildflower enthusiasts. Any meeting of native plant hobbyists will be a happy jumble of home gardeners with no training in horticulture, nurserymen with a special interest in wildflowers, and botanists and naturalists, either professional or self-taught.

Planting wildflowers in gardens and tended woodlands is not a new idea. After all, the first garden flowers were transplanted from the wild or grown from seeds or bulbs found in the wild. It is safe to say that the first flowers were domesticated because they were the prettiest plants around, at the least prettier than weeds, and perhaps fragrant. Some would have been "bee plants" grown to supply foraging bees with a nearby source of nectar and pollen.

Home gardeners have an easier time than botanists when it comes to distinguishing between wildflowers and weeds. To nonprofessionals, if a native North American plant is showy in bloom or graceful in foliage, even for a short period of time, it is a wildflower. Most nonprofessionals would expand the usual definition of a weed as a "plant out of place" to include all plants with tiny, nondescript flowers and awkward growth habits, even when they are part of the native plant population. Botanists prefer not to use the pejorative term "weed": they tend to group all wild, nonintroduced flora as "native plants." They refer to all introduced plants as "exotics."

All garden flowers were at one time wildflowers but have been so extensively hybridized and improved that they would have a hard time surviving if transplanted to the wild. Many have been so dwarfed and loaded with flowers that they are dependent on gardeners for supplementary plant food and water.

By definition, wildflowers are unimproved species. Plants within species are not as alike as peas in a pod. Individual plants or isolated populations often show quite a bit of variation from the plant designated as "typical," or "the norm," which has caused great confusion in nomenclature. This gene pool diversity is one of nature's devices for insuring survival of the tens of thousands of species in the wild. It also provides sharp-eyed plant breeders candidates for improvement and introduction as garden flowers or landscape specimens.

Always, there have been nature-oriented gardeners who prefer wildflowers "as is" . . . who appreciate their often spartan simplicity and informality. Almost as soon as the first colonists arrived here, these early naturalist-gardeners began moving wildflowers into their gardens by seeds, bulbs, cuttings, and transplants. Those with talents in botany began active seed, bulb, and plant exchanges with the Old World and with other parts of the Colonies. Some North American species were instant "hits." Others

(Right) One of Weesie's "affinity groups" incorporates blue Phlox divaricata; *white foam flower,* Tiarella wherryi, *the Japanese Solomon's seal,* Polygonatum odoratum *'Variegatum'; the groundcover* Epimedium x warleyense *and, foreground, hardy cyclamen.*

became the stuff of legends, such as the beautiful flowering shrub *Franklinia alatamaha*, sent to Europe and no longer found in the wild.

Native North American wildflower history and lore is really more about people than plants because it concerns the early plant explorers such as John Bartram, who gathered and sent seeds, plants, and bulbs to foreign collectors. In some instances, plants and seeds were collected on research, military, or strategic explorations of middle America and the West, by Audubon, Lewis and Clark, Fremont, and others. European plant explorers came over, either out of scientific curiosity or on commissions from wealthy collectors. Catesby, Michaux, and others are remembered by species they discovered. Thomas Jefferson broke with the reliance on exotic flowers for gardens and tried our native wildflowers at Monticello.

The incredibly rich and varied flora of the New World has enchanted European gardeners since the first boat returned with glowing descriptions of our plants and animals. To this day, interest in propagating North American wildflowers for garden plantings is stronger in Europe than in the United States. Our wildflowers are capable of getting started, surviving, and multiplying despite wide fluctuations in temperature and rainfall. Except for dryland species, ours are easier to grow in Europe than some of their more temperamental species are here.

The early involvement of Europeans with our wildflowers explains why, in colonial days, seeds of some North American species were shipped back to us for planting in gardens. The Europeans were growing species from all over North America, including Mexico, at their botanical gardens when our own garden seed industry was limited to a few industrious Shakers in the East. Some of the varieties had been selected for uniformity, larger flowers, and a better range of colors, but many looked essentially as they did growing in the wild. Thereafter, for many years, the emphasis among European and American seedsmen was on converting American wildflowers into improved garden flowers rather than on propagating wildflowers as Nature put them on this earth.

Wildflowers deserve all the attention they are now receiving, and more. Some rival garden flowers in beauty, durability, and ease of growth. They can add character and interest to otherwise bland seasonal grasslands, forests, and rocky slopes. With all of this going for them, why do so many gardeners slight them in favor of named cultivars of garden flowers?

Some of the resistance is the result of the "regionality" of wildflowers. Each species or subspecies gradually evolved to fit a certain rather narrow ecological niche, and some are not happy unless the grower can provide a similar environment in his garden or woodlands. You have to devote more thought to planting wildflowers and native trees and shrubs than to establishing garden flowers. You have to think of wildflower plantings as "restoring an original picture" rather than "creating a new picture," as you do with garden flowers.

Four developments during the last two decades have conspired to simplify the growing of wildflowers. First, several regional greenhouse-nurseries have begun to produce plants of a wide range of species of native wildflowers, trees, and shrubs for sale. They have worked the kinks out of propagation and can offer sound advice on landscaping with native plants. Second, certain wildflower groups have worked hard to popularize native plants, such as prairie wildflower associations in the Midwest, mountain wildflower groups in the Appalachians, and horticultural societies everywhere. Third, seed companies are promoting mixtures of wildflower seeds as an alternative to large expanses of high-maintenance turf grass. Last but not least, easy-to-follow books on propagating native wildflowers from seeds, cuttings, and division are becoming available.

More and more Americans are becoming concerned about preservation of the environment and the conservation of resources, including native plants. Some are concentrating on protecting or enhancing wildflower sites; others on establishing sanctuaries for wildflowers in their private or public gardens and woodlands. Others are pushing officials to establish wildflowers on roadsides and large open sites such as the land around airfields.

Before the term "conservationist" became stylish, Weesie Smith of Alabama combined her love for wildflowers and gardening with an intense and active concern for preserving irreplaceable sites. Her knowledge of southeastern wildflowers is so vast, her motives so simple and straightforward, and her personality so warm and sharing that it rubs off on everyone she meets.

Weesie's steep land features rock outcroppings that she has planted with native ferns and flowering plants.

*I*t is hard to envision Weesie slogging through the swamps of Alabama, or picking her way through deep, brush-clogged ravines to find and identify wildflowers. A tall, slim, gracious lady of great beauty, she charmed the *Victory Garden* audience when we featured her garden. With her education, energy, and natural talents, Weesie would have had little trouble running a sizable business. But she chose family life, gardening, and wildflowering.

In 1957, Weesie and Lindsay Smith built their present home on a deeply wooded, steeply sloping lot of more than four acres on the outskirts of Birmingham, Alabama. She laughed when she recalled how they had to convince their contractor that they really wanted to build on such rough terrain, and that they had to insist he remove only the trees that were in the way of the lane and the house. (In those days, contractors preferred to clear and flatten building lots.)

For a while, Weesie gardened conventionally, landscaping mostly the sunny areas around the house. She had already been bitten by the wildflower bug, but now she had the space to bring them into her garden. Over the years, she and Lindsay constructed winding paths throughout the heavy woods on her property, and removed dead trees to open up the dense canopy of foliage. Then began a continuing wildflower planting program that includes native plants from all over the Southeast and some related wild species from afar.

The *Victory Garden* TV crew taped Weesie Smith's wildflower garden at peak bloom time. I saw species that were new to me, including the forest understory tree, *Stewartia malacodendron*, also called the silky camellia, and *Luecothoe populifolia*. She had great swatches of the common herbaceous wildflowers such as deciduous ginger, and little clumps of rare plants such as terrestrial orchids. Down in a deep ravine, she had sunk plastic bags in the ground to create a boggy environment for southern rain orchids, *Habenaria clavellata*.

Weesie's gardening interests include more than native wildflowers. "Years ago," she said, "Lindsay and I built a 'pit greenhouse,' sunken into a hillside, with the south side open to the sun. We installed drainage tiles and insulating glass slanting toward the winter sun. Down in the concrete block pit, it is cool and dry, and almost never requires heat. I start seeds of wild species and cultivated plants under banks of fluorescent lights over benches, then move the seedlings to a bench beneath the slanted window to grow to transplanting size.

"That ten-by-thirty-foot greenhouse," he continued, "has the propagation capacity to quickly overload our property with wildflowers. So, I use much of the space to force cool-loving, winter-blooming pot plants such as freesias into bloom to use as holiday gifts."

Downslope from the Smiths' house are several terraces, supported by boulders removed during construction. On these contoured banks, Weesie has planted exotic rock garden plants and perennials such as tree peonies and the "roof iris," *Iris tectorum*. Odd little bulbous plants spring up through the rock walls, but she often has to replace them because of the depredations of chipmunks, mice, and voles.

Weesie refers to these areas as her "cutting gardens" because she relies on them to produce sprays for arrangements throughout the growing season. She calls a similar garden nearer the house her "cottage garden"; it receives more sunlight than any other site on the property.

"These tightly managed gardens look okay where I have them," she said, "but I choose carefully the wildflower species I plant close to the house. To me, most wildflowers look best in a natural setting, away from manicured lawns and flower beds . . . out where they appear to have been 'born free.' Conversely, I am very careful not to turn aggressive cultivated ornamentals loose in my wildflower area. The shade-loving woody and herbaceous exotics can become real pests, competing with native wildflowers. Two of the worst in our area are the ivies and vine myrtle."

Weesie was drawn into wildflowers in the late 1950s when her children were still small. She and Lindsay were, and still are, avid hikers and canoers and felt at home in the outdoors. Identifying wildflowers came naturally to Weesie, and during the first years of their marriage, she grew a few without knowing much about them. But she felt the urge to learn more about the environment, and especially Alabama soils, how they were formed, and how they influence plant populations. So, she completed several courses in natural and physical sciences, beginning with geology.

That was the scene when a wildflower enthusiast entered Weesie Smith's life—the late Eleanor Brakefield, a pioneer in the "dig and save" movement for conserving wildflowers threatened by construction projects. Eleanor persuaded Weesie to come along on a wildflower rescue expedition. In those days, dams were going up all over Alabama, often flooding priceless ecological niches; suburbs were expanding; freeways were being pushed through. Irreplaceable wildflower sites were being drowned, bulldozed, or asphalted over.

"I soon found myself caught up in the race to save whole populations of wildflowers from being wiped out," said Weesie. "From the beginning, I centered on saving shade-loving species of herbaceous wildflowers, shrubs, and small trees and transplanting them to our lot. Our property is heavily wooded and bringing in more sun-loving species than we could accommodate in our few patches of sunlight would have been pointless. I was already an experienced gardener, but I soon found that I had to learn a lot about each wildflower to succeed with it."

So began the gradual conversion of the Smiths' wooded lot into a wildflower garden. Weesie's studies in geology helped her to analyze native plant sites and to approximate them in her home garden. Cleaning out the invasive Japanese honeysuckle, muscadine grapevines, and cat-briers from four acres by hand-pulling familiarized her with every square inch of the property. She probed here and there and located dry, rocky outcroppings, moist seeps, and areas of deep, fertile loam.

"There were virtually no understory plants worth saving," she said. "So it simplified the removal of about four hundred dead pine trees, killed by pine bark beetles. Later, I contacted the city and commercial tree companies and found them only too happy to dump chipped wood and leaves on our property. I wheelbarrowed it into areas I had marked for planting wildflowers. It wasn't long before I had a deep layer of decaying organic matter over much of the forest floor, and was building paths of chipped wood.

"Our five children were busy being kids," said Weesie: "they helped a little, but I couldn't expect them to share my commitment to wild-flowers. I tried taking them on wildflower digs, but found the two incompatible. Instead, Lindsay and I diverted their energy into exploring northern Alabama.

"Lindsay helped by clearing honeysuckle and fallen tree limbs, but he was working long hours building his practice and couldn't go along on dig-and-save missions. After a while, I realized that wildflowering is basically a solitary pursuit, except when you are on field trips with like-minded enthusiasts. You can enjoy wildflowers without knowing much about them, but there are so many species that really knowing them can become a lifelong learning experience. Many gardeners have never ventured deep into woods and wetlands, and are more familiar with the bright annuals and perennials that grow in full sun. The rugged roadside flowers pretty well take care of themselves, but not the forest understory species. You can't just plant them and let them grow wild: they require varying degrees of management.

"When I advise gardeners on starting wildflower gardens," said Weesie, "I take them through a short checklist. I suggest that they first consider the duration and density of sunlight that falls on the site. Any site that receives a half day or more of full sunlight should be planted with

Weesie gathers fragrant freesias in her pit greenhouse.

sun-loving meadow flowers. The shade-tolerant species will do better beneath deciduous trees, but some have a tolerance for sun that doesn't appear in catalog descriptions. Densely shaded areas can be improved by limbing up trees or dropping and chipping unthrifty specimens."

Weesie has formed a conclusion about "shade-loving" wildflowers that has a lot of merit. She feels that many species are found only in the woods in the wild because of heavy competition from other plants out in the sun. She has found that many forest species will adapt to situations where they receive morning sun, and afternoon and evening shade. "But," she says, "they won't survive in the sun unless the soil is rich in organic matter and is kept moist." I think that Weesie's discovery opens up many possibilities for gardens that have little shade.

"Beginners need to locate different soil types on their property. Dig into the soil at various places on the site. If the soil is uniformly heavy, you may have to modify some spots with sand to suit the preference of some species for fast-draining soil. Southeastern soils are almost always acid and relatively poor, which suits most wildflower species just fine.

"There isn't much you can do to prepare soil beneath trees for planting wildflowers, other than raking the leaf litter to the side, spreading a two-inch layer of composted wood chips or pulverized pine bark as a mulch, planting through it, and pulling the dry leaves around the plants.

"Competition from tree roots is fierce; wildflower plants need help to get started on the forest floor. Fall is a good time to transplant wildflowers to wooded sites because the trees are going dormant, and rains will lessen the watering chore while getting plants established and well rooted. Spring is a poor time to transplant because the trees are leafing out and roots are competing for soil moisture.

"The forest landscape will become more natural looking as the stands of wildflowers thicken and spread from the few plants you plug in beneath trees. Contented wildflowers set seeds and reproduce abundantly.

A pea gravel walk leading to the pit greenhouse is bordered with the azalea R. 'George Taber' and Phlox divaricata.

Some species have backup systems for reproduction, rhizomes or bulbs as well as seeds.

"The big difference in just growing wildflowers and gardening with wildflowers," said Weesie, "is using landscaping skills to enhance their natural beauty. For example, whenever I acquire a new species, my first priority is to choose for it the best possible site, one with the proper amount of shade and moisture, and the most appropriate soil. We have both heavy clay and sandy soil on the place, which gives me some flexibility. Then, I look up at the forest canopy and down at the soil, and try to sense the effect of wind and winter exposure on the site. My aim is to do everything I can to start that new plant off right, because, once it is planted, I can't change its surroundings.

"I don't wish to make wildflower gardening seem difficult," she said, "because it is as simple as growing zinnias and tomatoes. It is just that the needs of most wildflowers are different from those of garden flowers. If beginners will take a little time to try to understand wildflowers, they won't be disappointed in their attempts to grow them. In the wild, each species adapts to certain soil, climate, and exposure situations; the trick in growing them is to try to duplicate those conditions in your own garden or woodlands.

"Let me back up," Weesie said, "and remind beginners in wildflowering never to remove plants or seeds from national or state parks or nature preserves. Actually, it is best to defer collecting until one knows for sure whether a species is abundant or rare. Generally, the summer-flowering meadow and roadside wildflowers are fairly abundant: collecting a few seeds shouldn't hurt. Just leave a few heads to drop seeds for next year's plants.

"I have to caution beginners about the 'localness' of many wildflowers. Only a few, and they are meadow flowers such as gaillardia, coreopsis, liatris, and phlox, will grow in varied locations around the country. For example, in Birmingham, we are on the southern edge of adaptability for species that are more at home in northern Alabama, Georgia, and Tennessee. We know from experience not to go into southern Alabama and bring back wild plants. They are accustomed to mild winters and more rainfall. Rarely will they survive our cold winters, tremendous variations in winter temperatures, and periodic droughts.

"This is why the first wildflower books you buy should be publications of your state wildflower or horticulture society or, at the most, books published for a discrete climatic region such as our Southeast. As you get deeper into the subject, you may wish to buy one of the college-level books published for each state or region, bearing the title of *Flora of* a particular state. These are heavy books, but you will need them when you begin delving deeply into wildflowers. They list and describe many species not found in general garden encyclopedias."

I asked Weesie which "surefire" wildflowers she would recommend as starter plants for woodlands. She reminded me that her recommendations would stand only for the Southeast and told me that the first plants she moved to her woods were:

- Bloodroot, *Sanguinaria canadensis*
- Blue phlox, *Phlox divaricata*
- Liverleaf, *Hepatica spp.*
- *Trillium spp.* (she now has fifteen species)
- Jack-in-the-pulpit, *Arisaema triphyllum*
- False Solomon seal, *Smilaceae racemosa*
- Solomon seal, *Polygonatum biflora*

I certainly concur with her choices, because the woods around my farm are rich in these species. One more I would add is a sun-tolerant plant with yellow and green daisylike flowers, *Chrysogonum virginianum*, usually found where a fallen tree has opened the forest canopy to let sunlight through. And the wild deciduous azaleas: they especially like moist soils along creeks and around seeps.

Weesie has mixed feelings about the current rage for "wildflower meadows." These are areas planted with mixtures of flower seeds made up of sun-loving native American species and exotics from other parts of the world, often laced heavily with grass seeds. "I would feel better about them," she said, "if they were made up totally of North American wildflowers, because I am wary of introducing species which could become invasive weeds, such as cornflowers. They are probably okay for yards where they are not likely to escape, but I'd rather see only natives planted along highways, where roadside plants might escape into agricultural land."

Weesie offered this advice to gardeners trying to propagate wildflowers or to increase stands on their property. "With my greenhouse and banks of fluorescent lights, I have an ideal setup for starting seeds and growing plants of wildflowers. However, a beginner could get by with one fluorescent light fixture in a cool corner of a basement or unheated room. Get fresh seeds if possible. Fresh seeds of many wild species will germinate within a week or two, but let them dry out and turn dark, and they may not come up for six to twelve months! If your supplier ships plants or bulbs, query them on the source; buy from only the specialists who propagate their plants and not from those who take them from the wild."

Weesie doesn't shy away from being called a "conservationist" as well as a wildflower gardener. "It took only a trip or two with experienced wildflower specialists," she said, "to convince me of the scope of ecological loss we were facing in Alabama. It was abundantly clear that very few people seemed to understand that it was irrevocable. And even fewer were doing anything about it. In all of northern Alabama, not more than a dozen of us were fighting for conservation. But we pulled others into a loose-knit coalition and began to press for the protection of significant sites. We began to log the locations of scarce species of wildflowers and, in the process, discovered some that were previously unknown.

"One of our most significant accomplishments was protecting unique ecological niches along the ravines in the northern sector of the Sipsey River wilderness. Lindsay and I had hiked through them and were convinced of their value. With help from all over the state, indeed from the entire United States, our coalition of concerned citizens was able to have some deep ravines set aside as wilderness area. These were all in the northern sector of the Bankhead National Forest; we were too late to save similar ravines in the southern sector; they were flooded by a dam impoundment.

"We hadn't been as successful in getting the ear of highway officials," she said. "Until recently, they seemed more interested in subduing the environment with herbicides than in putting wildflowers to work in beautifying roadsides." Fortunately, this is beginning to change.

Weesie told me that her wildflowering trips were fewer nowadays because of the demands her home gardens place on her time and energy. When we taped the *Victory Garden* show there, we were amazed that one person, with occasional help for heavy jobs, could manage such a large area of wildflowers. Weesie admitted ruefully that she is no longer expanding the garden but is concentrating on maintaining it. "There are days," she said, "when I think about removing trees to let in more sunlight for my wildflowers, then I remember that we need the shade to keep the house cool and to discourage sun-loving weeds from coming in. It's a trade-off.

"Nowadays, rather than rushing out on dig-and-save missions, I find myself spending more time at home, protecting my weak wildflowers from the more aggressive species, replacing plants or stands that have been damaged or wiped out by voles. Much of my time is spent pulling out and composting ferns. I think that, if I left our woods unattended, ferns would take over and run out most other species.

"Every now and then I get a pleasant surprise like a little patch of three birds orchids, *Triphora trianthophora*, which apparently came up from seeds. They grew in chipped wood I had spread on a path. The seeds may have been picked up in the bark of a tree dragged across the land during harvesting. The little orchids seem willing (or able) to grow only in the path, perhaps because no other plants are growing there. They come up, bloom, set seeds, and die back in five or six weeks, so I don't try to move them. I just block off a four-foot section of the path in late July."

Weesie shared with me some of the challenges and triumphs of collecting and moving wildflowers. "When the children were small," she said, "we had one of those huge station wagons. We'd load it with newspapers and canvas carrying bags and head for a dig-and-save site. We always asked permission to enter such rescue sites, unless the bulldozers were already going. Then, we'd try to get ahead of them.

"One of the conservationists active then, Eleanor Brakefield, taught me how to move wildflowers at any time of the year. She would worry a plant out of the ground to save as much as possible of the root system, lay it on a newspaper, fold the paper over the root ball, roll it up, soak the wrapped roots in water from a creek or seep, label the plant by species and location, and stand it up in a canvas bag. Sometimes we lugged plants for miles, sweating and swatting at mosquitoes, gnats, and ticks. It was thrilling when we crept down steep inclines on rough, rocky roads that were more like trails, but there were times when, with tires spinning and throwing gravel, I doubted if we would make it back up those hills!

"I had a good eye for spotting wildflowers . . . still do," said Weesie. "But another conservationist, Josephine Henry, beat us all. It would be fair to call her a plant explorer because she traveled all over the country identifying plants, recording their locations, and profiling their sites. On the few occasions I was lucky enough to travel with her, she would use binoculars to locate spots of color at great distances. When you are in such rough terrain that each step is work, being able to go straight to a patch of plants is a lifesaver."

1)

2)

3)

4)

5)

6)

Southeastern Wildflowers

A gallery of typical southeastern wildflowers from Weesie's collection: the Atamsco lily, *Zephyranthes atamasco* (1), grows from bulbs and likes light shade and moist soil. The Florida flame azalea, *R. Austrinum* (2), brightens open woods in midspring. *Phaecelia bipinnatifida*; the celandine or woods poppy, *Stylophorum diphyllum*; and the cinnamon fern, *Osmunda cinnamomea* (3). *Trillium luteum*, one of Weesie's fifteen trillium species (4). Green and gold *Chrysogonum virginianum* tolerates sun (5). *Hepatica americana* (6), liverleaf, a widely known early spring flower. Weesie reminds beginners that success with wildflowers depends on respecting their often limited adaptability. Most species are suited only to the particular conditions of soil, climate, and exposure of their region.

I asked Weesie about memorable "digs." She recalled the day she and Lindsay whizzed past a clump of wild red lilies on a bank alongside the interstate freeway they were traveling. She fixed the spot in her mind and determined to come back and see the lilies. So, the next morning, she told Lindsay she'd be right back and took off for the remembered spot. When she sighted the lily, she realized that it was just past an exit. She kept on going to the next exit, which proved to be eighteen miles down the road! Thirty-six miles later, she found the lilies, dug up just one, wrapped it in sphagnum moss, and sent it to a botanist friend, Joab Thomas, at the University of Alabama. He pronounced it to be a previously unknown species, more like *Lilium michiganense* than *L. canadense* or *L. superbum*, yet resembling all three. After more study, it will be classified. Perhaps it was fateful that Weesie dug that one bulb. The clump on the highway has disappeared, but their salvaged specimen is reproducing through stolons and can be perpetuated.

Weesie also recalled collecting on a 100-degree day near Peterson, Alabama. The site had long been used for field trips by university students in botany but was slated for obliteration, due to the construction of a new lock and dam. "We carried heavy canvas bags of plants for what seemed like miles through that heat and humidity. But it was worth it! We were saving plants of Alabama croton, a relic from the Silurian geologic era, and snow wreath, *Neviusia Alabamensis*, a beautiful little deciduous shrub.

"Later, I had to travel into central Alabama to rescue from a scheduled spraying with herbicide a plant I consider the star of my garden, a rare yellow ladies slipper orchid, *Cyprepedium kentuckiensis*. It has larger, slightly later flowers than the more abundant yellow ladies slipper, *C. pubescens*, and is lighter yellow in color. In my garden this precious plant has thrived and is multiplying nicely."

Weesie paused and, with a concerned look, told me, "I hope I'm not giving you the idea that I'm rushing around Alabama ripping off rare wildflowers. For many years, I got my plants solely on dig-and-save missions, where the plants would have been destroyed, along with their site. In those days, thirty years or so ago, virtually no nurserymen propagated wildflowers. Every now and then, I'd see advertisements in our *Alabama Farmer's Bulletin* for wild plants being sold by farmers. Usually, I would drive out to see the plants to assure myself that they were not an endangered species and, if not, that they were dug in a way which would insure survival.

"We in Alabama owe a debt of gratitude to two nurserymen for promoting nursery-grown wildflowers. Years ago, commercial 'collectors' would raid wild plant populations and sell them by mail or to pharmaceutical companies or mail-order nurseries. Some still do, and I deplore it. That's why I feel so grateful to my nurseryman friend, Tom Dodd, for popularizing all sorts of woody native Alabama plants, especially the azaleas and rhododendrons. And Dan Coleman, even though he never seemed to have enough plants in his nursery to meet the demand, brought several choice species into public notice. At first, they propagated the traditional ways, by cuttings and layering. It was so slow. Now, they use mist propagation and container culture to reduce the time from cuttings to sales size. Tom Dodd grows most of his native shrubs from seeds to maintain a wide gene pool and has evolved into a wholesaler."

I asked Weesie what advice she had to offer people who are just becoming interested in wildflowers. "The single most important step is to find a local wildflower society or a wildflower group in a local horticultural society. Then, begin going on field trips with them. At first, you may feel totally out of place, listening to the botanists and old-time wildflower specialists reeling off latin binomials and reminiscing about great field trips they have taken. They will be patient and sharing with you, and will show you how to use the picture book guides to identify species.

"Books and seminars are just fine, but they aren't sufficient unto themselves. I've never met an armchair wildflower specialist who knew what he or she was talking about. There is simply no substitute for time in the field, in the company of knowledgeable specialists. Most of these specialists are not botanists or biologists but come from all walks of life. Anyone who loves nature can fit into these groups.

"I wouldn't even dream of trying to plant wildflowers in my garden before seeing or studying how they, or a closely related species, actually grow in the wild. From that, I can make educated guesses on the type of soil, level of acidity, soil moisture preference, and sun or shade requirements of the plant."

Weesie Smith is grateful that getting to know wildflowers led her into the preservation movement. She feels that the two are inseparable; no one can know and love wildflowers without being concerned about their shrinking habitat. She feels blessed that her hospitable land provided a safe harbor for many wildflowers that would otherwise have been lost. But most of all, she values the person/plant interdependence that grows out of wildflower gardening—the pleasure they bring to her, year after year, in return for the time she took to learn their likes and dislikes.

More about Wildflowers

Most wildflower beginners aren't ready to become activists in wildflower conservation, and they aren't up to the more challenging aspects of propagation. They want to start with something simple, sure-fire, and inexpensive. Growing wildflowers from seed mixtures is the answer.

Planting Wildflower Seeds

One of the best ways to get to know the common varieties of sun-loving wildflowers is to plant a row or two in your food or flower garden, using a wildflower seed mixture. Start with at least an ounce or two of seeds to be sure to get a good stand and a representative number of plants of each species in the mixture. Sow the seeds in a row or band so you can tell where the flower seedlings leave off and the weeds begin. The mixtures contain both cool-weather and warm-weather annuals. Plant them in the fall or spring; summer planting won't give the cool-weather annuals a chance to show off before hot weather burns out the plants.

A gardening encyclopedia or a wildflower reference book will help you learn the names of the flowers in the mixtures: the references with color pictures will give you a better batting average. Some are common American wildflowers but many are rather obscure European species. Let the plants dry up at the end of the season; then pull them and scatter the seeds over the row. You should get a good stand of the stronger species the following year and another opportunity to identify those which baffled you at the first try.

Establishing large meadows of wildflowers from seed mixtures is a bit more complicated because you have to eliminate heavy stands of grass and weeds to get a good stand. Flower seedlings are small and comparatively weak, and strong grass and weeds can swamp them before they develop plants large enough to compete.

The success of wildflower seedings depends partly on the soil being rather poor, and not heavily loaded with seeds of grass that spread from stolons to make dense mats. Wherever the soil is naturally fertile, moist throughout the year, and seeded with grass, the grass will soon push out all the wildflowers, except the rugged species with large-enough plants to overgrow or thrive between tufts of annual grasses. Casual observers can get the impression that wildflowers prefer poor, dry soil. Not true. They grow there because Nature has adapted many species to grow on soils too poor, dry, or infertile to support a thick stand of stoloniferous grass. Some western wildflowers survive by growing in the open areas between clumps of bunch grasses.

Start a year ahead, during the summer. Plow and rototill the soil. Fumigate the soil to kill weeds, grasses, seeds, and root-rot organisms. Use a chemical such as Vapam or methyl bromide when the soil is warmer than 60 degrees F. If you are an organic gardener, cover the moist, tilled soil with clear plastic, batten it down tightly, and let the accumulated solar heat of summer kill most of the weed seeds. Allow six to eight weeks to "solarize" the soil. Alternatively, soak the area a few times and rototill when the soil is dry enough to work. Several tillings will kill many sprouting seedlings and greatly reduce the weed seed count. Planting thickly and tilling under a summer green manure crop such as soybeans will also help reduce the weed population. During soil preparation, incorporate limestone as indicated by soil tests, and a phosphate source. Incorporate a balanced fertilizer only if the soil is exceedingly poor or if it is raw subsoil. Supplementary nitrogen has a way of encouraging the bad guys to take over.

During the past few years, *The Victory Garden* has taped programs at several botanical gardens where wildflower meadows have been established. Consistently, the thickest stand of wildflowers, the greatest range of species, and the fewest weeds and aggressive grasses were seen where the soil had been fumigated. Furthermore, fumigated plots repeated better and longer; one still looked good after three years, requiring only the pulling of a few aggressive weeds before they set seeds.

After fumigating or "solarizing" large areas, work the soil into a seedbed and use a disc, spring-tooth harrow or rake to make furrows about 2 inches deep across the area. If you garden in zone 7 or south, scatter seeds at the recommended rate in late summer or fall, then drag the soil with a square of cyclone fence to cover seeds lightly with soil. You can either "water up" the seeds with a sprinkler or let them emerge with the fall rains. Either way, they will go through the winter as small seedlings and bloom the following year.

In zones 6 and north, get the soil ready and delay seeding until late fall, just before the soil freezes or early spring. Broadcast the seeds and cover them lightly with straw, not weed-infested hay. The mulch will prevent seeds from washing away and will reduce the loss to foraging birds. Few seeds will come up until late spring; the freezing and thawing will hasten and improve germination. The meadow will bloom the following season. However, some of the slow-growing perennials may form rosettes and not bloom for yet another year.

Starting and Transplanting Seedlings

An even better way is open to gardeners who are prepared to start wildflower seeds in flats. At the time you begin preparing the soil, fill shallow plastic or fiber "seed flats" with planter mix and plant them with seeds of wildflower mixes or individual adapted wild species. You don't need a greenhouse: start them under the shade of a tree, up on a table out of reach of pets and mice. Once the plants have grown enough to fill the flats with a mat of roots, and before they bloom, plant entire flats by scraping shallow holes into the prepared soil. Soak the holes before setting-in the flats. Consider the flats as "islands" of flowers scattered randomly across the prepared soil.

As the islands of flowers grow, water occasionally and cultivate in between them to kill emerging weeds and grasses. By late summer, many species will have completed flowering and will have set seeds. Discontinue cultivating and let the seeds drop or blow onto the bare soil surrounding the islands. Scatter a few wildflower seeds on the loose, bare soil to hasten the process of filling in. Wildflower islands can be transplanted in early spring, but this means you have to start seeds in a greenhouse or under lights in late winter.

A few enlightened nurseries have begun to grow what they call "plugs" of wildflowers, which are similar to the flats previously described, and are planted in the same way. They know how to start the species that are difficult or slow to germinate. Some offer plugs of individual wild species as well as mixtures of adapted species.

Some of the widely available North American species are easy to start and dependable in wildflower meadows: coreopsis, *Gaillardia, Rudbeckia, Ratibida, Bidens, Echinacea* or coneflower, *Liatris* or gayfeather, *Helianthus* or sunflower, *Phlox drummondi* and *P. subulata*, various lupins and fall-blooming asters are good examples. You can buy seeds of them from wildflower specialists, grow plants, and set them in colonies in meadows, the way they would grow naturally. This is the best way to establish a meadow of purely American wildflowers.

Planting in Shady Areas

A wooded landscape presents a different set of challenges and calls for a different group of wildflower species than sunny meadows. In nature, some forest floors seem hostile to wildflowers; others teem with them. In my climate zone 7, the richest concentrations of hardwood forest-floor flowers are on steep hillsides away from the afternoon sun, and they always seem to be thicker toward the base of the hill. Scientific research indicates that the degree of shade is not nearly as important as root competition for water. Slopes away from the afternoon sun don't dry out badly, and flowers on the lower end of the slope benefit from water seeping from in-soak higher up the hill.

This information suggests how you could grow wildflowers under trees with aggressive surface roots which suck the water out of soil. Rake the area free of leaves and loose duff and lay down a layer of spun-bonded synthetic "landscape cloth." Buy the cloth as wide as you can, because you will need to overlap joints 6 inches. Shred the leaves with a rotary mower and mix them with finely pulverized pine bark and moistened peat moss, mixed on a 3:1 ratio. Include a few shovels of topsoil from beneath the trees. Add a phosphate source but no limestone, and no nitrogen or potash fertilizer. Spread the organic mulch 3 to 5 inches deep over the landscape cloth, and you are ready to plant.

Planting seeds under trees is futile. Start with adapted plants purchased at a native-plant nursery. Spring or early fall transplanting should give you the best results. The landscape cloth should prevent tree roots from competing with the wildflowers until they get a good start. After three or four years, tree roots will find a way to grow into the moist mulch and you may have to fish around, find the heaviest of them, and snip them off with pruning shears.

Generally, the best competitors for forest-floor plantings are the hardy perennial species that come on with a rush in early spring, bloom, and restore their stored carbohydrates before the forest canopy shuts out the sunlight they need for growth and reproduction. In my climate, wild ginger, hepatica, blue-eyed grass, anemone, bloodroot, several species of wild violets, and two species of dwarf iris like hardwood forest situations. Several species in these genera will grow as far north as zone 4.

Some of the most hospitable forest situations are moist glens between trees where the light or dappled shade excludes most grass but allows summer-blooming wildflowers to thrive. The steep banks of healed ravines are ideal for plants such as *Trillium*, *Dodecatheon*, or shooting stars, which need more moisture than most wild species.

Landscaping with Wildflowers

An increasingly popular use of native plants is for surrounding intimate garden rooms, retreats, or sanctuaries in landscapes. You can go all the way and transform a thoroughly domestic garden by landscaping it entirely with native plants. Use shrubs for screening, medium-height to tall wildflowers for color, and low-growing wildflowers for groundcovers. Look for slow-growing plants that mature at small sizes. In the trees and shrubs you may have to settle for improved cultivars of native species. Your Cooperative Extension Service can supply you with a list of adapted native trees and shrubs. If the list seems uninspired, check your library for books on native plants of your region. Most of them will be about herbaceous wildflowers. Only a few will instruct you in landscaping with larger native plants. These definitive books will tell you how large a tree or shrub will grow at maturity, its rate of growth, and its soil preference.

When searching for native plants, write down a few facts about each contender: mature height and spread, season and duration of bloom, fragrance, attractiveness to butterflies or their larvae, fruit or berries for wild birds, fall color, winter bark and form of branches, special soil requirements, and water needs. If you live in an acid-soil area, stick with the species that like acid soil. Concentrate those which like moist soils around ponds or streambanks or near a water faucet. Make raised beds for the species such as azaleas that need perfect drainage. Leave generous spaces between trees and shrubs: give them room to grow. You will enjoy watching plants develop their natural form, and they will be healthier.

One of the easiest ways to use wildflowers is to set plants into mixed borders of perennials, shrubs, and roses. Many of the native wildflowers are just as beautiful as exotic cultivars; their inherent vigor enables them to survive where exotics could succumb to insects, plant diseases, and weather stresses. Collectively, more herbaceous wildflowers are planted in this fashion than in any other way. Gardeners usually start out with rugged species that will adapt to almost any garden situation, then gradually work their way into more demanding flowers. The lists given previously for meadow and forest floor plantings are good starting points. Native orchids and plants which require hosts to thrive are not for beginners.

Most nurseries display wildflower plants among other perennials and sort them out by sun- or shade-loving species. When you do find a native American species, it may very well qualify as a wildflower by definition, but won't naturalize well over much of the United States.

With this in mind, if you like the looks of flowering meadows planted with exotics, by all means plant them. But, not if your garden is near agricultural land; exotics can escape and become pests. Personally, I'd rather be selective and use only North American wildflowers, especially those native to my region.

I am optimistic that gardeners in the United States and Canada will come to appreciate the incredible variety and beauty of our native North American wildflower species and will demand plants or seed mixtures only of species native to their regions. When that day comes, the seed companies will be forced to mass-produce seeds of native North American wildflowers instead of garden flowers originally from other parts of the world.

If you want to know and grow wildflowers, it has to be more than a summertime romance. You can learn a bit by growing and observing a few species each year and you can benefit from seasonal wildflower walks sponsored by your state parks system. But you will become proficient by attending meetings of your local wildflower society or horticultural society. Go along on their walks in the woods and meadows. They know what is blooming, and where to find it. Hardly a bush, tree, vine, or groundcover escapes their notice. They exclaim just as jubilantly over common Jack-in-the-pulpit as they do over showy orchids. A plant doesn't have to be in flower for them to know it. They are naturalists as much as gardeners and will help you through the most difficult part of wildflower gardening . . . getting to know the plants. In their company it will be a pleasant voyage of discovery.

Lilies

Ruth and Hugh Cocker find southern Minnesota just right for their hobby of breeding and showing hybrid lilies.

*P*erhaps it is fragrance that makes lilies seen years ago linger in your mind like the memory of a lost love. Or their compelling presence: they draw attention away from lesser flowers by grace and perfection, by colors that make catalog pages pale by comparison. There is no blue lily, nor black, and I would hope never to see one. Give me, instead, the sunny yellows, strawberry and candy-apple reds, delicious pinks, and waxy whites. Throw in a few stripes, penciled or picoteed petals, spots and aureoles . . . and you have enough variety to fill a lifetime of gardening with joyful discoveries.

Combined with other flowers, groundcovers, or dwarf shrubs, or displayed against a hedge of conifers or hollies, lilies display their charms to best advantage. Their graceful flowering stems, elaborate as chandeliers, move in the slightest breeze and animate gardens. Some lilies have been refined so much that you can barely see the foliage between the flowers, but some blend into surroundings like a fawn in a sun-dappled glen.

(Left) The Cockers' lily evaluation plot dazzles the beholder on a summer day.

Were you to gather and plant bulbs from each of the ninety-odd lily species, then label each with its flag of national origin, your garden would look like a gathering of the United Nations. Then, you would discover that Northern Hemisphere nations from around the globe would be represented, but there would be not one flag from south of the equator!

About half of the species are native to the Asian landmass, about one-quarter from Europe, several to North America, and a few to Japan. One, the southernmost in origin, is native to the mountains of the Philippine Islands and was not discovered until the late 1940s. Doubtless, a few species remain to be discovered.

This enormously varied gene pool has given us some of the most beautiful plants in the world, so spectacular that the flowers were offered to propitiate the gods of ancient civilizations. But, secular needs were fulfilled as well as sacred: the bulbs were used for food and, later, for their medicinal properties. As human cultures mingled through trade and conquest, lilies began to cross boundaries. The Romans introduced Asian and Middle Eastern lily species to Europe as they fanned out to establish forts and footholds for the Christian religion. During the Dark Ages, monastery gardens sequestered the bulbs, which might otherwise have been eaten. Literature of the 1500s mentions *Lilium martagon*, a Turk's cap lily, and *L. chalcedonicum*.

In the 1700s, the eastern American natives, *L. canadense*, *L. superbum*, and *L. philadelphicum*, made their way to Europe. Importation to Europe of Japanese species such as *L. japonicum* did not begin until the 1800s. The lilies native to the western United States were little known until after the Gold Rush, but created a sensation when they arrived in Europe. Unfortunately, because of their demanding cultural requirements, they proved difficult to grow in Great Britain.

Plant explorers found and introduced *L. Henryi* and *L. leucanthum* in the early 1900s: the dauntless E. H. Wilson brought back *L. regale*, *L. Sargentiae*, and *L. Davidii* from Asia between 1905 and 1908. Shortly thereafter, *L. amabile* was introduced from Korea. Many bulbs perished in transit, forcing plant explorers to retrace their steps hundreds of miles back into mountainous terrain, to dig and ship replacements.

Early lily breeders made some significant crosses but lost them to diseases transmitted through vegetative reproduction. Had they known that disease-free lilies can be grown from seeds, more long-term hybridizing successes might have been reported during the 1800s and early 1900s, when other specialty plant species were rapidly being improved.

(Right) These un-named Asiatic hybrid lily seedlings bred by the Cockers are still under evaluation.

The Japanese had been improving their indigenous species all along, but mostly by selection, until they crossed. *L. martagon* from Europe with their own *L. hansonii*, to create the first of the Martagon hybrids. The hybrids had larger individual flowers, more of them, a wider range of colors, and extended life due to thicker petals.

The Boston nurseryman Charles Hovey reported making crosses in 1843, and the renowned plant breeder Francis Parkman made a three-way cross in the 1860s, using *L. speciosum*, *L. auratum*, and *L. candidum*. The Bellingham hybrids, incorporating mostly western North American species, were made in 1899 by Robert Kessler of Los Angeles, but languished until 1932 when they were introduced by the USDA.

Perhaps the most severe obstacle to the improvement of lilies was the lack of a strong, skillful, committed, and well-financed breeder/grower/marketer. But such a man, Jan de Graaf, came along in the late 1920s. He began working for, and later bought, Oregon Bulb Farms in the fertile Willamette Valley.

With so much untapped potential to exploit, Jan de Graaf set about directing the work of a crew of skilled plant breeders in making up to thirty thousand crosses every year. Prior to that time, no other lily breeder had made crosses on such a large and organized scale and embracing so many species. In the process, Jan de Graaf's hybridizers helped to establish the chromosome counts of the various species and to perfect ways to save pollen from early bloomers for use on late-flowering species, and vice versa.

The various lily species are relatively easy to cross. For some reason, they have not developed the elaborate defenses against cross-pollination that complicate the cross-breeding of other genera. In fact, the only defense of lily flowers is against self-pollination, undoubtedly Nature's scheme to prevent the gene pool from shrinking. Lily flowers display their reproductive organs with the innocence of little children and readily accept bee- and wind-delivered pollen from other flowers.

With Jan de Graaf, as with other breeders, success came as much from the courage to discard good, but not great, hybrids as from the ability to recognize and propagate the pivotal selections. He employed European know-how in freeing his foundation bulbs of viruses by production from seeds and popularized the term "strains" of lilies, meaning sibling bulbs grown from seeds. Strains produce lilies that are reasonably similar to each other, but not as alike as peas in a pod. De Graaf also produced cultivars of lilies by what we now call "cloning," vegetative reproduction from scales, bulblets, or stem cuttings. Cloning is mandatory in new award-winning cultivars, where each bulb has to produce a plant and flower almost exactly like every other one bearing the name.

De Graaf seemed to have a sixth sense for the colors, flower and plant sizes, and plant habits that were desired by both home gardeners and commercial growers of pot plants. Beginning with 'Enchantment' in 1942, De Graaf's "Jagra" line of hybrids became world famous. More than any other cultivar, 'Enchantment' marked the turning point in lily breeding. It remains the most popular lily hybrid worldwide. Among other famous Jagra cultivars and strains are the trumpet type Aurelian hybrids and the late-blooming Oriental hybrids. His 'Pink Perfection' strain, 'Red Band' hybrid, and 'Golden Splendor' are popular around the world.

In 1968 Jan de Graaf sold his business and, in succeeding years, the company lost momentum. Numerous smaller companies in the northwest United States, the Great Lakes area, and southern Canada moved in to capitalize on the swelling demand. Dutch bulb producers began growing the cultivars needed for the American market. At the same time, some private lily hybridizers began licensing bulb producers to increase their backyard businesses. Other lily enthusiasts, with promising seedlings from their own hybridizing, elected not to expand, but to keep their hobby secondary to growing and showing lilies.

The decision to begin breeding a specialty plant marks a turning point in the lives of hobby growers. Successful plant breeders have a special status at plant society meetings because other advanced hobbyists know how much forethought, work, and determination is required in crossing, evaluation, and follow-through. For Ruth and Hugh Cocker, lily breeding sets the pace of their days, the rhythm of their seasons, and most of the goals for their gardening.

Hugh and Ruth collect pollen from choice male parents to be saved for hybridizing.

*O*n a breezy June day, I visited Ruth and Hugh Cocker at their five-acre farmstead on the outskirts of Rochester. Their comfortable home is shaded by trees they planted shortly after buying the place in 1950. Black walnut and butternut trees line the approach drive. The most obvious feature is an impeccable half-acre patch of closely spaced lily beds in the side yard and another smaller field of lilies and perennials in the back. Hugh told me that, if all the rows in the beds were lined up end to end, they would measure amost two and a half miles!

Anchoring the farmstead is a neat red haybarn built by Hugh . . . an artifact from the days when he raised and showed Shetland ponies. More than two dozen grazed their pasture at one time. Now, the barn comes in handy for storing lily bulbs in sand over winter.

The Cockers have always been hard workers. At his boyhood home in Canton, Minnesota, Hugh helped his parents with general farming as well as with their spring business of growing and selling bedding plants, perennials, and gladiolus bulbs. Moving to Rochester after finishing high school, he went to work part-time for Ruth's parents in their business, Whiting's Flowers. Ruth and Hugh married while he was serving the air force as a gunnery instructor in B-17s in Florida. The noise battered his hearing. Hugh jokes, "The phone keeps ringing in my right ear, but I've learned not to answer it."

Home again, Hugh worked full-time at Whiting's and after-hours did carpentry. In 1973 he was employed by the city of Rochester as head gardener for the Plummer House estate garden. He and his crew brought the neglected grounds back to their original beauty. He retired in 1986 to devote full time to growing and hybridizing lilies.

Ruth is a small, wiry, brisk woman who chuckles a lot as she recalls her lifelong involvement with plants. "There were few child labor laws in the late twenties and early thirties," she said. "My parents were good to me but, as soon as I was big enough to help, they put me to work with an older brother delivering vegetables to rooming houses in Rochester. Even back then, Rochester was a national medical center, and families would stay in the rooming houses to be near loved ones. We would wash and trim radishes, carrots, onions, and rhubarb, and load them into a coaster wagon. Dad would give us a ride in the morning on his way to work. We would make the deliveries door to door, and there were lots of rooming houses in Rochester. When we were down to odds and ends, we'd pull the wagon home.

"At age eight, I was assigned one street corner adjacent to a Rochester hospital, my older sister another. Every weekday during the summer, I would make up bouquets from buckets of flowers my parents grew, and sell them for twenty-five cents to people visiting patients. Early on, I learned not to put fragrant flowers in hospital bouquets, because the scent can bother sick people. To this day, I have to force myself to recognize fragrance in lilies as a trait desired by most people."

Ruth never lost her interest in growing flowers for florists. Today, sales of stems of lilies, coral bells, balloon flowers, baby's breath, and statice help to pay for their lily hobby.

In the early 1960s, Ruth had become interested in hybridizing daylilies and had worked up to twelve hundred experimental hybrids in her trials. Then, their orbit intersected that of lilies.

"Mentally," she said, "we had been preparing to explore lilies for some time. Back in 1967 we had joined the North American Lily Society. A friend, Louise Koehler, cemented the decision when she gave us eleven of her unnamed hybrids. We loved them and still do. But, it was Earl Tesca, a crusty, opinionated hybridist, who showed us how to recognize potential in lilies and to settle for nothing but the best."

Ruth and Hugh loved working with the lilies. Eventually they offered to move Earl Tesca's collection to their farm. Until his death, Earl continued to work in the lily trials, teaching the Cockers what he knew about hybridizing and lily culture. His breeding emphasis had been on the early "Asiatics" which he felt had the greatest potential for northern home gardens and for cutting. Ruth and Hugh offered to register any of Earl's hybrids in his name, and have honored their promise.

The sudden acquisition of several thousand lily bulbs, representing more than four hundred species and crosses, forced Ruth to make a wrenching decision. "I knew I couldn't work with both: one had to go," she said. "When I made up my mind to get out of daylily hybridizing, I sat down in the middle of my 'babies' and had a long cry. Then, I got up, and dug and bagged all my plants of 'Hems', fifty plants per bag. I hauled those bags all over town and gave plants to schools, county and city parks, and 4-H clubs, hoping to create an interest among youngsters in growing daylilies. And, do you know that, to this day, I can still recognize my hybrids growing around Rochester public gardens and homes!"

Ruth and Hugh gradually transformed what they had learned from Louise Koehler and Earl Tesca into their own set of criteria for breeding lilies. Each breeder has his own vision of "the perfect lily" and, realizing that it is not likely to be achieved with one masterful stroke of the pollen brush, settles for a long-range program of gradual improvement.

The secret of successful lily breeding is to recognize good parents and to know the traits they pass on to progeny. It isn't as simple as it may appear. Some characteristics are linked to others; some are recessive, others are dominant. You can even get entirely different results when you make a "reciprocal cross" by changing roles between the male and female parents.

The time-honored route to gradual improvement is to start with a desirable parent that has a particular shortcoming. The breeder tries to replace that trait with a more desirable characteristic from another species or hybrid by crossing. If the result is promising, but not sufficiently attractive, the breeder may "backcross" to intensify the desirable trait. All of this takes time, careful and critical note-taking, and a great deal of luck. Yet, it is infinitely superior to random crossing.

I asked Ruth if there is a shortcut to recognizing good parents for hybridizing. "If there is, I wish someone would tell me," she said. "I know that certain lines set seeds well and I tend to use these as female parents. And I know that certain lines produce lots of variation when used as male or pollen parents. I don't mind sharing that kind of information with other lily hybridizers because, even if they duplicated my crosses, they would probably get different results. Any new lily hybridizer is going to plow old ground for a while until he or she discovers parent lines that 'notch' and produce interesting offspring."

Ruth took me through the steps of hybridizing lilies, a simple operation because the reproductive parts are so large and easily accessible. She forced apart the petals of a nearly open flower, reached in with her fingers, and pulled off the anthers with their load of unripe pollen, to emasculate the flower. Then, she covered the female stigma with a little square of aluminum foil and squeezed down the corners to form a cup. "Easier and faster than bagging to keep out foreign pollen," she explained, "and hardly visible except from close up.

"In two or three days the stigma will be covered with stigmatic fluid and sticky—receptive to pollen," Ruth explained. "I harvest pollen from desirable male parents just before it is mature enough to shake loose. I catch it in little rectangular snap-top plastic boxes like those used for faucet washers. After the pollen has dried for a day or so, I outfit each box with its own short-handled cotton swab. The pollen will keep all season in the refrigerator; I understand you can freeze it, but I've never needed to do that."

Ruth showed me how to hybridize by transferring dried pollen from one of the storage boxes to a receptive stigma. She removed the protective aluminum foil, pollinated the stigma, and replaced the foil to exclude windblown or insect-vectored pollen from a different source. I

1)

2)

3)

4)

5)

6)

Hybridizing Lilies

The Cockers demonstrate the steps of hybridizing lilies. Pollen from desirable male parents is collected, labeled, and boxed, then stored in the refrigerator (1), where it will keep all season. The female parent's receptive stigma is swabbed with pollen on a Q-tip (2); afterward Ruth covers the stigma with a square of aluminum foil to keep out foreign pollen. The cross is labeled with the code numbers of the parents (3), then Ruth records the cross in the "Stud Book" (4). When the pods are nearly ripe, the seeds are shelled out (5). The seeds from one hybridized pod are planted in a single pot (6). These seedlings are ready to be separated and transplanted into garden rows for growing to evaluation stage.

thanked her and started to move on, but Ruth stopped me and said, "Hold on, Jim; we're not through yet." She wrote on the tag the date of the cross and the code numbers of the female plant and the pollen donor, then looped the tag over the completed cross.

She told me that she goes back later and looks for crosses that have "taken," those that show swollen ovaries, indicating successful cross-pollination. Only about one-third of Ruth's crosses take; these are entered into her "stud book," a permanent record of pedigrees. For ease of retrieval, crosses are entered alphabetically and numerically. Regrettably, some of the seeds from crosses don't germinate: these failures are also noted in the stud book for future guidance.

I asked if they have tried any hybrids between species. "No, we leave that to the scientists who understand how to manipulate genes and germ plasm. Interspecific crosses are difficult. We find plenty of potential for improvement just in crossing within the same species," said Ruth.

When I asked the Cockers for their checklist for evaluating new hybrids, they told me that "everything was in their heads," and commenced pouring out information as fast as I could take notes:

"We look first for color and flower form. You might describe it as 'overall impact.' This first screening can be done on the first or second year of bloom and will eliminate 90 percent of the hybrid seedlings. An entirely new color is highly unlikely, so we look for clarity of straight colors and new combinations of markings and background colors. Earl Tesca preferred only a few strong colors, and 'spotless' at that, with no markings or spots on petals. We don't have a bias against any color, and our taste runs toward the modern bicolor or tricolor patterns and spots.

"We look for symmetry, width of petals, lively texture, and number and conformation of flowers that is new for that particular class. There are places in every garden for upright, outfacing, and nodding blossoms; open-faced, flaring, or reflexed. Size isn't everything; the maximum overall impact can also be attained by greater numbers of rather small individual blossoms. Bright colors aren't everything; we've found some lovely pastels.

"Plant height has to be in scale with the 'inflorescence,' or the total frame of flowers. Short plants tend to be more wind-resistant but, if they are dwarfed too much, you can't cut the inflorescence without weakening the bulb. So, our preference is for vigorous, medium-height plants.

"Our experience in flower shows and selling cut flowers conditions us to look for flower substance and holding power. We want flowers that look crisp week after week in the garden and that will hold well when cut for arrangements. The thickness of petals has a lot to do with this.

"Flower colors should not fade with age or sunlight; we call this trait 'color-fastness.' We grow all our lilies in full sun so we can judge this factor critically.

Hugh and Ruth show me their early-flowering Martagon hybrid lilies. Note the pendant blossoms.

"Of late, we have been breeding for more flowers per stem, that open sequentially. Some of our lines have as many as five buds per stem branch, as opposed to the usual two or three. This means that lilies will continue to bloom longer and, with deadheading of spent blossoms, will last longer in arrangements.

"We watch for endurance of bulbs; they should come back year after year, increase strongly, and not tend to die out. With this screening, we also cull out the hybrid seedlings that tend to be severely hurt by late spring frosts.

"Out in the open, and not staked, out lilies are exposed to high winds and thunderstorms. We look for strong stems that don't break or topple, and that recover quickly after being bowed down by rains. We don't have many lily diseases in Minnesota and, with our preventative spray program, we don't let virus-carrying aphids get a start. Consequently, most of our selection for disease resistance is done by eliminating the lines that show susceptibility to leaf spots and bulb rotting.

"As for earliness . . . at first, we were taken with the extra-early Asiatics but found that they emerge too early in the spring. The growing point can be frozen so badly that the bulb will not bloom or even may die. Consequently, we are gravitating toward second-early and later types to lessen the damage from late spring frosts.

"Most of our breeding is with the Asiatics and the Martagons, neither of which has much fragrance, if any. To introduce fragrance to these lines, we would have to cross them with the later-blooming Trumpets or

Orientals and backcross to restore earliness. We don't have the time for such an ambitious project."

Actually, Earl Tesca's passion for perfection has, in a way, delayed the introduction of a line of lily hybrids under the Cocker name. "We respected Earl so much," Hugh said, "that we felt obligated to continue evaluating his hybrids and to register the outstanding lilies after his death. That took several years.

"We have registered only one of our own hybrids, 'Carolyn Marie', named after one of our daughters. We have six or so more ready to register with the Royal Horticultural Society in England but have been vacillating. Now we are sure enough of our own judgment in lilies to say, 'Okay, this is the best we can do in improving this class . . . perhaps the best anyone in the world can do. The time has come to register our own hybrids, increase and introduce them.' Meanwhile, we will continue hybridizing in other classes."

I asked Ruth and Hugh how many lily awards they had won. Ruth gave one of her chuckles and asked, "Do you really want to know?" Then, she proceeded to drag out enough silver to start a mint, plus a cut-glass award from Czechoslovakia, a bronze medal from Poland, and fancy porcelain plates in presentation cradles. Ribbons were laced together like fish on a stringer; they weighed so much that Ruth grunted when she hoisted them up to show me.

"It has gotten to the point that people expect Cocker seedlings to win in the classes where we specialize," said Ruth. "We never take lily shows for granted, however. We are fortunate to have thousands of lilies from which to choose, and we cut and condition stems carefully. For local or regional shows, we cut stems early in the morning, tag them with cultivar names or code numbers, stand them in glass milk bottles filled with water, bag each head, and load them into our van for transport. National conventions of the North American Lily Society are another matter. When we have to fly, we reduce the number of stems over what we usually show, pack the stems carefully, and check them as baggage.

"As for stem length, it doesn't hurt the bulb to cut stems. Just leave about a third of the stem and leaves for photosynthesis. We have cut stems from the same bulb year after year and have noticed only a slight decrease in the size of the plant and spray of blossoms. However, you can kill bulbs by taking the entire stem when cutting. We had a severe hailstorm one summer, which stripped some plants of leaves. We lost a number of these, and the damage would be comparable if you cut off stems at ground level.

"When we are setting up for shows we cut off a bit of each stem to balance the stem length to the size and optical weight of the blossom truss. We advise home gardeners to nip off the anthers of lilies they bring in the house because the pollen can stain clothing and tablecloths. We

Ruth loads up for a show. The carrying trays hold lily stems in bottles of water.

The Cockers have amassed an impressive collection of trophies from their participation in lily shows.

don't do that for shows, of course, because blossoms must be complete for judging. We find that sun-warmed water is taken up by cut stems faster than cold water right out of a tap.

"Our satisfaction really doesn't come from winning lily shows. Sure, we'd like to win "Best in Show" at the NALS someday, but aren't going to fret if we don't. We get our kicks out of renewing old friendships at local, regional, and national shows, including many lily people from Canada and other foreign countries. We love shoptalk and sharing lily know-how with people just getting into lilies as a hobby plant."

We talked about the place of lilies in landscaping. The Cockers' home landscape reminded me of "the shoemaker's children." It is neat and attractive, but includes no lilies. "We forget about taking care of the lilies we plant around the house," explained Hugh, "so we concentrate our lilies in the test plot." But, they have a good feel for how to use them massed in exhibition beds, or mixed with perennials and annuals for flowering borders. Their lectures on lilies explore the many ways lilies can be used in home gardens.

"In lectures," said Ruth, "I always tell home gardeners that they shouldn't believe everything they read in garden books. For example,

Surrounded by lilies, Ruth and Hugh point out 'Rochester'. The white is 'Mont Blanc'; the yellow in the foreground is 'Earl of Rochester'.

books will tell you to group three to five bulbs of the same lily cultivar to make 'drifts' of the same height and color. That's good if you can afford it. But, good lily bulbs are not cheap. If you are on a tight budget, you can buy one each of several kinds, space them widely, and let each bulb increase to make a drift. Sure, the recommendations for planting tall kinds in the back and shorter kinds toward the front always apply, and you shouldn't mix colors indiscriminately. But, it's no problem if you make bad combinations; just wait until late fall and move the bulbs."

Ruth added, "I prefer to see lily bulbs interplanted with low-growing annual flowers or nonspreading perennials. Lilies don't really hit their stride until the second or third year after planting. The filler flowers help to cover the bare dirt while the lily clumps are thickening, then the lilies begin to shade the ground around them. This serves to keep down weeds and reduce evaporation of water."

The Cockers are blessed with deep, fertile, sandy loam soil. Much of their nutrient supply comes from decaying organic matter. Ruth and Hugh gather and work in leaves saved by friends in Rochester; consequently, their soil is in beautiful condition. However, to maintain a good level of mineral nutrients, they top-dress a light application of balanced fertilizer around April 1, before the lilies begin to emerge.

The high level of organic matter may explain why they have been able to replant the same area in lilies for several years with no outbreaks of bulb diseases. It also increases the speed and depth of in-soak of rainwater and encourages root proliferation by bulbs. On the flip side, it also encourages all sorts of rodents: moles, voles, gophers, mice, and shrews. But their talented cat, Dixie, kept them under control until her demise. Even the abundant rabbits gave their yard a wide berth. Deer are all around but have bothered them only once, when they browsed a few seed pods. Then, Ruth got some human hair from the beauty shop and tied balls of it around the lily plots; it did the job.

Hugh offered this advice to gardeners who are just beginning to grow lilies: "In the North, the weather in late fall may be so wet and cold that planting becomes impossible, and you will have to store bulbs until spring planting time. When it happens to us, we store our common bulbs in boxes of sand in the barn. They freeze solid but it does no harm. However, we pack our most valuable bulbs in plastic bags without holes, fill them with moistened peat moss, and seal them tight. We store the bags in a refrigerator in the basement, set at about 40 degrees F. to keep the bulbs from freezing. In tight bags, the bulbs hold without sprouting until we can prepare the soil in April.

"Spring planting works fine for us," said Hugh, "but there is a solid reason for planting in the fall when possible. Lilies have contractile roots that anchor them like holdfasts. Being accordion-pleated, contractile roots can increase or decrease in length. They can pull shallow-planted bulbs down to a depth where the bulb feels comfortable. I think that adjustment goes better in the fall, when the soil is loose and moist."

The Cockers use Treflan pre-emergence herbicide to maintain clean beds, and mulch with pine needles. In our walk through their plantings I saw Ruth remove only three weeds, all so small that I didn't notice them until she stooped to pull them out.

"You have to keep an eye on the clumps," Ruth cautioned. "After a few years, five on the average in Minnesota, the clumps will thicken up so much that they will begin to run down in vigor. The stems will be shorter than is normal for the cultivar, and look puny. The plants are doing everything but waving and shouting at you to signal that it is time to lift, divide, and replant them. We wait until the frost has killed the tops in the fall before digging and replanting."

Hugh grinned at that thought and said, "Some of those big old clumps of lilies will give you a struggle, especially if the soil is wet. A big clump can weigh twenty pounds, dirt and all. You have to lay it on the grass and blast the soil off with a spray of water before you can see and get at the individual bulbs. I can usually pull the bulbs apart but sometimes have to use a sharp knife. We don't have bulb disease or nematode problems in southern Minnesota, so there is no need to dip or dust our bulbs with fungicides or insecticides."

As we walked through their lily trials, the Cockers pointed out plants with brown lower leaves, evidence of late frost damage. Some plants were oddly stubbed-off, their flower buds apparently blasted. "It's the very early ones that get hurt badly by late frosts. They look unhappy, but will survive and develop new flower buds for next year," said Hugh. "That's one reason why we like the mid-season Asiatics; they emerge a little later and usually escape frost damage."

Ruth and Hugh pondered and waffled for a long time before answering my request for a short list of starter varieties for beginners. (When you know and love so many cultivars, it is genuinely difficult to boil down the list to a few.) At last they agreed on these selections:

- 'Connecticut King': Yellow with orange center, midseason.
- 'Black Beauty': Dark crimson with white edge, late.
- *Tsingtauense:* A species lily, orange, early; it prefers partial shade.
- 'Henryi White': Blooms just after midseason.
- 'Carolyn Marie': Wine-colored, midseason.
- 'Claude Shride': A dark red, early Martagon hybrid.

"Where winters are severe, stay away from the class of lilies called Oriental; they are not hardy. Avoid the unusual species lilies until you get a feel for lilies; with certain species you have to practically duplicate the conditions under which they grow in the wild."

With their tremendous and varied experience, the Cockers have long held memberships in local, regional, and national organizations, and have served them well. Hugh was President of the Northstar region of NALS for two years and served two three-year terms as a Director. Ruth was Secretary of the Northstar region for two terms. Over the years, their lily patch has given the Cockers rest from their busy schedules and restored their psyches.

Thomas Jefferson said, "The greatest service which can be rendered any country is to add a useful plant to its culture." Perhaps the Cockers' deep enjoyment of their hobby springs from the value their work will have for future gardeners.

More about Lilies

Buying Bulbs

The first order of business, if you are interested in growing lilies as a hobby plant, is to send off for catalogs from specialty suppliers of lily bulbs. Freshness of bulbs is very important to success in growing, and the best place to get fresh, carefully harvested bulbs is from mail-order suppliers.

Specialty bulb growers will ship you new crop bulbs as soon as possible in the fall or early winter, after digging. They can't do it any earlier, because bulbs shouldn't be lifted until the foliage has turned color. The major United States producers of lily bulbs are in the Northwest, where digging of the Asiatics doesn't begin until late October and, for the later Orientals, not until well into November.

Gardeners in northern states are then faced with shipments that come in after the ground is frozen. Experienced lily growers anticipate the late delivery. They prepare lily beds in advance, dig the holes, cover the soil with mulch to keep it from freezing, and slip the bulbs in the holes when they arrive.

Growers in Holland, where lily bulbs mature even later than in the United States and Canada, have to wait until spring to ship and sell over here. This causes no great problems with home gardeners because, when spring-planted, good-quality bulbs will bloom the same growing season. However, the plants won't be quite as vigorous the first year as those grown from fall-planted bulbs. Gardeners should be wary of bargain-priced lilies, for while mail-order lily specialists price their bulbs according to size, small bulbs can be sold at retail to novices without their knowing that they will take longer to measure up to their bred-in capacity.

Lily bulbs are a difficult product for mass marketers to sell in the spring, because the bulbs begin to sprout shortly after they are displayed in a warm area. They are sometimes packed in plastic bags, which force the sprouts to turn and twist. Such distorted growth will usually produce a stunted plant that will rarely bloom the first year.

Experienced local nurseries know to pot up lily bulbs when they show signs of sprouting in the package. Some will offer plants in full bloom for transplanting to the garden, but these are not a good buy. All that top growth will stress the root system when the plant is set in the garden, and the plant may not survive. Young, green containerized lilies will adjust much faster and better when transplanted.

Lily Classifications

Lily enthusiasts have organized lily hybrids and species into ten "divisions," which are internationally accepted. Ideally, all catalogs and labels should carry the name of the division, because the excellent European books on lilies refer to them frequently and they are used in lily shows. Of the ten lily divisions, five are important in North America. If you have only the cultivar or strain name, here are some hints on finding its proper division:

Asiatic Hybrids. Most of this germ plasm is from species originally from Asia. The goal of hybridizers has been to create early-blooming, adaptable, short-to-medium-height, disease-resistant plants. The colors range from pastels to bright and include a few dark shades. The only shortcomings of this division are lack of fragrance and a decided preference for the cooler weather of the northern and midwestern states. The NALS describes these as "the early-blooming and easy hybrids."

Martagon Hybrids. Taller than most of the Asiatics, the Martagon hybrids have pendant Turk's cap blossoms and whorled leaves. In favored locations, the Martagons will spread into large colonies and naturalize. Colonies have been known to live for more than a century. Slower to get started than the Asiatics, the Martagons prefer about the same climatic conditions.

Trumpet and Aurelian Hybrids. These generally tall, magnificent lilies bloom after most of the Asiatics are spent, and are second only to them in popularity.

The powerfully fragrant Trumpets are recognizable more by their petals than by blossom form. The petals have a waxy sheen and dark-colored outer surfaces: purple, brown, or green. The newer Trumpets, especially, are easier to grow than the Orientals. Within this division are cultivars with blossoms that look not at all like trumpets, that are, instead, bowl-shaped and outfacing, pendant, or nodding. Some have open-faced flowers, with petals flaring back from the center attachment.

The early Trumpet hybrids utilized *L. regale* × *L. sulphureum* crosses to get golden and sulfur-yellow colors. Jan de Graaf made hundreds of selections from *L. leucanthum* (centifolium), then crossed the best of these with *L. Sargentiae, L. sulphureum,* and *L. Brownii.* The most significant results were the cultivar 'Pink Perfection' and the large, varied class called the "Aurelian hybrids." This division of lilies is intermediate in hardiness between the Asiatic and Oriental hybrids. Most cultivars are fragrant; the flowers are borne in large trusses.

Oriental Hybrids. Easily recognizable, these have enormous individual blossoms. The first crosses were between *L. speciosum* and *L. auratum,* and many hybrids have since been developed from this approach. Later, *L. auratum* was crossed with *L. japonicum* and *L. rubellum* to get plants with less massive frames. Out of these crosses came the "Imperial Strain," which added gold center bands to petals, expanding the color range of the basically deep red, pink, or white flowers. The most recent hybrids within the division include genes from disease-resistant species or from the short, large-flowered, upfacing *L. nobilissimum.*

In North America, the Oriental hybrids perform best on the West Coast and in favored locations in the East and Upper South. They grow well in warmer parts of Great Britain but even better in New Zealand and cool zones of Australia. They are not nearly as cold hardy as the Asiatics, but will tolerate hot weather better, if given afternoon shade. Their elegant presence brings entirely different reactions from viewers than do the saucy, bright-faced Asiatic hybrids. They have an innate dignity. Thus, they have to be sited with greater care in the landscape than do the Asiatics.

Species Lilies. If you could see the species lilies growing wild in native populations, you could understand why you cannot satisfy the requirements of all species with one garden soil, one site, one feeding and watering regimen, and one schedule and method of propagation. Most grow in rather cool areas, at specific latitudes, altitudes, and sun exposures. The North American Lily Society recommends that, despite the fact that some of the true species lilies are easy to grow, novices should start with the hybrids, which are less demanding. The species lilies range in size from miniature to head-high and require research to appreciate the great range of choices. A good place to look up species of native American lilies is in wildflower books for your region.

Planting

Have your soil tested before preparing soil for lilies. Most lilies prefer a soil pH range of 6.0 to 6.5, but the Oriental hybrids prefer somewhat more acid soil in the range of pH 5.0 to 6.0. The pH of soil can be lowered (made more acid) by working in 1 pound of agricultural sulfur per 100 square feet of sandy soil, or twice as much for heavy clay soil. Apply yearly until the desired pH level has been reached. Except on vegetable garden soil, which contains residual nutrients from fertilizers, mix in 3 pounds of 5-10-10 fertilizer per 100 square feet.

Lily bulbs can be sunk into the soil in open spaces between low-growing conifers, dwarf rhododendrons, or groundcovers, where they will benefit from the organic litter and from their roots being in the shade. Incorporate a little fertilizer and, if needed, lime, before planting.

When your bulbs arrive, you can dust them lightly with captan fungicide or dip them in a Benlate solution. If they look dry and a bit shrunken, put them in a sack of moistened peat moss for a few days until they plump up. If your bulbs arrive with the roots trimmed off or rotted, send them back. Well-rooted bulbs will start off much faster and give better first-year performance.

Follow the directions received with the bulbs for spacing and planting depth. The rule of thumb is to cover the bulb with soil to a depth twice that of the *diameter* of the bulb. (Lily bulbs are usually rather flattened from top to bottom.) When you see recommendations to cover bulbs with 6 to 8 inches of soil, they are the type that forms a root system on the stem above the bulb, as well as contractile roots below the bulb. Conversely, when you see directions to cover bulbs with 2 to 4 inches of soil, they are the type that forms roots only at the bottom of the bulb, or are of a species that will rot if planted deep.

If you decide to plant "on the flat," you will discover that the bottom of your planting holes will be below the level of the surrounding soil, not the best situation for drainage. Instead of digging holes, work up the soil in the bed and buy some bags of planter mix. Set the bulbs on the top of the prepared soil and pour the planter mix over them to cover the bulbs to the recommended depth. This is a fancy way of building a raised bed, but it elevates the bulb to warmer, drier soil levels where the drainage is better.

As you plant each bulb, mark it with a more or less permanent label. Drive in a stake 3 to 5 inches away from each bulb of taller varieties.

Fertilizing

A preplant application of fertilizer won't be enough to feed lilies through the growing season unless your soil is quite fertile. Typically, lily enthusiasts side-dress a low-nitrogen fertilizer on the soil around lily plants as soon as new growth begins to show: 2 to 4 tablespoons per plant should suffice. Be sure not to get any fertilizer on the foliage. One or two foliar feedings with water-soluble fertilizer before flower buds form may work better on sandy soils.

Pests and Diseases

Several minor leaf spots may attack lilies in zones 7 and 8, and elsewhere during wet summers. They are not critical but can disfigure foliage. In northern and midwestern areas the only major fungus disease is botrytis or gray mold, a muggy weather problem, which starts as spots on the leaves and gradually involves flower buds. Micronized copper sprays are effective. Wide spacing between plants and siting lily beds out in the open helps lily foliage to dry faster and to minimize foliage disease.

Even more important, spray at the first sign of aphids. Keep weeds pulled too; some weed species can harbor cucumber mosaic virus and transmit it to your lilies through aphid vectors. If any foliage looks mottled, light green against dark, dig out and discard the bulb without delay. Mosaic virus symptoms are nothing like nutrient-deficiency signs, light or off-color foliage. Try supplemental feeding if you are in doubt: foliar feed or drench around plants with fish emulsion or one of the water-soluble fertilizers high in potash; they are labeled for feeding ornamentals.

Dividing and Transplanting

Don't move or divide lilies unless there is a good reason for it. However, taking up lilies to speed up increase is a different matter. As plants mature, young plants will begin to come up, growing from new bulbs that form around the mother bulb. In the fall, you can dig these young bulbs and spread them out in drifts or use them to start new lily beds. Tiny new bulbs may get lost if you transplant them into the landscape, unless you label them carefully.

The stems of some lilies run for some distance underground before turning up one to two feet away from the old bulb. This is an especially good habit among low, rather open shrubs, which act as an understory, even giving stems some support. These are called "stoloniferous" lilies after their underground stems. The American lilies with stolons form new bulbs on the ends.

Some species, such as *L. tigrinum*, set numerous bulbils—little dark, shiny beads—in leaf axils. These can be taken when they begin to loosen prior to dropping off, and rooted to make new bulbs. Or when the foliage turns brown, you can bend the stem over at the base, cover it lightly with soil, and new lily plants will grow along the stem the following year. You may see small bulbs forming right at the surface around stem-rooting hybrids; if so, heap up a few inches of soil to cover them until they are large and well-rooted enough to take up for division.

Certain lilies can be increased from bulb scales. Plunge the scales with the scar down, in trays of moist vermiculite to root, or alternate layers of scales with layers of moist vermiculite in a plastic bag. Bottom heat will speed the process but, since you will be doing it in late summer, you probably won't need extra heat. Tiny bulblets will form around the scale and, when these begin to show green shoots, detach and pot them up in a seed flat mix to grow to the size of a quarter before setting them out in a nursery row.

Hybridization

Watching lilies develop and bloom from bulbs you planted and nurtured is thrilling, no doubt about it. But, the ultimate thrill is to become the proud hybridizer of a seedling lily that is more beautiful than either of its parents. Don't bother with haphazard crossing; instead, start with one of the newly introduced polyploids. They have extremely complex genetic backgrounds, which enhance your chances of developing a fine new hybrid. Just make sure that the catalog listing says that they are fertile.

To succeed in crossing polyploid lilies, you need to play a little "numbers game." The chromosome number of the gametes of most lily species is 12. Normal or standard lilies are diploid; that is, they have a chromosome number of 24. Triploid lilies have a chromosome number of 36, and the chromosome number of tetraploids is 48. Your best results will come from crossing diploids with diploids, triploids with triploids, and tetraploids with tetraploids.

Lily catalogs lump all cultivars with more than the normal chromosome number under the catchall term "polyploid." This classification developed only recently and includes some of the most exciting new lilies seen in many years.

Peppers

Fun, fellowship, community service, and creative satisfaction are harvested along with Ann and John Swan's Pennsylvania pepper crop.

(Left) The colorful sampler shown here displays some of the sweet, mild, pungent, and hot peppers grown by the Swans.

Peppers are one of the most important food crops in the world, but you'd never know it from looking at typical produce counters. One small bin of green stuffing peppers and a few jalapeños in the gourmet section would be representative. However, as you travel south through Mexico and into the Caribbean and Central America, you enter the homeland of peppers. Peppers everywhere! Fresh, dried, pickled, roasted, fried . . . mostly hot, but many with subtle flavors that are wasted on us Norte Americanos.

Whoever first referred to the genus *Capsicum* as "peppers" started a confusing situation that seems insoluble. The name "pepper" was already being applied to *Piper nigrum*, the tropical spice pepper, before explorers brought back garden peppers from the New World. Most Europeans refer to garden peppers correctly as *"Capsicums,"* but it seems doubtful whether the Latin name will ever catch on here.

Collectively, sweet and hot peppers may rank second only to tomatoes among garden vegetables worldwide. In many nations, hot peppers are the single most important condiment. Use of garden peppers in the United States, mostly fresh in salads, is "small potatoes" compared to other parts of the world. The use here is increasing, thanks to the promotion of golden and mature red sweet peppers and the increasing interest in Mexican, Southeast Asian, and Pakistani cuisines, which call for hot and mildly hot peppers.

Peppers spread all over the tropical and semitropical parts of the world with the early explorers. The seeds are easy to keep and transport, and will remain viable for several years. Curiously, the "hottest" cuisines in the world are not found in the New World, where garden peppers are native, but in Africa, Pakistan, Thailand, and China. Many countries offer side dishes of fiery pepper sauces and vinegars, so that diners can season foods to individual tastes. It is possible that the bland taste of the basic foods of these countries led them to welcome the addition of hot peppers for seasoning.

Early explorers reported that Amerindians grew peppers for more than flavoring. They appreciated hot peppers as an appetite enhancer, an aid to digestion, an expectorant, and an aphrodisiac. When the Europeans arrived, peppers had long been domesticated. However, a few wild stands survive, and are harvested annually for vine-dried hot peppers. Old-timers in the South maintain that homemade sausage made with hot peppers keeps better and that peppers tame the taste of wild game. No self-respecting truckstop in the deep South is without bottles of red "Louisiana hot sauce" and pickled hot peppers on every table. The hot, vinegary juice from pickled peppers is used mostly to flavor boiled mustard and turnip greens.

Peppers were first reported in North America in the Florida and New Mexico gardens of Spanish garrisons. Soon thereafter, numerous varieties of both sweet and hot peppers arrived with planters from the Caribbean settling in the South. Yet, seeds of sweet peppers had arrived early with colonists from Great Britain, France, and Holland, and spread south and east with frontier expansion. This may account for the overwhelming national preference for sweet peppers.

Thomas Jefferson planted peppers at Monticello, perhaps ordering seeds from Bernard M'Mahon's catalog. In his 1806 offering, M'Mahon states: "The capsicums are in much estimation for culinary purposes . . . the 'Large Heart-shaped' is the best." He named other varieties: 'Cherry', 'Bell', and 'Long-podded'.

Taxonomists have squabbled over the botanical arrangement of the genus *Capsicum* for centuries. One of the major drawbacks to classifying the various varieties by species was that most of the United States taxonomists and agricultural botanists were at northern universities. In short-season

areas, culture of the late-maturing sweets and hots was difficult, and growing of the true tropicals was impossible. However, in recent years, with the aid of laboratory techniques such as electrophoresis, taxonomists have been able to distinguish the subtle differences among species.

Classifying peppers is difficult partly because pepper plants cross so readily. Fortunately, wild specimens of certain pepper species can still be found, which gives scientists a starting point. They have been able, working with ethnobotanists, historians, and archaeologists, to project the centers from which the various *Capsicum* species spread throughout the world.

Hortus III lists only two *Capsicum* species as important in North America, *C. annuum* and *C. frutescens*. Five "groups" are listed under *C. annuum*; these include virtually all the sweet and nontropical varieties of hot peppers. Within *C. frutescens* is the Tabasco pepper, the source of the heat for the best-known brand of Louisiana hot sauce, which is fermented for a year before bottling. Vinegar-pickled hot peppers are often of the 'Serrano' variety or of 'Tabasco'. Certain of the tropical species or forms won't grow well in this country because they developed under specific conditions of night length, duration of season, and day and night temperatures that we can't duplicate in continental United States gardens.

Everyone, it seems, is more aware of peppers these days. The press coverage generated by the many chili cookoffs, which have now spread coast to coast from the original in Terlingua, Texas, has helped. People everywhere are recognizing and using sweet peppers as well, to add color and flavor to salads, and for their high vitamin content. Still, we have only just begun to appreciate the great variety and potential of the many easily grown pepper varieties and hybrids. Elizabeth Snyder, in her book *Uncommon Fruits and Vegetables*, puts it this way: "With the Mexican and Southeast Asia food explosions in this country of late, we had best begin to make an effort to understand which [pepper] is which and how to use them."

A good place to start would be the produce stand of a grocery serving Mexican-Americans or Southeast Asians. You'll see fresh fruits of the bluntly conical, black-green 'Jalapeño'; the slender, twisty 'Red Chili'; the considerably longer and milder 'Anaheim' or 'New Mexico Chili', or the variably hot, horn-shaped 'Hungarian Yellow Wax'. Dried pods of 'Ancho' and 'Poblado' will be for sale for making powders, and the small, pungent, fruits of 'Serrano' and 'Bird Pepper'. Few of the varieties popular in Southeast Asia and Pakistan are seen here; emigrants from those countries have adapted pretty well to the Mexican varieties.

There is, as well, a big difference in flavor of the various kinds of sweet peppers. Connoisseurs agree that the best flavors are not to be found in the big, blocky bell peppers sold on produce counters, but rather in the medium-sized tapered or horn-shaped peppers such as 'Gypsy' hybrid or the sweet strains of 'Hungarian Yellow Wax'.

Each sweet, mild, or hot pepper variety has its own distinctive flavor; these flavors change with maturity, and in cooking, drying, or pickling. Pepper enthusiasts have learned to tune their tastebuds to the nuances. For John and Ann Swan, a flirtation with peppers more than thirty years ago has blossomed into an infatuation that adds zest to their lives.

John and Ann prefer to allow their sweet peppers to ripen red before picking.

John and Ann Swan of West Chester, Pennsylvania, are the kind of people who have fun growing any kind of plant, be it a flower, vegetable, tree, or shrub. They are good-natured, sharing people who have developed into crackerjack home gardeners and are enjoying every minute of it. Peppers are one of the plants that add spice to their lives and those of everyone around them. Red, yellow, green, purple . . . sweet, mild, hot, and fiery peppers; name a variety and chances are they will have grown it. In their big garden, their pepper patch dominates.

Plunked down in the middle of a large raised-bed food garden, their pepper patch gives the Swans room to try a few new varieties each year, while supplying pecks of peppers of their favorite varieties. The food garden is only the beginning of a beautifully integrated landscape. Flanked by huge, curving beds of perennials and decorative herbs, their side-yard area melds into spacious peninsulas planted with shade-loving species, mostly native plants. In the background are great trees. Atop a rise above the food garden are a culinary herb garden and a sizable wildflower meadow garden. All around the house are choice shrubs, groundcovers, and bulbous plants. The Swans are serious gardeners, no doubt about it!

English born and brought to the United States in infancy, John credits some of his love for flowers to his mother, "who loved to gather and arrange great armloads of flowers, like a proper Englishwoman." Not so with Ann Tucker Swan. Born in Bermuda of an English mother and a Bermudian father, she came to the United States with John as a war bride after World War II. (John was stationed in Bermuda with the U.S. Army Air Corps.) Ann, who describes with relish her growing up as "the only girl on an island with a school for boys," came by gardening from both sides.

Ann's father founded and headed up the Nonsuch Island Training School for wayward boys. They were taught numerous skills, and gardening was, perforce, high on the list. Imported food would have been too costly to satisfy the appetites of growing boys. Her parents taught Ann how to prepare the eclectic foods of Bermuda, reflecting cuisines that merged on the island: British, African, Portuguese, and Caribbean.

In particular, Ann learned how to use peppers to make food more interesting.

"Our friends in Bermuda included people from many parts of the world," recalled Ann. "Each grew his or her own kind of heirloom peppers, sometimes several kinds per family. They pickled the small, red, very hot 'bird peppers' in sherry or rum and used them as condiments for fish chowders and stews. A dash of either of these hot sauces made a memorable Bermuda version of the Bloody Mary. Bermudians grew and used lots of cucumbers, as do I, and put them up as spicy pickles, sometimes with hot peppers. In Bermuda, all surplus vegetables were preserved; the cost of imported food provided incentive."

Gardening had to wait while John finished his degree in English at the University of Pennsylvania and Ann began a career at Smith Kline Laboratories in Philadelphia. "I wasn't good at waiting," said Ann; "I soon had an office full of plants!" John went to work in marketing communications at the DuPont Company. Thirty years ago, they bought a lot near West Chester, Pennsylvania, and later expanded it to three acres. They named their mini-estate "Frogmore" after a famous manor house in England.

"It was not until we began building our house that we took a close look at the land," said John. "We had wondered why the property was strewn with rocks and was rougher than the surrounding farmland. Then, an old farmer in the neighborhood told us that our land was the site of an abandoned dump for rock rubble blasted from a serpentine stone quarry. Ever since before the American Revolution, and up until the early twentieth century, chunks of rock had been hauled from the quarry to our lot. In some areas of the lot, rock was thirty feet deep! We had been unable to recognize the extent of it because of a tangle of underbrush, vines, shrubs, briars, and trees. The saving grace was a cart trail that wound through the piles at ground level, and a more or less rock-free area where we built our home. The old trail, which led down to a creek in the back, became our woodland garden.

"My back still aches," said John, "at the memory of the rocks Ann and I removed and piled aside to make room for our first food garden. That experience taught me why the settlers in this area built homes of stone . . . they needed a place to put them when clearing their fields!" Ann added: "We hauled in soil and dumped it over the rocks; we grew beans and corn at first, stuff we could direct-seed. Neither of us had done large-scale gardening, so we began with simple crops. Our first failure was asparagus; it just didn't produce well for us. Early on we began composting, as my father had taught the boys to do on Bermuda. John and I could get lots of manure locally, loads of leaves from our trees, and field hay from our open pastureland. Years ago, we began saving and recycling all garden refuse and kitchen scraps."

In their then-new garden, Ann could hardly wait to get started growing her fondly remembered peppers, especially the tiny, very hot bird peppers. She sent to Bermuda for seeds and began what has proven to be an absorbing hobby of evaluating hot, mild, and sweet peppers in the garden, and preparing or preserving them in many ways.

"Our friends considered me slightly balmy," Ann said, "until they tasted my bird peppers pickled in sherry. Just a few drops turns bland dishes into party foods!" Her days of sailing a ketch from Nonsuch Island to mainland Bermuda for shopping showed in her description of refilling empty pepper-sauce bottles. "As the tide goes out, pour in more sherry. The flavor will hold through one complete refilling."

A plant of 'Cubanelle' pampered by the Swans with a plastic pot reservoir, a wire cage, and salt-marsh hay mulch.

"I can't get the same kind of sherry we used years ago on Bermuda, but from all the kinds I've tested, one seems to approximate the taste I remember . . . Taylor's Golden Sherry. It is neither too dry nor too sweet.

"John helped me so much with my pepper hobby and, later, as I branched out into herbs," Ann said, "he built a thousand-square-foot vegetable garden on a slope so steep that he had to terrace it with railroad ties, three high at each step. I wheelbarrowed and dumped in soil mixed with spent composted manure from a nearby mushroom grower.

"After we completed that job, he and I tackled the piles of stones around the place." As Ann spoke, I tried to imagine the number of man and woman hours needed to load, move, offload, and set the thousands of stones in evidence. They were neatly laid without mortar, in back-sloping walls. I estimated the walls at about five hundred feet total, ranging in height from two to four feet. The stones have begun to collect a patina of moss, lichen, and ferns. Here and there, choice perennials are chinked in. Carefully chosen prostrate shrubs and creeping groundcovers break the stark gray-green lines.

"If only we had been able to afford a tractor and a scoop loader," John added, "we could have finished the job in a year or two. But, we were young and strong. The hard work, year after year, may have been a blessing. We still have the energy and endurance to do whatever we wish, be it gardening, volunteer work, or travel."

Their shared excitement crackled as they told how they discovered a wild pepper on an island in the Galapagos Archipelago. "On the side of a still-active volcano, at some distance, partly hidden by tall grass, we caught a glimpse of pepper red. We picked our way through the underbrush and, sure enough, found a tall, shrubby, pepper plant with small pods. It was the first wild pepper we had seen in our travels and we had to have it for our pepper trials.

"We brought seeds home and grew plants, only to find our Galapagos pepper was a promiscuous little devil. After only one generation, we lost the original line due to natural crosses with other varieties. One of those accidental crosses, it turned out, was a 'keeper,' a small-fruited pepper we named 'Frogmore' after an estate in England. We are still growing it.

"Many of the exotic pepper varieties are available from seeds ordered from specialty catalogs. We've picked up seeds of local varieties in Ecuador, and have found a few more wild kinds," says John. "Friends give us some; that's how we got started with 'Rocotillo'; it came from Puerto Rico. We order seeds of Mexican and southwestern specialties from Seeds and Plants of the Southwest, in Santa Fe, New Mexico, and from Horticultural Enterprises in Dallas. Stokes Seeds in Buffalo is another good source with a wide selection of sweet and mild peppers. The Pepper Gal in Largo, Florida, has an interesting list as does Park Seeds in Greenwood, South Carolina."

The Swans' pepper patch, which is planted on terraces, ascends a steep slope.

Ann is delighted with an heirloom pepper they were given by a friend who found it in South Carolina. It is one of the distinctive small-fruited hot peppers native to the tropics and has adapted to temperate climates. It is a different species from standard hot peppers: the foliage is smaller and the plants bushier. No one knew its name, so they dubbed it 'Ethel Jane' in honor of the person on whose property it was found.

"Space is limited in our garden," John said. "Before we order seeds, we decide how many fruits of each variety we will need to grow for our own kitchen and for the Pennsylvania Horticultural Society's 'Harvest Show.' Then, we project how many plants we'll need to produce them. Finally, we add a few varieties that we've never grown before. After dropping the varieties that were unsatisfactory or indifferent the previous year, that brings us up to twelve to fifteen varieties, three to ten plants per variety. That's all we have room for in the food garden. Ann plugs a few plants of the more ornamental hots into sunny perennial beds, and that relieves a bit of the pressure for space.

"I always draw a plot plan of the vegetable garden so we can rotate crops," John continued. "We don't like to plant peppers in the same location two years in a row. We don't rely on memory; a plot plan reminds us of what we planted, when and where, from year to year."

John does most of the propagation for the Swans' garden. "I start pepper seeds in the basement beginning the second week in March," he said. "I plant three seeds per cube in Jiffy 7s, which I buy a thousand to the case to save money. When the seedlings have their first set of true leaves, I scissor out the surplus and leave one strong seedling per cube. Pepper seeds germinate best at 70 to 75 degrees F. I get good results by setting trays of moistened and seeded Jiffy 7s in the furnace room for germination. I cover the trays with sheet plastic to keep moisture in and marauding mice out.

"As soon as the seeds show green sprouts, I remove the plastic and move the trays of Jiffy 7s to fluorescent-lit shelves and grow the plants to the six-leaf stage at about 65 degrees, 60 at night. Then, I do something that I feel makes a real difference in pepper growing. I pot up the Jiffy 7 plants in four-inch plastic pots filled with a half-and-half mixture of screened soil from the vegetable garden and a potting medium named 'Pro-Mix.' I don't sterilize the soil used in the mix; so far, we've been lucky not to have any root rot in our plants.

"After three or four weeks, the seedlings will have filled the pots with roots but, in an average spring, won't be pot-bound. At that season of the year, we begin listening to the weather-band radio. We really need to get our pepper plants in the ground around May 15, after hardening off for two weeks, in order to maximize production. So, around May 1, weather permitting, we begin setting trays of plants outside, along a sunny, sheltering wall. Wind is the real villain; if it kicks up during the day, we cover the plants to keep the stems from being damaged. If the temperature drops, we bring them indoors. Every cold night we bring them in. We have learned that you must not allow pepper plants to become shocked by cold temperatures or whipped and weakened by drying winds.

"We can actually see the plants changing as they harden off. The stems and leaves thicken and become stiffer. The leaves turn dark green. New internodes are short. We know that, when we set a hardened-off pepper plant in the garden around May 15, it won't be shocked by transplanting.

"We've developed a system of transplanting that works for us. Our soil is fluffy and weed-free from tilling in late fall and adding composted manure from a mushroom grower. We line out rows three feet apart and set pepper plants thirty inches apart, to get the maximum number on each terrace. How we set them in makes a big difference, we feel.

"Hooeee!" I sample Ann's dried and powdered hot peppers for the TV cameras during The Victory Garden's *visit.*

"We mix a handful of 5-10-5 granular fertilizer into the quart or so of soil excavated to make a planting hole. We set the plant in just deep enough to match its soil line with the surface of the garden soil, perhaps half an inch higher. If the plants are overgrown due to weather delays, we straighten out girdling roots before planting and backfilling.

"Next, and we may be the only gardeners doing this, we cut the bottoms out of six-inch nursery pots and set them around the pepper plants, small end down. We twist them this way and that to sink the bottom rim one and a half to two inches deep into the soil. These pots shelter young seedlings not only from cutworms but also from stem-whipping winds. They reflect and concentrate heat, and give us a reservoir for watering. We pour water into them slowly, to avoid washing soil around. Those bottomless pots are one of our 'secret weapons.'

"Another secret weapon is a stack of large, rigid, empty three-gallon plastic nursery pots we stow in the garden house. If night temperatures threaten to fall below 50 degrees, we cover pepper plants with inverted pots. We're not so much concerned with frost after May 15 as we are with the chilling effect of cold wind and cold rain. We didn't have to buy the containers; they came with perennials and shrubs we purchased.

"As anyone knows who has grown peppers," John said, "they sit still for two or three weeks after planting, regardless of the weather. Nothing

1)

2)

3)

4)

Protecting Peppers

The Swans employ an arsenal of techniques to protect their peppers until harvest. Bottomless plastic one-gallon pots shelter new transplants from wind and cutworms, as well as reflecting and concentrating heat (1). Baskets and nursery containers cover pepper plants against late spring frosts (2). Old shutters supported above plants reduce the stress from extremely hot weather (3). Old madras bedspreads pulled over cages protect plants against fall frost (4).

you do will make them add size. I think that the plants are developing roots like crazy. When the soil warms in June, the plants take off and grow with a rush. Some of our hot varieties don't put on much growth until late July.

"When fast growth starts, we set a cage around each pepper plant. The cages serve three purposes: they keep plants from toppling in windstorms, they minimize breakage of brittle limbs, and they keep our feet from compacting soil near the plants. We have tried growing peppers without cages but lose production to toppling and breakage. We like redripe peppers and let so many fruit hang on the plants that they are especially vulnerable to breakage.

"We make pepper cages of the reinforcing wire mesh used to strengthen concrete; it works much better and lasts longer than the thinner, less substantial fencing such as dog wire. All our cages are eighteen inches in diameter. We make some of them thirty inches high for short varieties and some forty-eight inches for taller peppers. The net height is six inches less because we snip out the cross wires on the bottom ring. That leaves spears that stick into the ground to prevent the cage from tipping over in a storm. The cylinders last for nearly ten years; we're on our second set. In late June we dress two to three inches of salt marsh hay over the entire vegetable garden, for moisture retention, weed control, and reduction of soil temperature. Salt hay is particularly good because it holds up for a long time, contains no weed seeds, and does not support fungus diseases."

It's important not to cultivate around pepper plants. Instead, hand-pull weeds growing around the plants and rake soil out of the walkways to pull up around the plants and to bury weed seedlings.

John continued: "The mulch really helps our plants to withstand extreme heat and dryness. During a heat wave, some of our sweet varieties, especially 'Gypsy' and 'Cubanelle', looked as if they were about to die. Watering kept them barely alive but didn't seem to help the problem. We laid old louvered shutters across the tops of the cages and the shade saved the plants. Hot weather always reduces fruit set, except on the hot varieties, even though we water deeply every two or three days. Peppers can stand only so much heat and dryness."

The Swans rarely find it necessary to give their peppers supplementary fertilizer. "The 5-10-10 we mix in at planting time is enough to produce a good crop on our soil," said John. "The mushroom compost, being composed mostly of straw and horse manure, probably contributes most of the other nutrients needed by vegetables. If I see an occasional plant growing slowly, I will give it a shot of liquid plant food, but never of a high-nitrogen analysis."

I asked Ann how many peppers they harvested from the seventy plants in their garden, and which was the most prolific variety. "I have no doubt we lose some production," she replied, "by minimizing picking until the 'Harvest Show' in late September. Even so, we get up to five pounds of fruit per plant, especially from 'Cubanelle' and 'Gypsy'. Some of the hots such as 'Bird' pepper, 'Thai Hot', and 'Tabasco' have hundreds of fruits but they are so tiny and hard to pick that we are lucky to get half a pound per plant.

"Personally," Ann said, "I much prefer red-ripe sweet or mildly hot peppers over the immature green fruit. The flesh is sweeter and thicker. And, since I roast, sear, or sauté most fruits rather than eating them raw, the thick mature skin slips right off. I am willing to sacrifice yield for such quality. As it stands, the day before the 'Harvest Show,' every inch of space on the basement floor and the family room is covered with baskets of ripe peppers, labeled by variety. By the way, I clip off large-fruited peppers with a pair of sharp Felco shears. Snapping or twisting them off can break limbs.

"After the show, we concentrate on preserving all the peppers we can before hard frost," Ann said. "Light frosts don't worry us because we lay old cotton bedspreads over the crops. The Madras spreads are rather light, but rarely blow off, and they dry out quickly after a rain. We've tried the new spun-bonded floating row covers, but they tear on the cages and are hard to anchor. I hate the way they feel when they are wet! I'd rather dry the bedspreads on the vegetable garden fence, fold and store them between frosts."

The plants' heavy foliage canopy in the fall tends to shield the lower half of the plant and, often, the fruits that are borne down low. Even though a light frost can blacken the outer shell of foliage, you can continue to pick peppers for a while. But frost makes a warm-weather vegetable act like a wounded deer; it may run for a while but is doomed to a short life. You'd be better off either picking all the fruits before a frost and freezing them, or pulling the entire plant and hanging it in a cool basement to supply you with fresh peppers for up to a month.

"A killing frost doesn't ordinarily come before mid-October, so we have about three weeks to harvest and preserve our pepper crop. We freeze 'Gypsy' or 'Canape' diced, or halved and seeded, along with whole fruits of the pungent 'Rocotillo'. The 'Jalapeño M' fruits, we pickle. We lay fruits of the thin-fleshed hots on old window screens and dry them in the furnace room. Fortuitously, we turn on the house heat at the same time we need heat for drying.

"I hate the dry hot pepper flakes served in Italian restaurants and pizza parlors!" said Ann. "I prefer a powder I make by grinding and mixing selected hot and mild peppers to taste. I try to make my mixtures hot, but not so hot as to kill the flavor."

She showed me how she prepares hot pepper powder for the Philadelphia unit of The Herb Society, which sells it as a fund-raiser. She combines flavorful mild peppers such as 'Fushimi' and 'Zippy' and removes the calyxes (caps) from the dried fruit. Then she adds about 10 percent by volume of a very hot dried pepper such as 'Thai Hot', 'Bird', or 'Tabasco'. She runs these through her food processor, tastes the mixture to be sure it has the right degree of heat, then runs it through her blender to make a fine powder. She seals the powder tight in small bottles to preserve the flavor, labels and dates them, and they are ready for use. I tasted some of Ann's blends and, to this old hot-pepper lover, they seemed just right!

I asked Ann if she wore rubber gloves when working with hot peppers. "No," she replied, "the flush of heat I get from the active ingredient makes my arthritic hands feel better. But I always take out my contact lenses because the flying powder will bring tears, despite my laying a damp towel over the food processor and blender."

For her pepper jelly, another fast-selling item for their fund-raisers, Ann prefers to use mature red fruits of 'Gypsy' and 'Canape' hybrids, or 'Hungarian Yellow Wax'. They tried the paprika variety 'Szegedi', but it lacked production. They shy away from the large-fruited bells because

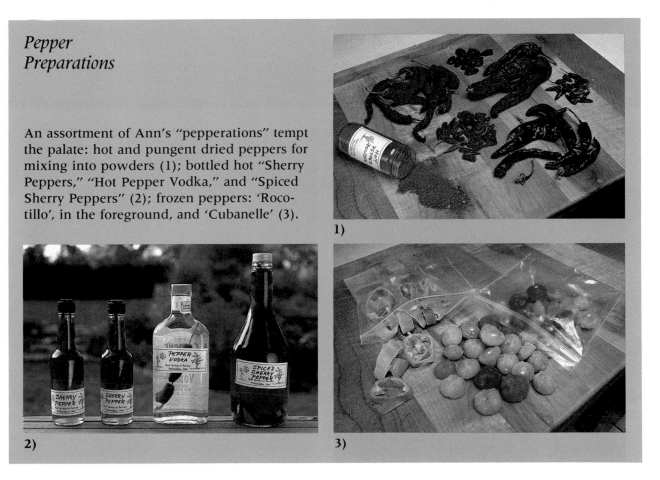

Pepper Preparations

An assortment of Ann's "pepperations" tempt the palate: hot and pungent dried peppers for mixing into powders (1); bottled hot "Sherry Peppers," "Hot Pepper Vodka," and "Spiced Sherry Peppers" (2); frozen peppers: 'Rocotillo', in the foreground, and 'Cubanelle' (3).

1)

2)

3)

the flat-topped fruits tend to catch water and rot. She finds other uses for mature red peppers; for her, 'Gypsy' makes fine pimiento peppers for canning. Others, such as the mildly pungent 'Anaheim TMR 23', she chars, removes the skin and seeds, stuffs into pint plastic containers, adds a pinch of salt, applies lids, and freezes. Thawed, they are in a handy increment for adding to cooked dishes.

One of Ann's newest but most popular productions are pickled cocktail peppers of the 'Rocotillo' variety, flavored with dill. These are funny little pungent, but not fiercely hot, peppers, flat like flying saucers. Green when immature, they turn yellow, then red when ripe. She mixes the three colors for pickles.

Also new are experimental hot mustards made with powdered dry 'Habañero' and 'Thai Hot' peppers. Ann is perhaps best known for the Bermuda specialties, sherry pepper and rum pepper. To make them, she stuffs tall, slender jars one-third full of red-ripe fruit of small, thin-skinned hots such as 'Bird', 'Tabasco', 'Thai', and 'Ethel Jane', fills them with sherry or rum, caps them, and lets them sit in the dark for at least a month before use.

Ann gave me two more pepper recipes before I left their pleasant company. "For breakfast, try 'Cubanelle' peppers sautéed in light olive oil. Serve them with grilled tomatoes. And for a pepper jelly that will take the blue ribbon, use red-ripe bell peppers and add either horseradish or freshly ground ginger."

The Swans' hobby has given a new focus to their travels and has attracted a new and expanding circle of friends who swap pepper seeds and stories with them. They have been at it so long and have researched peppers so thoroughly that they just might be the best-informed amateur pepper growers in the country. I think they are, and I hope they keep on growing and sharing for many years.

More about Peppers

What's in a Name?

The names of the *Capsicum* species and groups are complicated, but there is a reason for it. Long ago, seeds were transported from centers of origin in the New World to distant points where distinct "varieties" evolved or emerged from selection by man. If you could grow plants of a taxonomic variety side-by-side with representatives of its original species, you would see few differences except for those achieved by primitive methods of selection. Plant scientists can make the connections, however, despite the differences, by comparing similarities that only taxonomists can appreciate.

Eventually, when a taxonomic "variety" becomes sufficiently uniform and true to type, it may be given a "cultivar" name, which is botanical argot for "cultivated variety." Were you to compare cultivars with their original species side-by-side, you might see great differences in the size, shape, and number of fruit, plant habit, season of production, and disease resistance. Yet, taxonomists can look closely at antecedents and descendants and see their relationship.

So, there may be types of peppers for which three entities exist: the original species, the crudely improved and variable variety, and the greatly improved modern cultivar.

For maximum clarity, cultivar names should always appear in single quotation marks such as 'Yolo Wonder' or 'Anaheim Chili'. Few seed catalogs follow this modern nomenclature and prefer merely to capitalize the first letter of the cultivar name or to print it in boldface. Further confusing the issue, seedsmen also prefer to refer to their open pollinated strains of vegetables as "varieties" rather than cultivars.

Dr. Jean Andrews's book, *The Domesticated Capsicums*, contains a chart of domesticated pepper varieties which could be considered a *Capsicum* family tree. The apparent redundancies in naming are unavoidable. Explanatory notes have been added.

● *Capsicum annuum* var. (variety) *annuum:* Representative cultivars would be 'Jalapeno', 'Gypsy', or 'Park's Whopper'. Most of the sweet and hot peppers popular in temperate climates are in this group.

● *Capsicum annuum* var. *aviculare:* A representative cultivar would be 'Chiltecpin'. The bird peppers are in this variety. The plants are generally tall, open, and rather small-leaved, and the fruits are tiny, variable in shape, and very hot.

● *Capsicum baccatum* var. *pendulum:* 'Kellu-uchu' and 'Pucauchu' would be representative. These varieties do not perform well at our latitudes.

● *Capsicum chinense* var. *chinchi-uchu, habañero,* and *rocotillo:* Habañero and rocotillo are late maturing, but can be grown at our latitudes. The plants are rangier but otherwise superficially similar to popular varieties of *C. annuum.*

● *Capsicum frutescens:* Representative varieties would be *tabasco* and *uvilla grande.* Both have erect, quite hot fruit on large, late plants.

● *Capsicum pubescens* var. *rocoto:* No mistaking these plants: the leaves have a faintly furry look and appear thinner than those of our garden peppers. Not well adapted to temperate climates.

The *Capsicum* family trees don't show 'Habañero' and 'Rocotillo' as cultivars, even though seeds are available under these names. I believe it is because these are primitive and highly variable varieties from which other named cultivars were later selected. Any Jamaican, for example, can tell you that their version of *habañero* — some call it 'Scotch Bonnet' — can differ in hotness and flavor from village to village.

You won't find many hybrids among the hot peppers, but you may encounter the term "strains." A given variety may have several different strains, depending on who grows the seeds. Each producer has his own specifications for the variety, and selects toward it, when choosing seed parents. After a few generations of selection, his strain may differ from the original, yet will still look enough like it to pass. For example, certain strains of 'Hungarian Yellow Wax' are distinctly nippy while others are perfectly sweet. You can't tell the difference without tasting them. Sometimes, strains become accidentally mixed by field-crossing with another variety. That can result in mild-flavored peppers in a supposedly hot variety or—surprise!—hot peppers in a supposedly sweet variety.

Adaptability

I can remember when peppers were the prima donnas of food gardens. Those old varieties sulked in hot weather and cold: if the temperature didn't suit them, they would blossom, but wouldn't set fruit. The new hybrid peppers perform well in all the contiguous states, but the bearing season in the northern tier of states, even with the aid of heat-trapping mulch, is rather short.

When you order pepper seeds or plants, remember that peppers originated in or near tropic latitudes. If you garden in an area with short or cool summers, choose the early varieties or hybrids, those that will mature in sixty to sixty-five days. This means you can't grow the great big stuffing peppers because they mature rather late. Take heart: the smaller-fruited hybrids are more productive anyway, and often are better flavored.

Mulching

Peppers respond well to mulches but what you use depends on the average soil temperature in your garden during the summer. Peppers like warm soil, but not hot. The hot varieties of peppers can tolerate hot soil, but would yield better if mulched to hold down maximum soil temperatures. This is why John and Ann Swan's salt marsh hay mulch produces good results for them. Such organic mulches are recommended across Middle America and farther south and west, rather than plastic.

Plastic mulches, however, work better in northern zones such as 4 and 5 and the upper edge of 6. They trap solar heat and keep the soil warmer than in surrounding areas. Experiments in Duluth, Minnesota, confirm that clear plastic mulch is most effective in their cool climate, applied after the soil warms up, and covered with organic mulch later for shading. Weeds will grow beneath clear plastic due to the warmth, humidity, and transmitted light, but the organic mulch will shade them out.

Black plastic mulch is not recommended for zones 7 and south, unless you run drip irrigation tubes under it and spray-paint the areas over root zones with flat white. In warm climates soil temperatures can rise alarmingly beneath black plastic, particularly on dry, sandy soil, and can stress plants by killing the roots in the surface layer beneath the plastic. The white paint reflects sunlight and reduces soil temperatures. White plastic mulch is available but is expensive.

Buying Seeds and Plants

Pepper enthusiasts soon learn to order pepper seeds from companies that conduct field performance trials in a climate similar to theirs. Their "average plant height" figures can be relied on. Field trials also reveal the varieties or hybrids that are more tolerant of heat, cold, drought, or wet soil than others, and resistance to locally serious plant diseases.

Pepper breeders believe there is a genetic linkage between the ability of peppers to set fruit at low temperatures and at high. One appears to go with the other, to a point. There is a threshold of heat, about 86 degrees F., beyond which the bell or sweet peppers won't set fruit. You can expect peppers not to set fruit, when temperatures remain cooler than the low 60s for extended periods.

Pests and Diseases	Certain pepper hybrids have been bred for resistance to locally prevalent plant diseases. Your State Cooperative Extension Service will list these in their "Recommended Varieties" publications. They name resistances to specific diseases rather than, as some seed catalogs do, merely using the general and not particularly enlightening term "disease resistant."

One of the features we at *The Victory Garden* advise new gardeners to look for in pepper varieties is resistance to tobacco mosaic virus disease, TMV. This virus can cripple pepper plants, shut down their production, and make the plants look distorted and mottled. Many old bell pepper varieties have no resistance whatsoever, but most hot peppers have high levels of resistance. There are degrees of resistance: steer clear of any variety or hybrid labeled as "Tolerant of TMV"; you need maximum resistance in peppers, not merely tolerance.

Peppers have few problems with insects, but leafhoppers and thrips can rasp foliage and cause fruiting buds to drop. These can be controlled by spraying with insecticidal soap. A few species of larvae such as tomato fruit worms can bore into peppers; these are more difficult to control; your County Agent can suggest spray programs.

Planting

Peppers benefit from 2 to 3 percent organic matter in the soil, just enough to make it accept and store water, and to keep it biologically active. Too much organic matter can result in runaway release of nitrogen in warm weather, with resultant lush growth and inhibited fruit set. Peppers also like raised bed culture and drip irrigation; during dry seasons, drip irrigation can produce significant yield increases over watering by sprinkler.

Don't overplant peppers. Two or three plants will keep the average family in salad and stuffing peppers all summer long, and one plant of hot peppers will suffice. That leaves room to try new varieties and hybrids, and I hope you will. The incredibly beautiful ornamental peppers make fine heat-resistant plants to set among your garden flowers. Not all catalogs will tell you whether their ornamental varieties are hot or sweet; most are hot.

Boosting Yields

You can increase pepper production in many ways: by wrapping pepper cages with clear plastic for a few weeks after planting (leave a chimney for warm air to escape), by picking fruits weekly to reduce the drain on plant vigor, by installing drip irrigation, and by growing them with the aid of plastic mulch in cool climates. Some gardeners save plastic milk jugs, cut out the bottoms and remove the caps, and set them over young plants. The idea is to shield the plants from cold wind and rain and to accumulate a little heat to make them grow faster than unprotected plants. It works, and it also keeps out cutworms.

Most people miss out on one of the major advantages of peppers. They are so productive that only a plant or two of each variety can give you all the fruits of one kind that you can eat or put away for winter. Why plant several bushes of one variety of pepper when you can mix them up and have many different fruit sizes, shapes, colors, and flavors? Just one season of growing peppers will convince you that they really are easy to grow, and will inspire you to experiment with a wide variety. You'll have the makings for international cuisines and good old American cooking right at your fingertips!

Index

Page numbers in *italics* refer to illustrations

soil preparation: adding sand, 46, 81, 153; fumigating, 68, 192, 193; and purchased topsoil, 21, 34; "solarizing," 192, 193; tilling/rototilling, 20–21, 24, 25, 192, 193, 228. *See also* compost; fertilizers; lime/limestone; mulching materials; pH (soil); planting mix; raised beds; *individual plant varieties*

Solomon seal (*Polygonatum biflora*), 186; (*P. odoratum*), *176*

sooty blotch, 106. *See also* diseases

southern red cedar. *See Juniperus*

southern yew (*Podocarpus*), 151

spider mites. *See* pests

spraying: daylilies, 62, 68; dwarf conifers, 151, 153; environmental concerns and, 81, 105–106, 115; Extension Service suggestions for, 27, 111, 115, 237; fruit trees, 105–106, 108, 113, 115; lilies, 207, 216; peonies, 165; rhododendrons, 27; roses, 78, 80–81. *See also* diseases; pests

spruce. *See Picea*

squirrels, 151. *See also* pests

statice, *128*

Stewartia malacodendron (silky camellia), 180

Stylophorum diphyllum (celandine poppy), *189*

sugar maple (*Acer saccharum*), 144. *See also* maples

sulfur, agricultural, 215. *See also* pH (soil)

sumac wood, 100

sun: colors faded by, 61, 206; need for protection from, 23, 24, 34, 113, 172, 231; sun-loving or -resistant plants, 34, 36, 64, 90, 182. *See also* heat; light, fluorescent; shade

sunflower (*Helianthus*), 193

sweet briar (*Rosa eglanteria*), *88*

sweet marjoram, 133. *See also* herbs

sweet woodruff (*Gallium odoratum*), 6

tarragon, French, *122. See also* herbs

Taxus (yew), 151; *cuspidata, 148*

teasel, *128*, 130

temperature tolerance. *See* frost or cold weather; heat; winter-hardy plants; *individual plant varieties*

thrips, *See* pests

Thuja (arborvitae), 151; *occidentalis* (dwarf), *136*

thyme, 125; dwarf cultivars, 150; English, 133; lemon, 125. *See also* herbs

tilling. *See* soil preparation

"tipping back." *See* pruning

tissue culture. *See* propagation

tobacco mosaic virus (TMV), 237. *See also* diseases

tomato fruit worms, 237. *See also* pests

topiaries, 139, 140, 141, 144

transplanting. *See individual plants*

Trillium, 186, 194; *luteum, 189*

Triphora trianthrophora (orchid), 188. *See also* orchids (wild)

Tsuga (hemlock), 151; *canadensis* (dwarf), 44, 149, 153

verbascum, 122

vermiculite. *See* planting mix

vine myrtle (as weed), 181

violets (wild), 194

voles, 113, 181, 188, 211. *See also* pests

watering and drainage: daylilies, 62, 64, 65; dwarf conifers, 146, 152, 153; fruit trees, 106, 114, 115; herbs, 126; hostas, 40, 45, 46, 48; lilies, 216; mulching and, 21, 106; peonies, 167, 171; peppers, 231, 237; rhododendrons, 21, 23, 24, 25, 26, 27; roses, 81, 90, 91; wildflowers, 183, 193, 195

weeds and weeding: daylilies and, 68; edgings and, 46; "exotics" as pests, 87, 181, 195; herbicides and, 34, 46, 113, 212; hostas and, 31, 34, 46; landscape cloth and, 91, 113;

manure and, 114; mulching and, 80, 113, 114, 193, 231, 236; and pepper plants, 231; and wildflowers, 176, 181, 187, 188, 192, 193

weevils. *See* pests

white pine blister rust, 102. *See also* diseases

wildflowers, 174–195; adaptability of, 185; books about, 185, 191, 192, 194; climate preferences, 178, 182–183, 185; collecting from the wild, 181, 182, 185, 187–188, 190, 195; definition of, 176; drying, 121; fertilizing, 192, 194; history of North American, 178; landscaping with, 178, 179, 181, 184–185, 194–195; mulching, 184, 193; pests, 181, 183; planting seeds, 192–193; propagating (vegetative), 178, 181, 187, 191; purchasing, 179, 186, 187, 190–191, 193, 194, 195; seed-grown, 181, 184, 187, 188, 191, 192–193, 195; site selection, 182–185, 194; soil preferences and preparation, 183–184, 192–195; transplanting, 184, 188, 193, 194; watering and drainage, 183, 193, 195; weeds and, 176, 181, 188, 192, 193; as weeds, 187; "wildflower meadows," 186–187

wilting, rhododendron, 27. *See also* rhododendrons

wind, protection from: hostas, 40, 45; pepper plants, 228, 229, 231, 237; rhododendrons, 23, 24

winter-hardy plants: peonies, 162, 167, 170; roses, 86, 87, 89. *See also* frost or cold weather

witches' brooms. *See* dwarf conifers

wood chips or shavings. *See* mulching materials

wormwood. *See* artemisia

wreaths/wreathmaking. *See* herbs

yarrow (herb), *128*

yellow root (herb), 100

yew (*Taxus*), 157